Pusher Myths:
Re-situating the Drug Dealer

by
Ross Coomber

Published in the United Kingdom 2006
by Free Association Books
London

© Ross Coomber 2006

British Library Cataloguing in Publication Data
A catalogue record for this book is available from the British Library

Produced by Bookchase, London
Printed and bound in the EU

ISBN 1853439487

For Liza, Jake and Ellie

Contents

Preface and Acknowledgements

The first thing to be said about this book is that it is *not an apologia* for drug dealers. It is undoubtedly true that some drug dealers will conform to much, if not all, that has been attributed to the image of the drug dealer over the last one hundred years or so and we have ample criminal justice based evidence of the existence of many violent, ruthless and unscrupulous members of the drug trade whose operations are openly brutal. This book is neither an attempt to deny this nor to suggest that such individuals are in some way misunderstood. However, just because some such individuals exist and are the most visible of those supplying illicit drugs, it doesn't mean that all, or indeed most, drug dealers can be usefully understood as conforming to this stereotype. When subjected to greater scrutiny there are in fact many good reasons for suggesting that most common assumptions about drug dealers and drug markets are ill-informed, often incorrect and overly simplistic. This is not however an easy thing to say or write about. Drug dealers are one of the most despised groups in contemporary western society and rarely engender any sympathy or concession to their character. The images that we have of them moreover – as this book will show – are highly durable and resistant to change even in the face of contrary evidence.

This book does however counter most common assumptions about what drug dealers are; what they do, and why they do them, and seeks to understand why drug dealers are seen in the ways that they are. In this sense this book has been very hard to write, for in some quarters, some of the conclusions that are reached could be misconstrued as being 'soft on drug dealers' and that is of course anathema for many under almost any circumstances. It has also been a difficult book to write in terms of making decisions about the content and level at which to pitch the material. On the one hand the book relates a number of detailed pieces of research that I have carried out over the last ten or so years that feed directly into the various debates covered but it also critically re-examines current drug field literature and attempts to draw out rarely considered themes within that literature or to situate them differently. This means that the book, partly at least, is non-introductory. On the other hand there is much by way of history and context that is absent from drug dealer and drug market literatures and to make the book fully explicable I have included some information and background that will help readers new to the drug market literature understand from where contemporary debates have emerged and developed. At times, for those familiar with the literature this may seem like an overly indulgent overview but I firmly believe that too much by way of broader historical and cross-cultural contextualisation is missing from the literature in this area. I make no apologies therefore for my 'combined' approach.

In chapter one this has led to a new reading of some well covered themes in the drug literature in relation to the development of drug controls. A history of the development of controls over drugs and drug users is well established by researchers such as Berridge and Edwards (1987) and Musto (1987). What is less well established, particularly regarding any early history, is the parallel but reasonably distinct development of controls and perspectives over the suppliers of such drugs within national borders – the drug dealers. Particular emphasis is given to how the 'Chinese experience' is writ large even in contemporary perceptions of the drug problem and what might result from a problem unrestrained. This conventional notion however is being increasingly questioned by contemporary scholars of Asian history and the 'new history' that is developing is much more consistent with experiences in other cultures and more enlightened understanding of the effects of addiction. Chapter one thus provides a general setting for the book in that it tries to show that many contemporary images of the drug dealer are an historical product of circumstance; beliefs around what drug such as opium, heroin and cocaine *do* to people, of morality movements and of an appropriation of other negatively viewed 'outsider' groups such as the Chinese and the criminal, but also the pedlar, the huckster and the quack. Having an understanding of some of the problematic aspects involved in the formation of those contemporary images hopefully provides a basis upon which to more easily read critiques of the various drug dealer and drug market behaviours and stereotypes dealt with in the next five chapters.

All of the research that this book is based on really emerged from some initial exploration into the 'fact' of dangerous adulteration – almost a standard assumption for some – following an overdose or unexplained 'drug related' death. This research blossomed into more and more enquiry around drug cutting practices, and then as a consequence, the minutiae of a range of other drug dealer practices and behaviours within the drug market. Close scrutiny of dangerous adulteration practices led me to find that little that is commonly believed about the cutting of street drugs such heroin, cocaine and ecstasy was commensurate with either the available evidence nor that which I went on to produce. In the course of my research into cutting practices a number of other common beliefs about what drug dealers *do* and why they do them came under the microscope, particularly those relating to the essentially predatory nature of the drug dealer: dealers giving away free drugs to children to get them 'hooked'; dealers standing at the school gate; dealers putting addictive drugs like heroin in other street drugs such as ecstasy, again to get them surreptitiously hooked. Closer scrutiny again revealed that these long held, widely believed linchpins for drug dealer behaviour, although culturally embedded, had little by way of substantiating evidence to support that they happened – more damagingly that they were often underpinned by rationales (for example, about how *addictive* drugs were, or how people *become* addicted) that were themselves faulty. Chapter two, which looks at a range of these issues, provides a detailed discussion of their place in the public consciousness and how we might better understand drug market behaviour such as the provision of 'freebies' and credit as part and parcel of market consolidation and customer relations rather than a means for predatory action on the uninitiated.

By exploring and revising what it is that drug dealers can be generally understood to do regarding the cutting of street drugs, the provision of free drugs and the way that they operate within the market generally another long held and particularly pernicious belief about drug dealers could be explored – that of the Blue Star LSD Tattoo. This particular urban legend, or hoax, or rumour, manages even today to circulate around towns, cities around the world almost unabated. Drawing on most of the drug dealer images and activities explored in earlier chapters, this rumour reinforces beliefs of the other activities and creates its own fear. It gains its credibility because, in circular fashion, the event it describes is supported by existing beliefs about what drug dealers do, the rumour then in turn proves that that is the case by reporting an event that is happening that demonstrates it all to be true. Each of the behaviours covered in the book suggest an evil individual – who else could do the things that they do? In part they do these things because, many of them, have been changed by the drugs they use and sell, they have been transformed. The primary way that individuals have been historically represented as transformed in writings on drug effects is in terms of losing their humanity and becoming amoral beings. Often coupled with examples of violent outcomes the drug user has commonly been depicted as particularly unpredictable and aggressive. Drug markets by extension have been depicted as exceptionally violent places and those that inhabit them to be rightfully feared as unscrupulous, dangerous and capable of any crime against those they come into contact. Again, through a certain level of circularity this belief reinforces those of dangerous adulteration and other predatory behaviour because these are the likely results of the amoral and uncaringly vicious. By reanalysing what drug markets actually look like, by revisiting what kind of individuals actually make up drug markets and drawing on a raft of research that undermines such views chapters five and six re-evaluate the extent to which drug markets really can be understood to be essentially violent and drug dealers to be similarly so.

The end result is a book in which it is suggested that neither drug dealers nor drug markets conform, either in their entirety or, probably, even generally to most of the key aspects thought to characterise them. I reiterate the point made at the very beginning of this introduction: this book is not an apologia for drug dealers. It does however argue that much that is thought about the workings of *the* drug dealer and *the* drug market and the way that they are commonly characterised is misconceived, based upon assumption, ignorance, prejudice and overly homogenised stereotypes that ignore the complexity of each. Acknowledging complexity and misinformed perspectives should never be confused with a failure to stand tall, the opposite is in fact true and paying lip service to simplistic images that are politically palatable is, of course, the easy option.

Note on Terminology

The term addict and addiction is often preferred in this book. This is because there is nothing essentially derogatory about the term addict although there is no doubt that it at certain times it has been hijacked to some extent to mean something essentially bad. Attempts to 'rescue' the drug user however have resulted in overly clinical and perhaps overly pharmacological (e.g. drug dependence) terminology or terminology which is too non-specific (e.g. problem drug user) particularly when the population being referred to is an addicted population. I choose to use these terms with nothing more than neutral connotation and the sense that addiction 'proper' is more than simple dependency but also encapsulates lifestyle, career and elements of choice.

Acknowledgements

This book has been some time in coming. From May 2001 I was lucky enough to spend a year with my family in Sydney Australia, researching and writing. The book was already contracted to a publisher and the research I was carrying out there (with Lisa Maher) was complimentary to the enterprise. On my return to England however I found myself moving to a new job and as a consequence away from London to Devon. Settling in took a while and it took a sabbatical (for which I am grateful) from my usual duties at the University of Plymouth to finally enable me to complete it. During this period of transition the original contract for the book vanished in a mist of publisher mergers and I therefore thank Trevor Brown of Free Association Books for taking on the risk under his admirably titled 'Publish and be damned' catalogue that encourages the publication of titles that some publishers might shy away from. This book arguably comes firmly within that category. The book itself is a consequence of over ten years researching the issues covered but is in fact the result of twenty years spent in the 'drugs field'. In that time I have benefited enormously from numerous colleagues with whom I have worked, collaborated debated and disagreed. The many ideas in the work that are presented here, are, in all fairness the ideas of many people, represented in many pieces of research. How I have put them together and the emphases that I have chosen can only however, be blamed on me.

I would like to thank – once again – Liza my wife for putting up with the difficulties that an enterprise such as this tends to produce and by extension my children Jake and Ellie. Without their support and love (and ultimately, patience) I could not have finished it.

A number of people have commented on the chapters and provided me with valuable insight – and for that I am grateful. In particular, I am once again grateful to Liza who read everything and provided discerning comment. I am also grateful to (in alphabetical order as all comments were gratefully received) the following individuals who read chapters or sections at various times and provided support and feedback: Adrian Barton; David Best; Jon Caulkins; Ric Curtis; Bruce Jacobs; Bruce Johnson; Lisa Maher; Karen McElrath; Steve Miles; Lauren O'Connell; Nigel South; Paul Turnball and Travis Wendel. A thank you also to Cliff Shephard, who, over games of pool and general imbibing, provided a different context within which to muse over the book's production.

Publisher and image acknowledgements

The image on the cover of this book is: M.C. Escher's "The Scapegoat" © 2006 The M.C. Escher Company-Holland. All rights reserved. www.mcescher.com

The LSD blotter images of 'Felix'; 'Mickey Mouse'; 'Snoopy' and 'Tin Tin' were reproduced with the kind permission of the Blotter Barn project all © 2006 Blotter Barn. All rights reserved.www.blotterbarn.com

Portions of chapter two have been reprinted with kind permission from the *Journal of Drug Issues* (2003) 33(4): 939-962. Portions of chapter three have been reprinted with kind permission from *Addiction Research** (1997) 5 (3): 195-212 and *Addiction Research* (1997) 5 (4): 297-306.

Lyrics in chapter two from the *Old Dope Peddler* (1953) reproduced with kind permission from Tom Lehrer ©

*Now Addiction Research and Theory

Chapter 1:

The historical development and rationale for the image of the 'evil' drug dealer.

This new stereotype of a drug dealer has become a staple of popular culture, the *very embodiment of evil*... Such men are portrayed as driven by greed and utterly indifferent to the pain from which they profit (Murphy, et al 1990 my emphasis).

What do we envisage when we hear that someone 'uses drugs'? The drug is of course heroin ... 'the evil heroin, dispensed by the Mafia through the vilest of criminals, the pusher (Krivanek, 1988: 181).

As the quotes heading this chapter suggest, contemporary depictions of the drug dealer are of particularly evil, amoral individuals. They deal in death and they care not that they do so. Indeed their very 'will to wealth' means they unscrupulously pursue any means to satisfy their greed regardless of the broken lives that may result from their activities. Governments, criminal justice authorities, community groups, parents, teachers and welfare workers among many others condemn the dealer in a manner perhaps only paralleled in recent times by the treatment of child sex offenders. Such broad based opprobrium to the drug dealer and the extent to which it is felt is reflected in criminal justice approaches to drug supply where in many countries around the world the penalty for being convicted of being a drug dealer can be more severe than for almost any other crime – including murder. Media portrayals can be unrelenting and we are left in no doubt of the character of the individuals that they are referring to. Yet, as this book will try to show, many of the stereotypes attached to those that deal in illicit street drugs are difficult to sustain for the vast majority of those that would be classified as drug dealers, whilst some such stereotypes are simply untrue. Although an attribution of evilness suggests the problem of the drug dealer lies in individual pathology – they do the things they do because they are 'bad' people (or in some versions because the drugs turned them bad) – this attribution of evilness itself needs to be understood within a broader historical and contemporary context.

This chapter then is concerned to explore how those who supply drugs have been historically understood and how the specific contemporary represen-tations we are familiar with then developed. To do this we have to explore how drugs and drug users have been conceived of and received historically as well as understand how various social and political forces have impacted upon the development of drug controls and as a consequence those that supply intoxicants and illicit drugs. The modern idea of the 'drug dealer' is a relatively new phenomenon, only in existence since around the turn of the twentieth century when the supply of substances such as opium and cocaine first became heavily restricted in the US[1]. The image of the drug dealer however didn't simply materialise from the metaphorical ether in response to those flouting the new laws. Prior to this, a range of historical events, spiritual and scientific movements, and particular prejudices had combined to produce a modern world view of drugs such as heroin and cocaine, and those that 'peddled' in them, and it is these that influenced how the modern day drug dealer came to be seen. As such, it is these events, social movements and prejudices that we will now explore to give us a better understanding of why certain images of the drug dealer predominate. The reasons as to why they persist however, is a broader issue that will be dealt with in ensuing chapters.

The historical spread of intoxicating substances

The history of humankind, to some degree at least, has almost universally involved the use of some kind of intoxicating substance (Weil and Rosen, 1998). Invariably, the substance or substances initially used by any one group, community or society would have derived from whatever was available locally.

This resulted in the use of significantly different types of substance, methods of use and levels of integration into the lives of those that adopted their use (Rudgley, 1995; Coomber and South, 2004). Many groups for example integrated the use of intoxicants (from alcohol to powerful hallucinogens) into religious or spiritual ceremonies whilst other intoxicants were integrated (in both celebratory ritual and prosaic patterns of consumption) into the day to day lives of nearly all of those in a community (alcohol again, but also opium, among others). In some societies the use of an intoxicant may have been only moderate and highly circumscribed whilst in others, the same (or similar) substance was used copiously with few social or other sanctions attached to its use. Thus we find that the use of intoxicants has found differing levels of acceptable use in different communities but that the extent of use and of acceptability has not always been predictably related to the relative strength of the intoxicant or the degree to which it is psychoactive. Beer, for example, was once drunk in a manner now alien to modern life and sensibility for most Northern Europeans for whom it was one of the primary sources of nourishment:

> An English family in the latter half of the seventeenth century... consumed about three liters of beer per person daily, children included...[moreover] remember that breakfast as a rule consisted of beer soup, a now forgotten dish Schivelbusch (1993:22-23).

Even today in many parts of rural India and Pakistan, opium continues to be used in a range of customary and traditional ways. New born babies are given a piece of opium to welcome them into the world whilst at various stages of the life course, different types of opium use signifies both practical (e.g. medicinal and/or to relieve fatigue when working) and symbolic (e.g. rites of passage) aspects of rural Indian life (Ganguly, 2004). As with opium use in India early forms of intoxicant use tended to find a 'natural' level of use[2] and be more or less meaningful to the group in question. In addition, most groups in earlier times would have been literally unaware of the existence of other intoxicants and indeed often even of other cultures or ways of life beyond their own geographical borders.

Exposure to different forms of intoxicants and other substances, such as spices – as with disease previously confined to specific regions – would have come about initially through war and occupation, early trading and immigration. In his *Social History of Spices, Stimulants and Intoxicants* Schivelbusch (1993) for example refers to the how the Crusades (11th Century on) led to the unexpected adoption of numerous 'luxurious' aspects of Arabic civilization including many new oriental seasonings. This exposure and adoption later blossomed into unprecedented international trade. War and trade therefore has been instrumental in exposing new 'contacts' to new products, new practices and ways of living.

Not all such contact however leads to adoption of use and Courtwright (2001a:53) has pointed out that it is to some degree a mystery as to why some substances became 'global products whilst others remained local. Even those that have 'travelled' and consequently been adopted their reception has often been mixed – particularly by those in power. At different times in different locations some newly introduced intoxicants have been received positively whilst at other times considered to be dangerous or even sacrilegious. This is true even of substances that today are barely recognised as drugs with psychoactive and other effects such as tea and coffee (Gossop, 1996). Roden (1981: 21) for example tells of a seventeenth century reaction to coffee use in Istanbul where: 'For a first violation the punishment was cudgelling. For a second, the offender was put into a leather bag, which was sewn up and thrown into the Bosphorus'. Matthee (1995:33) similarly relates how in the late fifteenth century Rodrigo de Jerez – a member of Christopher Columbus' crew – was 'brought before the Inquisition, accused of sorcery, and imprisoned for seven years' for smoking tobacco, whilst in 1604 King James I of England denounced tobacco as repulsive and dangerous and discouraged use by taxation.

The specific histories of newly introduced intoxicants thus build to a more general history of mild to extreme reaction. Further, we can see that although newly introduced substances were not always met with open arms, respective reactions were about how a particular substance was *understood* and what effect it was *perceived* to be having on those that used it. In some cases it would be a simple (over)reaction to a new behaviour or activity not seen before or understood – as with the Inquisitors who on seeing de Jerez spewing smoke from his mouth accused him of consorting with the Devil. Such opposition is often easily resolved and on release from prison de Jerez was no doubt a little upset to find that tobacco smoking had become an established custom in Spain (Matthee, 1995). In other cases however reaction has related to the various economic, social and political contexts in which the substance was newly introduced – or *who* it was being used by. The prohibition of coffee in Istanbul for example was a reaction to coffee houses being seen as hotbeds of dissent and places of congregation for radicals. At other times, to the present day, 'outsiders', 'deviants' and non-indigenous populations have commonly had their choices of drug use questioned, prohibited and punished by way of mistrust, prejudice and racism. In the West in particular, as we shall see later, the use of opium, cannabis and other substances (including tea, coffee and even chocolate) has been subject to particularly intense forms of moral condemnation much of it based on the font of protestant asceticism as well as lay and professional judgements on the beneficial (or otherwise) effects of the substance in question (Berridge and Edwards, 1987; Matthee, 1995; Schivelbusch, 1993).

It is perhaps with the earliest sanctions – where they occurred – that we see the first associations of substances being related to 'others' and 'otherness' – a theme we shall return to shortly – and the sense that either foreign drugs are unnatural or that unfamiliar drug use by foreigners is often a sign of their failings or weaknesses, failings that the 'home' population doesn't want to be tarnished with. As regards the the *supply* of problem substances, early condemnation and punishment related to intoxicants tends to focus on the *users* and little by way of control appears to have been focussed mainly on traders of intoxicants. This is a situation that graphically altered during the nineteenth century when attention became focussed on British traders as illegal and immoral suppliers of opium to China. Opium in fact has played a central role both in shaping events around the control of drug use as well as the way that contemporary drug dealers have come to be perceived.

Opium – from wonder drug to problem drug

It is important to have a sense of how views of opium (and opium traders/suppliers) have shifted over time. Opium has a long history and most of it has been a relatively unproblematic one. Mentioned in written form as early as 800 B.C., it has been referred to from early times as a sedative, a hypnotic and as a treatment for various ailments such as earache and eye ailments, and Hippocrates (4th to 5th century B.C.) also refers to its many medicinal benefits (Kritikos and Papadaki, 1967). Awareness of its dangers but also of its therapeutic properties permitted opium to take almost unparalleled position in terms of its therapeutic application both for those that self-medicated, and for those who were treated more formally, in many countries around the world. By 1680 the physician Thomas Sydenham was moved to famously remark: 'Among the remedies which it has pleased Almighty God to give to man to relieve his suffering, none is so universal and so efficacious as opium' (quoted in Saunders, 2000). Opium was thus well considered.

In England, the early to mid nineteenth century saw opium used in a range of ways: to quieten children, for sleeplessness, as remedy for excessive drinking, and as treatment or relief for all manner of pains and illnesses for which there was no other effective relief such as rheumatism, gout, coughs and colds, cholera, toothache and diarrhoea. For most people there was no access to meaningful medical help and many in fact did not trust what medical practice existed (or indeed afford it) and as such opium was the primary form of socially sanctioned self-medication – truly the 'opiate of the people' (Berridge and Edwards, 1987: 37). It was sold in numerous forms both home made and commercial:

> Families had their own private recipes which the shopkeeper made up. It was laudanum and ipecacuanha for coughs in one Hoxton family, laudanum and chloroform...in another area. Twopenceworth of antinomy wine with twopenceworth of laudanum for whooping cough was a remedy passed on in a Woolwich family (Berridge and Edwards, 1987: 30).

and,

> There were opium pills (or soap and opium, and lead and opium pills), opiate lozenges, compound powder of opium, opiate confection, opiate plaster, opium enema, opium liniment, vinegar of opium and wine of opium. There was the famous tincture of opium (opium dissolved in alcohol), known as laudanum, which had widespread popular sale, and the camphorated tincture, or paregoric...There were nationally

famous and long-established preparations like Dover's Powder...[and the list continues at length] (Berridge and Edwards, 1987: 24).

In addition to chemists it was sold freely from corner shops, backstreet grocers, wandering cart sellers and even by the 'wives of factory workers [who] often kept a small shop to supplement the family income' (Berridge and Edwards, 1987: 25) and its sale was almost totally unrestricted. In some parts of the country, such as the lowland Fens that part covered the counties of Norfolk, Lincolnshire, Cambridgeshire and Huntingdonshire, opium use was so normalised that it was drunk in tea, given to children for teething, used for energy when labouring and even put routinely into beer before drinking it. In short opiate use was ubiquitous and its forms and uses various.

It is only with the confluence of a range of forces from the early eighteenth century through the mid to latter stages of the nineteenth that opium came to be seen in a different, more problematic light and its pre-eminence became tarnished. This early history of how opium became problematised, particularly in the UK and US, has been well covered by a number of prominent authors in the 'addictions' field (Berridge and Edwards, 1987; Musto, 1987; Harding, 1998; Parssinen, 1983; Courtwright, 2001b) and a number of key themes are evident. For Berridge and Edwards for example, the early history of opium control in the UK is writ large in the histories of medicine and pharmacy and their attempts to professionalise prescribing and supply, the growth of the Public Health movement and a mix of concerns over drug use that were located in class (and finally race) antagonisms, Puritanism, and fears around the effects of the drug itself.

A slow shift in the perception towards opium in the UK started in the early nineteenth century with the publication in 1822 of Thomas De Quincey's *Confessions of an English Opium Eater* and the realisation that the use of opium for 'stimulation', enjoyment and non-therapeutic reasons was perhaps not uncommon. Although it triggered only nominal interest at the time (probably because, as Berridge and Edwards point out a blurring between therapeutic and recreational use would have been the reality for many people) it did sow the seeds of doubt about proper and improper use (moral and immoral use). Physicians at this time had also started to question the ubiquitous use of opium and many, given its attendant dangers – particularly the danger of overdose – queried its relatively unconstrained use (Harding, 1998). During the early to mid-nineteenth century concerns over opium overdose deaths, working class practices of 'child-doping' and working class 'stimulant' use – much of which was overstated or ignored comparable practice among the middle-classes – provided the burgeoning professions of medicine and pharmacy with ammunition to lobby for greater control over *who* should prescribe and supply opium (Berridge and Edwards, 1987). At this point in time however, the need for progressive control wasn't obvious to everyone or necessarily desired. In 1844 for example *The Lancet* professed doubt that the English would countenance the 'despotic' restrictions that had been introduced in St Petersburg – the clear labelling of laudanum (Dikötter et al. 2004). Slowly however, starting with the 1868 Pharmacy Act, access to various poisons and medicines (including opium) became subject to restrictions of access from medicine and pharmacy as they both increased their professional standing and power. With those, albeit minor restrictions, a dawning realisation began in the popular consciousness that the wonder drug – otherwise why control it – had its problems. For some politicians and commentators of the time the worst excesses of these problems were manifest in the experience of China.

The Opium Wars and the Chinese as victims of early 'pushers'

The 'Chinese experience' and the Opium Wars are historically very important to understanding about the foundations of contemporary drug control and perspectives on drug suppliers.

In the nineteenth century China appeared to provide a graphic example to many, and the emerging anti opium movement in particular, of the ways that a substance such as opium could render useless those that used it and by extension the society it spread through. Within China itself those who dealt or traded in opium became a special focus – with death being the ultimate penalty (Waley, 1968) – whilst to observers the 'Opium Wars' that took place in the mid-nineteenth century also signified that 'outside' forces could be complicit in the spread of unwanted drug use and that such supply should only be understood as reprehensible and immoral.

Opium was banned in China for the first time in 1729. The ban was a officially a response to anecdotal reports from the coastal provinces of Southern China regarding problem recreational use of opium mixed with tobacco and then smoked. Tobacco itself – introduced by Europeans in the early seventeenth century – had already been subject to numerous bans but, as in many other places, it soon became firmly part of Chinese culture. The initial formal reaction against tobacco however shows that China was comfortable with the banning of foreign substances and their demonisation: 'a more heinous crime [tobacco smoking] than even that of neglecting archery' (citation from Dikötter et al. 2004: 26). When the practice of opium smoking was introduced in the mid-seventeenth century – again by Europeans – it took place against a backdrop where opium had been used (eaten and drunk) in China for medicinal purposes for a number of centuries. It was only with exposure to this new form of use by European (probably Dutch) traders that led to reported problems (Dikötter et al. 2004). Initially seen as a barbaric 'foreign' activity, recreational opium smoking and the behaviour it was thought to engender was literally seen as 'unnatural' to the revered Confucian way which taught, amongst other things, adherence to cultural and traditional norms as well as virtue through temperance (Yu, 1998). New forms of drug use, as we have seen, often engender extreme reaction and alternative means to pursue intoxication which do not conform to traditional mores will not be accepted by all and some will see them as a threat to the way of life they hold dear. As early as 1720 one such reaction that conjures numerous contemporary stereotypes of current day heroin addiction; of the drug pusher, and of calls for a tough response can be found in a message sent to the Yongzheng emperor in 1720 (he would become Emperor of China in 1723):

Opium is produced overseas, and the foreign merchants who import it as medicine derive a lucrative business from this trade...Shameless rascals lure the sons of good families into [the habit] for their own profit...Privately run inns are established, where [smokers] congregate at night, only to disperse at dawn, leading to licentious behaviour. The truth is that youngsters become corrupted by smoking it until their lives collapse, their families' livelihood vanishes and nothing is left but trouble. If one is intent on extirpating this evil, one must tackle it at the root by ordering the imperial officials...to be strict in prohibiting the trade (cited from Dikötter et al. 2004: 34).

From here then the conventional story of opium and China revolves around how, with prohibition poorly enforced, use escalated from increased 'importation' of the drug, initially from the Portuguese but then from British controlled India and became the bane of Chinese life (Bello, 2003). In 1729 for example, in the region of 200 chests of opium were being 'imported' into China but by the 1830s this was in excess of 20,000 chests or 1,400 tons (Trocki, 2004). By 1906 the imperial government was claiming that 27% of the male population were addicted to opium (McCoy, 1991) whilst some have even (uncritically) asserted that up to half of the Chinese population were opium addicts by 1907 (La Motte, 1920). The Chinese formally continued to oppose the importation of opium and in time enlisted external help in doing so. Commentary from the Chinese state, local officials and later, numerous non-Chinese commentators, particularly missionaries who preached on the nefarious effects of opium on individuals and society was increasingly common (Baumler, 2001). By the time of the two infamous 'Opium Wars' (1839-42 and 1856-60) China had already officially stated, both domestically and internationally, that opium was destroying the very fabric of Chinese society and that this pernicious evil with its foreign origins – Britain in particular – and was to blame for the 'poisoning' of China (Baumler, 2001).

This is a conventional view that has long gone unquestioned, as Madancy (2001:436) has critically noted:

> It has long been axiomatic among historians of late imperial and early Republican China that opium was a plague on the Chinese people – sapping their willpower and stamina, weakening the military, draining the Qing treasury while padding the coffers of the colonial Indian government, and reinforcing China's international image as an empire in decline.

Axiomatic indeed and yet there is much about this period in Chinese (and drug control) history that is absent, poorly analysed and in fact has only recently begun to be questioned with any rigour. The extent to which China was really affected and devastated by opium has only begun in recent years to be strongly challenged. Newman (1995) for example has shown that the consumption of opium in China was widely integrated into all manner of social activities and consumed moderately and occasionally, as well as habitually, by many. Just as in India and other parts of the world opium was also used (as it is today) functionally by many workers to help them survive the harsh work conditions they had to endure. In short opium was used widely and for practical medicinal and cultural reasons as well for recreation. It is thus untrue (and only those with scant knowledge of opium would have believed otherwise) that opium was *essentially* problematic, inevitably addictive and that it destroyed all that it touched – all linchpins of traditional views of how Chinese opiate use should be understood. Whilst it is true that many Chinese saw opium as a threat to all they believed important (Madancy, 2001; Waley, 1968) others, drawn from all rungs of society saw it differently. There were opium houses for all social strata with some so luxurious as to attract the most important of customers and attendance in the prosperous Jiangnan region 'was as common as going to inns and tea-houses' (Dikötter et al. 2004: 61). As such, many of the statistics that normally attempt to show the extent of addicted consumption (because conventional understanding only perceives opium use in terms of addicted use) underestimate the levels of everyday normalised use that occurred and that opium was indeed consumed in ways that were perceived as unproblematic. Dikötter et al (2004) argue that the focus on the foreign variant of opium (for much was being produced domestically) must be understood from the wider social and political context. As with Berridge and Edwards' (1987) view that middle-class perceptions of 'stimulant' use of opiates by the dangerous classes became feared in England and created exaggerated drug scares, Dikötter et al argue that a similar situation was evident in China during the eighteenth century and that even at the beginning of the nineteenth century opium smoking was relatively rare and largely confined to a few coastal provinces. In addition, Bello (2003) has argued that domestic production of opium in China was not insignificant and that by the 1830s a large proportion of the population in south-western China were reliant on producing opium themselves and that numerous local economies were often dependent on this localised production. Moreover, and somewhat ironically, given the traditional version of events, Bello suggests that this clandestine cultivation of domestic opium had become more firmly established due to Chinese central government policy itself. The policy of diverting more and more revenue from the localities to the centre to drive imperial expansion in the seventeenth century had, he argues, the effect of garnering local opium cultivation and the informal economy to compensate for its effects – a primary reason for the failure of prohibition in such localities (Bello, 2003).

There was more to these conflicts however than simply concern over opium use. Briefly[3], the two mid-nineteenth century 'Opium Wars' need to be understood within the specific international economic and political context of the time. In particular, attention has to be paid to the severe imbalance of trade with China that had long been considered problematic by the British and other Western trading nations that was continuing to build. This imbalance was due in part to the strong demand for Chinese goods, especially tea, by the West, but it was also exacerbated by the fact that China was a largely self-sufficient economy that showed little interest in Western goods. In addition, China had a comparatively closed trading system that effectively prevented the opening up of markets in China to outsiders – other than through smuggling – and had excessive import taxes on legitimate goods, exacerbating the problem even further.

Albeit through smuggling, opium was one of the few products that the West had been able to exploit that had 'evened' up the trade imbalance. Not surprisingly this was a thorn in the side of the Chinese government both economically and politically and by the 1830s, with the ruling Chinese authorities also dealing with internal economic and political problems as well as an effective (and embarrassing) undermining of their foreign policy through the smuggling of opium, the issue built up to a point where it became a symbol of much more than simply problems revolving around the use of opium. With opium causing a seriously worsening reversal of the balance of trade that threatened the Chinese economy itself the Chinese felt forced into a corner by the British who were formally pushing (sometimes quite antagonistically) for the rights to extend trade (legally) into China and by the perceived worsening problem of opiate addiction. The Chinese response to this situation was to begin to enforce its prohibitions on opium more rigorously than previously and to impound British trading ships, confiscate the goods therein and restrict the liberty of those associated with the trade (Gelber, 2004). Such actions ultimately led to the first of the two wars. The outcome, largely due to the superior firepower and organisation of British and

Western forces was a comfortable defeat of China, its humbling and a forced liberalisation of trading relations with the West. Opium as a consequence became a legitimate article of trade. Lest we forget, at this point in time opium was a legitimate and relatively unproblematic article of trade for the British and most other nations. It was, as we have already seen, being consumed voraciously by the British and the Dutch but also the Germans and many others. So at that particular moment in time (effectively) forcing the Chinese to trade in opium would not have had the same symbolic effect on nations beyond China that many conventional writings of that history suggest, it did take on however, as we shall see, greater significance in retrospect.

There is a serious issue here: opium became understood in China as highly problematic yet we have already seen that different substances can be portrayed in the most venomous terms in one location at one point in time whilst being accepted if not lauded in other locations and moments in time. There is little evidence that opium was devastating China in the way that is conventional wisdom yet we might surmise that this is neither necessary to produce internal and international concern amongst the Chinese people and those beyond. Recent scares around heroin in the UK in the 1980s and around crack cocaine in the US were often full of exaggeration and myth, highly misleading and often incorrect (Reinarman and Levine, 1997) but this did not prevent them from impacting significantly on media representations, political debate and action and on how users and drug dealers were punished. As we shall see as this book continues, the power of suggestion, 'knowledge' and rumour are powerful devices. The position on opium – just like the 'position' on crack in the mid-1980s would have gone relatively unquestioned in eighteenth century China and beyond. Contrary scientific evidence was either ignored or unavailable and once the ball of prohibition against 'drugs' gets rolling it often picks up speed for the claims made against them strike at the very heart of popular fear and anxiety. It is not insignificant to point out that most of those writing at the time, regarding the effects of opium on China, accepted such vitriol and unsubstantiated hearsay uncritically but none-the-less paved the way for contemporary understanding of the problem. Those that followed, mainly historians by training and reliant for the most part on official documents and narratives from the time, had no reason to doubt the nature of the problem as it was presented because such images of opium (or opiate based drugs) have remained common fare even today (McElrath and McEvoy, 2001; Faupel et al. 2004). It remains the case that even today most of those (re)writing the history of opium and China are doing so from a relatively ignorant position vis-à-vis literature from the drugs field and are unaware how their new histories are increasingly commensurate with contemporary understanding of how and why drug control has emerged in the West and that it is often the case that the power of drugs to devastate in the way suggested for China is massively overstated.

Overall then, nineteenth century China provides a significant backdrop for much of how the drug problem is understood today around the world. Early propaganda around opium, fuelled by anecdotal reports led to exaggerated stories of the power of opium to 'ruin' individuals and communities. In classic scapegoat fashion a declining Qing empire chose to lay the blame of much of its decline at the door of opium on the one hand and the barbarian British (and other foreign suppliers) on the other despite some internal reliance on domestic production. Outsiders were portrayed as force-feeding the Chinese population with opium. They were undermining the great nation economically – by draining much needed resources from the country in exchange for a relatively useless article of trade that would, literally, go up in smoke – and socially and culturally by encouraging and facilitating the pernicious practice of opium smoking. Unsurprisingly many Chinese were incensed by this trade and demonised (literally 'foreign devils') those involved – a move that could only gain credence and moral support in the wake of two wars where a once great nation was easily humbled and embarrassed and then forced to legalise a substance it wanted to prohibit. The image of a country torn apart by opium is one that has rarely been questioned and in the mid to late nineteenth century (and ever since?) it provided ammunition for those intent on cleansing society of intemperance through inappropriate substance (including alcohol) use.

The Anti-Opium movement

Despite earlier protestation from China, concerns about opium use in India, revelations of non-medical 'luxuriant' and 'stimulant' use from the rich and the 'dangerous' classes respectively, the decisive shift in thinking around opium in the UK only came in the last quarter of the nineteenth century. Formed in 1874 the Society for the Suppression of the Opium Trade (SSOT)

– a Quaker funded and founded organisation – had as its primary objective a campaign to end the British controlled forced exportation of opium to China. Underlying the Quaker's understanding of the opium problem was their essentially ascetic perspective on the world and of opium. For the Quakers an individual's 'soul' and the path to a righteous life were protected by good moral behaviour and this included the avoidance of activities and behaviours that were unnecessarily lavish. Thus, moderation and denial of self-indulgence were considered virtuous and spiritual whereas excess, lack of discipline, and over-indulgence, were morally reprehensible. As Harding (1998: 4) has noted:

> Their objection to the trade lay in the belief that opium, when consumed for non-medical purposes – i.e. gratuitously and not for a specific ailment – was evil; and that the Chinese government, recognising this, had a right to block its importation on moral grounds.

As an anti-opium movement the SSOT was remarkably influential. It produced pamphlets, published a monthly journal organised high profile meetings, and lobbied parliament. In addition its General Council had forty-six highly eminent members (including the Earl of Shaftsbury) to raise its profile and standing. At the same time as the SSOT was proselytising its ideas of why opium use was unhealthy and problematic for society a new view of non-medical habitual opiate use was also making headway in the medical field, a view that saw the non-medical use of opium as a failing of the will. This overlapping of the medical and the spiritual (Berridge and Edwards, 1987) meant that two powerful forces – one scientific the other spiritual were both essentially defining addiction, and the effects of opium, in a way that was in-distinguishable from each other (Harding, 1998) – as a weakness and failing of moral will:

> ...at first to stimulate and afterwards to depress; to remove this depression the individual must take another dose – a habit of taking the drug is thus established. The nervous system suffers, the mental powers enfeebled, the moral faculties perverted, and there is an inability to distinguish between truth and falsehood (Nineteenth century physician Lauder Brunton cited from the Quaker journal *Friend of China* (1892): in Harding, 1998: 10).

By 1906 thirty years of lobbying by the SSOT, along with the coming together of the scientific and the spiritual views of opium addiction, the British Parliament, undivided, agreed to bring an end to the Indo-Chinese opium trade – a trade now considered morally indefensible (Bean, 1974).

The American Temperance movement

Although discourses about the virtues of moderation and desisting from excess can be traced back to Plato, Aristotle (Young, 1988) and even Confucius (Hamburger, 1959) what is important in understanding any particular historical positioning on such notions is the context within which such discourses emerge. The American temperance movement, closely allied with other prominent reform movements of the time such as the antislavery and women's rights movements, was a highly popular movement (Gusfield, 1986). The campaign was committed to proselytising that alcohol in all its forms was 'evil, dangerous and destructive' (Levine and Reinarman, 1991), that it led to compulsive and addictive use and the ruin of the moral mental and physical health of all those who drank it. Indeed just about all social problems were laid at the feet of alcohol – unemployment; violence; criminality; economic depression and more – and by 1850 it was common for temperance supporters to be espousing prohibition (Levine and Reinarman, 1991). The temperance movement of course was later instrumental in bringing about alcohol prohibition in the United States (1920 – 1933) but from the early nineteenth century its influence steadily grew on a number of areas of American life – including that of the opium problem (Schafer et al. 1972). Given the position of the US as a world power at this time this was not unimportant. This positioning took on greater significance when, on acquiring the Philippines from Spain in 1898 as a result of the Spanish-American War (1898 – 1901), the US also inherited an 'opium problem' of its own. The 'discovery' of more than 190 'opium dens' in Manila alone consequently resulted in a 'crusade against opium' (Moynihan, 2002; McCoy, 1991) from both the US and Philippine anti-opium movements and to prohibition being enacted on American 'soil' for the first time, between 1906 and 1908. Prohibition however did not prove straight forward. The problem for the US then became how to control prohibition in the Philippines when the trade from nearby China was essentially undermining of it. The result was a further moral crusade (Aurin, 2000) led chiefly by the protestant, anti-opium campaigner Bishop Charles Henry Brent (Brecher et al. 1972). Direct communication to President Roosevelt led to the US instigated organisation of the first international opium commission in Shanghai in 1909 (which Brent chaired) – a move that signalled the beginning of international drug control agreements and attempts to control the production, trade and supply of (principally) opium and cocaine (Carstairs, 2005; Bean, 1974; Musto, 1987; Bruun, Pan, and Rexed, 1975).

In addition to temperance concerns in the US there were other pressures building up on opium not too dissimilar to those taking place in England[4] vis-à-vis concerns around self-medication and non-medical use and the problems this was perceived to cause both individual and society:

> Resolved, That the State Board of Health be requested to make an investigation concerning the sale and use of opium, in various forms and preparations, with a view to ascertaining the extent of the evils arising therefrom; whether such use and evils are increasing, and, if so, the manner and cause thereof, and what remedies for such evils may be proposed; and to report the result of such investigation to the General Court (Statement to the Massachusetts State Board of Health, 1889. Quoted in Terry and Pellens, 1928).

Moreover, as in England the issue of race had become increasingly associated with problem drug use, and for the purposes of this chapter, how drugs were distributed and the otherwise innocent lured into the evils of drug use.

Racism, prejudice and otherness and the drug dealer

The history of cumulative drug control cannot be divorced from issues of otherness and race. Outsiders in the form of the working class scared the middle-classes with their 'stimulant' use of opium in England and the US at varying points of the nineteenth century (Berridge and Edwards, 1987; Spillane, 1998). Class fear and reaction regarding drug use also features subsequently in the early twentieth century and again in the 1950s, 1960s (Courtwright, 2002; Bean,1974) and the 1980s (Green, 1998; Miller, 1991). In each case the resulting outcome was moral outrage and calls for greater controls. Where this otherness has been combined with race the outcomes have been particularly meaningful (Bullington, 1998; Musto, 1987; Woodiwiss, 1998; Berridge and Edwards, 1987)). Specifically in relation to drug dealers Boyd (2004: 397) has said: 'Drug traffickers are constructed as 'outsiders' that threaten the world order of white, middle-class protestant morality. They are depicted as dangerous, out of control, and a threat to the nation, the family and white women's morality'. In the last quarter of the nineteenth century, Chinese immigrants in England and the US in particular were subject to media, literary and official stereotyping and as a consequence, a certain amount of public concern. By the end of the nineteenth century the infamous 'opium den' served to consolidate nefarious images related to the effects of opium, risks of contagion, risk to society and racial prejudice. In England, numerous literary references (Dickens; Wilde; Conan Doyle; Kipling; Doré and Jerrold) provided, from 1870 on, graphic description about what occurred behind the doors of an opium den and the problems they caused. The dens were portrayed as squalid, those that ran them as 'cunning and artful Chinamen' and to be populated by the 'dazed and helpless, jabbering in an incoherent manner' (London County Council Inspector cited in Berridge and Edwards, 1987: 199). They were portrayed as a threat to the local community and as likely to infest (spread) such usage wider than the local community.

The 'myth' of the opium den however is once again a lesson in the history of how opium came to be seen as a menace and how particular social problems can be constructed and added to the mix of uninformed hysteria around drug use. In London's East End where the dens were said to be located it seems that the number was small, perhaps no more than six even in 1884 and the actual amount of smoking of opium that was taking place in London to be 'minute' (Berridge and Edwards, 1987). This is not to say that opium smoking on a recreational basis was not more widespread amongst Chinese immigrants and seaman but that its 'organisation' was far less than was commonly supposed. Moreover, even where there were Chinese houses providing access to opium smoking there is scant evidence to suggest that they resembled the descriptions (or rather, interpretations) handed out by many and that in fact, scaremongering apart, there is little evidence to suggest they caused any problems – either for those indulging (who integrated opium use into their daily lifestyle, a lifestyle that included long hours of work) or for the close community (Berridge and Edwards, 1987). In the US the situation was slightly different and not for the first time (and certainly not the last), perceptions of opium, those that used it and the 'dens' in which they were used would have had a symbiotic relationship with those across the Atlantic. Sensationalised accounts in both nations would feed and substantiate accounts in the other. One thing that was different however was that in the US 'there was a den in every major city, and practically every western town' (Courtwright, 2001b: 72) due to the greater levels of Chinese immigration there since the mid-nineteenth century – many having been attracted to the 'gold-fever' of the era. In San Francisco in 1875 the first 'anti- narcotics law' was instituted to suppress the opium dens, laws that were then instituted in other towns and States (Gieringer, 1999). Such a law was however still out of kilter with general thinking at the time whereby an individual's drug use was largely seen as a private matter. Opium smoking (almost exclusively a Chinese pastime), only became a problem when the Chinese became a focus, or scapegoat, for the widespread economic ills of the time (Musto, 1987; KCBA, 2005). In 1887 the smoking of opium by the Chinese but, significantly, not white Americans, was outlawed. In addition to fears around the spread of addiction were beliefs that 'drugs encouraged sexual contact between the races and threatened the purity, even the survival of the white race' (Woodiwiss, 1998: 14) mirroring similar concerns in the UK (Kohn, 1992). Associations with problem drug use also affected other populations:

> Concern about drug use in America arose from distinct associations of certain drugs with unpopular and vulnerable societal sub-groups – of opium with the Chinese, of cocaine with "Negroes," of alcohol with urban Catholic immigrants, of heroin with urban immigrants and of marijuana with Mexicans – and from the claim that a myriad of foreign enemies were using these drugs against the United States. Propaganda often contributed to popular understanding of drugs more than factual or scientific accounts (KCBA,2005).

There appears to be little evidence that the opium dens of England or of the US really were like the heinous stereotypes that portrayed them. This is a situation that seems crazy. Yet, as Morone (2003) has shown, America was no stranger to exaggeration and (re)action in the face of constructed fear and perhaps this episode in drug control history is not as unusual as it at first appears, particularly if it is taken as an example of the ways that morality helped shape American sensibilities and institutions. Morone (2003) provides numerous examples – including ones around temperance – but perhaps an example from a different 'area' helps to show how 'facts' can emerge, fear can escalate and 'truths' go unquestioned. Thus, in relation to the furore over the 'white slave episode':

> Panic spread across the nation. Dangerous young men prowled the countryside. They lured young girls into ice-cream parlors, wooed them, whisked them off to the cities, and sold them into sexual slavery. By 1910, experts reported, sixty thousand women a year were perishing in brothels. Heartbreaking screams for help echoed unanswered, in the urban night...Popular tracts warned young women away from Italian fruit stands, Chinese laundries, German skating rinks and – most dangerous of all – the Eastern European Jews...When the moral champions finally marched into the sex districts, the enslaved maidens laughed at them. There were no iron bars on the brothels, no Jews skulking behind doors, no sixty thousand perishing country girls (Morone, 2003: 2).

The opium den however does provide us with yet another link in our chain towards our understanding of where contemporary notions of the drug dealer come from – some of which are embedded within it rather than simply sitting on the surface. In the opium den sat the predatory, untrusting, devious, unscrupulous and deceitful Chinaman and provided all that was needed by way of defining 'who' the drug dealer or drug supplier was. This was an image that was brought to fulsome life in a range of genre and media but is perhaps writ largest in the many novels of Sax Rohmer such as *Dope: A story of Chinatown and the drug traffic* (1919) and the later *Tales of Chinatown* (1922). Rohmer, in another of his creations, the character Fu Manchu, personified fears of the 'Yellow Peril' and the threat to western society and its values that Chinese (and Japanese) immigrants were represented as embodying more generally.

Pedlars, peddlers, hawkers and quacks – the use of popular signifiers

By the 1920s the expression 'dope peddler' was the primary descriptor for drug sellers in the US. Pedlars, peddlers, hawkers, hucksters, hagglers, cadgers – all related terms for itinerant dealers in goods. The signifier of 'pedlar' however has a complex history and the connotations it conjures (or has done historically) are mixed. Romantic notions of the pedlar depict a salesman (they were usually male but not always) often on foot (hence the derivation from 'ped' or foot) that brings new goods to outlaying areas making a simple living (Anderson, 2000). There were of course many hard working pedlars of many types of useful goods that were honest, trustful and trusted. Many pedlars would take the same route year in year out, become known by those they travelled past and even stay with them. Less sympathetic depictions imbue the word with meanings that signify someone looking to cheat and swindle to make their money and to swiftly disappear. As in all walks of life, there were of course also those dishonest pedlars who, on seducing trust and taking advantage of it, would then vanish never to be seen again. Other important associations relate to the fact that peddling has long been associated with Jews (Naggar, 1992). In the Middle Ages, this in part related to the way that Jews were excluded from various guilds and crafts leaving them few choices of employment (Hunt and Murray, 1999). At the end of the nineteenth century in the US, peddling represented an opportunity to new immigrants, often Jews, due to the fact that there was little needed by way of setup capital to get started and the association has continued in this way (Kosak, 2000). Concerns over pedlars has also long attracted a great deal of early legislation often designed to protect local businesses against travelling outsiders who paid no local taxes and thus drew resentment from numerous corners (Friedman, 2004) and to protect locals from the dishonest (House of Commons Journal 1802; Monmouth County Records, 1994). A final negative association to couple itself to peddling came in the early part of the twentieth century with the perceived (middle-class) need to shift away from a form of street based retail practice that was represented as old-fashioned and stifling of progress, to one that was modern and progressive – indoor retail and suburban shopping (Wasserman, 1998).

The archetypal stereotype of US western 'medicine pitchmen or showmen' perhaps sums up how the pedlar has been seen and in relation to the dope pedlar even more so. From roughly 1800 to 1940 the medicine pitchman would travel all across America selling potions that promised health and cures but delivering only hope and then disappointment (Anderson, 2000). A similar relationship was held (and indeed there is often a blurring of distinction) between such people and those labelled quacks in the eighteenth and nineteenth centuries. The distinction between quacks and real doctors however, was also not always so straight-forward. Porter (2003) for example has shown how some labelled as quacks were as well qualified as those doing the labelling and were often not necessarily employing any less a scientific approach, nor sincerity to their actions than so-called 'real physicians'. There is much in the popular imagery of quacks and quackery from this period that did however help pave the way for contemporary imagery around dope pedlars and contemporary drug 'pushers'. Stereotypically they were seen as:

> ...illiterate, ignorant, often foreign, commonly Jews. They possessed no medical abilities. Their much trumpeted arts and arcane, pills and potions, were at best worthless, and all too often, positively deadly draughts. They laid claims to miraculous powers, encyclopaedic learning, wonder cures...But all this was utter bunkum. For they were nothing but liars, cheats, and impostors (Daniel Turner, 1718 cited in Porter, 2003: 16).

Porter makes the point however that quacks were always 'other people'; that no practitioner was themselves a quack but lots of others were. The 'doctors' people visited were not perceived by them as quacks but those that others visited perhaps were. All however were aware of the existence of quacks (because warnings of them were all around) and that they needed to beware them. In real terms for Porter, 'quacks' existed in the sense that there was:

> [a] real-life scatter of operators – who worked, of course, within the fields of force and the lexicon of meanings stipulated by [medical] orthodoxy...[but also] there were swarms of dealers in medicine, just as there were traders in trinkets and chapbooks, in victuals and drink, in lodgings and entertainment; quacks were regular tradesmen if they were irregular doctors (2003: 29).

In other words there was an image of 'who' quacks were and 'what' quacks 'did' and a character attributed to them which was largely immoral and distasteful but this image is largely 'phantom' – something that as we shall see has future echoes as well.

The following quote from the *New York Times* in 1908 sums up much in the way that signifiers became amalgamated:

> The "coke peddler" is a familiar figure in the back rooms of saloon dives throughout the country and every "red-Light district" has a store that caters especially to the "coke" and other "fiends". The use of "coke" is probably much more widely spread among negroes than among whites. "Heaven dust' they call it. Its use by negro field hands in the South has spread with appalling swiftness and results. there is little doubt but that every Jew peddler in the South carries the stuff, although many States have made its sale a felony.

By the 1920s then the term dope pedlar (or by then – commonly 'peddler' for this latter spelling is associated more closely with trading in *illicit* goods) was imbued with a complex mix of negative imagery. Each word had its own baggage: peddler drew on a historical and contemporary mistrust of the itinerant street seller; the 'phantom' behaviour of the quack; backwardness and (for some) the stigma of Judaism. Dope itself was associated with a whole range of immoral acts and the capability to reduce its users to shadows (both in soul and body) of their former selves – a true evil.

The 'Dope Rings' and Drug Traffickers

Although, as we have seen, concerns around opium grew slowly during the nineteenth century and the themes of moral degeneracy continued to develop by the early twentieth century in the US at least it was reaching a crescendo. Analysis of media output of this time reveals a shift in the discursive understanding of drug use and addiction from unfortunate habit to being 'increasingly described as the root of all social evil' and that by '...the mid 1920s, anti-drug reformers were describing America's "narcotics problem" in apocalyptic terms (Speaker, 2002). At the root of this apocalypse was a new 'monster' (Speaker, 2001) – the drug trafficker:

> Whenever things get a little dull in town, the drug ring sends men and women to the villages and farming communities and these men and women establish agencies in strange, unlooked-for places: cafes, livery stables, garages, ice cream parlors—everywhere. We have no deadly

mist here creeping up from any low and fetid ground, but we have this drug traffic, as deadly, as cruel, and as rapacious as Creeping Johnny [malaria] ever dared to be. Would you like to see him face to face, this Creeping Johnny that is menacing us and our children with his slow, silent, smiling, cruel, secret advance? That you can never do, for it is part of the secret of his power that he himself is always invisible. But come with me, into the Street of the Living Dead, and I will show you some of his victims (Annie Laurie, famous reporter for numerous William Randolph Hearst newspapers/publications, October 1921, cited in Speaker, 2002: 202).

Stories recounting similar tales where the young were being preyed upon and where human destruction was left in the wake of those that peddled drugs became regular media fare, with Laurie's 'series' alone running on the front page of the *Examiner* for several weeks. The Hearst crusade ran side-by-side with those of William Hobson and the Head of the Federal Bureau of Narcotics, Harry Anslinger. The result, when combined with numerous other temperance activities elsewhere, was a persistent onslaught on the sensibilities of the American public in relation to illicit drugs. In particular, the American public (and somewhat by default – much of the rest of the English speaking world) was subjected to claims about what drugs such as heroin, cocaine and cannabis did to those that used them. In this there was no ambiguity and there was no room for confusion. In relation to cannabis for example Anslinger claimed that it turned the sane mad after just a few uses, that those under its influence would murder (strangers; own family; police), kidnap, rape and torture (Speaker, 2001; Anslinger, 1937). Likewise for morphine:

Morphine addicts...are mild and harmless while their systems are full of morphine....Take it away from them and they are wild beasts of savage cruelty, absolutely impervious to any human pity or sympathy of any kind. Many of the most brutal murders in America have been committed under the urge for morphine....A harmless, good-natured boy of 17 will take two or three sniffs of "snow" and turn into a cold-blooded, cruel, bloodthirsty bandit, ready to hold up his own father and kill his own mother to get money enough to go out and buy some more "snow" (Laurie, 1927 – cited in Speaker, 2002).

The user becomes a monster, and for the first time a clear sense of the monsters that prey on the otherwise innocent comes into play. Hearst was clear on this: 'The key to control, he said, was to "GET AFTER THE RATS,"..."Seek them out where ever they hide," he continued, "and show them no mercy" (cited in Speaker, 2002: 203). The theme continued to build through the 1930s, waning at times during the 1940s but returning when a new drug scare hit the headlines. In 1951 one dealer in New York received a record sentence and the reportage left no doubt as to the justification:

> he is worse than a murderer who shoots and kills and that is the end of it. But this type engages in the business of selling drugs, even to youngsters, for profit. He kills hundreds of people slowly, day by day. He is in the business of killing people, slowly but surely." Before sentence was imposed, Sol Gelb, defense attorney, requested that the court not be swayed by "hysteria" in the imposition of sentence. Angelet when arrested last Dec. 22 was described by the police as an "associate of a Harlem narcotics syndicate of 2,000 drug peddlers who preyed on school children for the purpose of making them addicts." Angelet had a record of previous arrest. His convictions as a second offender allowed the sentence to extend beyond ten years, the limit for narcotics cases (*The New York Times*, February 28, 1951).

The production of the modern 'evil' drug dealer

Although, a broad amalgamation of images centred on drug users and drug suppliers (often blurred and combined) had emerged by the 1920s it wasn't until there was a clearly distinguishable entity that the modern conception of the drug dealer could start to take definite shape. This was in part reliant upon the existence of a distinct entity in law. In the US for example, in addition to a focus on the 'underworld', early twentieth century persecution and prosecution of drug 'sellers' had also often focussed on control over pharmacists and physicians who continued to supply cocaine and opiate based products (Spillane, 1998; Trebach, 1987). The enactment of 1914 Harrison Act however restricted supply by those professions even further, ultimately prohibiting their supply even for medicinal purposes. Many doctors were subsequently persecuted and imprisoned for supposedly[5] having supplied narcotics to drug addicts illegally whilst others lost their livelihoods from the adverse publicity that even failed prosecution brought with it (Brecher et al. 1972). Although ambiguous in its reading the Act was seized upon by law enforcement officers who interpreted it so that any doctor or pharmacist caught prescribing 'opium or coca leaves, their salts, derivatives, or preparations' to maintain or alleviate symptoms of addiction could be prosecuted. Although not initially clear on paper it was clear that law enforcement was determined to stop the supply of such drugs to those dependent on them. The tensions were resolved in 1924 when the Harrison Act was tightened up such that heroin was banned for any kind of medicinal use at all (Brecher et al. 1972). In the UK a different context produced different outcomes and whereas in the US the penal approach won out, in the UK the result was somewhat more mixed. The 'British System[6]' as it became known was a compromise between liberal supply and outright prohibition that was to last relatively unscathed for over forty years. Although the Home Office pursued an overtly penal approach in the early 1920s (Berridge, 1984) and passed the Dangerous Drugs act in 1920 in order to establish this in law, by 1926 the medical profession had won back certain privileges. The Rolleston Committee established the right of the medical profession to prescribe cocaine and opiate based (including heroin) medication where they deemed it appropriate in the management of the 'disease' of drug addiction and, of course unlike the US even today, for pain relief. In reality, and unlike in the US, the outcome of this policy compromise in the UK affected relatively few people as the numbers involved at this time were quite small (Berridge, 1984). The 1920 Dangerous Drug Act did however provide the broad framework within which the supply of drugs, outside of the medical profession, was illegal.

Unsurprisingly, one effect of prohibition in the US, by strangling the licit prescription and supply of heroin and cocaine was to create and establish a black market in these drugs and by default their sale by the unlicensed and unqualified. In the UK a black market for heroin, other opiates and cocaine, failed to materialise in part because prescribing was permitted and also because there was too little demand for one of any significant size to survive. None-the-less in this new context of international and local controls over drugs such as opium, morphine, heroin and cocaine, where licit supply was for the first time unambiguously prohibited, the drug dealer proper was born and he was located unequivocally outside of medicine and the law.

The 1940s and 1950s

In the UK, until the 1960s, there was barely anything resembling a 'drug problem'. It was what Spear (1994:6) referred to as 'The quiet times'. Convictions for possession of cannabis in 1945 for example were a paltry four. By 1950 this had risen to 79 but it wasn't until 1962 that the figures managed to get above 500 (Young, 1971). The picture for opiates and cocaine is slightly different in the sense that convictions were more numerous but ultimately, in terms of there being a problem, the situation was similar. As regards opiate and cocaine use between 1926 and 1945, although there were 2,139 convictions, around 15% of these were in professions (doctors, nurses, chemists, dentists) where access to the drugs was relatively easy (Bean, 1974). The average age was over 40 years with relatively few (13%) being under 30 years. There were few demands for strict penalties and most (75%) were fined £5 or less. In the 1930s Great Britain, somewhat meaningfully, tended to report to the League of Nations that 'drug addiction is not prevalent in Great Britain' (Bean, 1974: 99) and even by 1958 over 80% of all known addicts were listed as therapeutic in origin.

In the US the situation was greatly different. The US continued to enact various domestic legislation often based upon the kind of scaremongering used by the Federal Bureau of Narcotics and crusaders such as William Hobson in the 1920s. The early 1950s in fact saw penalties raised and toughened and often linked (in the context of the McCarthy era) with Red China flooding the US with heroin (Musto, 1987). In 1956 the Narcotic Control Act 'even permitted juries to recommend the death penalty for those convicted of sales to minors, an indication of the symbolic endangered-youth issue' (Courtwright, 2002:13). Despite this however, in terms of general trends, there followed a period until the late 1960s and early 1970s where the drug problem was redefined away from issues of supply and towards that of demand (Carstairs, 2000). Emphasis shifted away from tough penalties towards that of treatment and rehabilitation, away from punishing 'bad' people and towards helping those that were 'sick'. One consequence of this was that the mood against drugs such as cannabis, and drug users in general softened. In this sense, even in the US where the drug problem was larger than in many other western nations and was associated with inner-city non-white groups and crime, there was a period stretching from the late 1950s to the late 1960s where concerns around drugs (at least in comparison to that which had preceded it) was moderated (Musto, 1987). This was all to change at the end of the 1960s when concerns over the new 'problem' drug users around Europe and the US, in a less liberal political context, meant that drugs and those that supplied them once again became a major focus.

The 1970s and 1980s a significant shift in emphasis?

For some commentators the criminal justice, policy and popular media emphasis on drug sellers didn't actually arrive until the late 1960s, 1970s and 1980s. Green (1998: 114-115) for example argues that in the UK:

> [Referring to the late 1960s] The street level pusher, however, was in the process of being demonised, constructed in the media as preoccupied with corrupting and debauching the young and innocent (seedy characters hanging around school gates), desiring only to create new addicts in order that their own cravings for drugs be satisfied' [and that] 'the notion of the trafficker emerges in its fully fledged demonic cloak during the "law and order" informed 1980s.

Brownstein (1999), for the US, suggests that prior to Nixon in 1971 and Reagan in 1982, the war on drugs was focussed on users not dealers and it was only with the consolidation of the supply side approach to the war on drugs in 1989 (ONCDP, 1989) that the war on dealers was finally declared. Whilst, for modern sensibilities it might seem that the modern drug dealer emerged from images of organised crime trafficking in drugs in the 1970s and crack sellers in New York in the 1980s, and that the new wars on drugs were a break from the recent past this is an exaggeration. Carstairs (2005) for example refers to the 'three cumulative stages' of international drug control and that supply control policy actually sandwiches that of demand control and user criminalisation that characterised the mid-twentieth century. In part, for the US, this may be explained by what Boyd (2004: 51-53) has described as a period where there was a break in temperance ideology which emerges again with the latest drug wars (of Nixon and Reagan) which were a conservative reaction to the 'liberal antiauthoritarianism of 1960s' and about 'getting back' and protecting family and other traditional values. It is true enough to say that a re-invigorated campaign against traffickers and dealers took off in the latter part of the twentieth century. Also, that it had its own antecedents and even new foci – such as the prevention of money laundering and interventions in producer countries – but it is untrue to say that this was either essentially new, uninformed by a past history or that the demonisation of the 'pusher' was in the *process* of construction. As we have already seen the essential elements needed to construct the 'demonic cloak' had long been in formation and even if a clearer 'ideological distinction between the two (users and dealers) emerged in debates in the 1960s' (Green, 1998: 112) it did so only against a backdrop of shifting sands where the dealer was already a clear entity[7]. This (UK) picture is partly muddied (for Green) because for the UK at least, as Lewis et al (1985) points out, until the 1960s an illicit drug market didn't really exist and there would have been little direct reference to them in the media or in policy debate. Images were largely therefore drawn from historical representation and from the US where the ideological distinction had existed for much longer (cf. Waldorf, 1973). The distinction though was easily made when such a market arrived – images were 'off the shelf' – not newly formed.

Contemporary images of the drug dealer

What conclusions then can we come to about the historical formation of images around the drug dealer and/or trafficker? To start with we can see that they are inextricably bound to concerns over drug users and (often) the introduction of new substances (or ways of using extant ones) but that they are none-the-less distinct from these in some important ways. It is certainly the case that concerns about supply usually follow concerns about use and that depending on the broader economic, cultural or political context (rather than any intrinsic property of the substance in question) will be more or less reactive. As we have seen, historically the introduction of a new substance can be met with fear and reaction only to become accepted and integrated into day-today life or it can slowly over time be part of parcel of normal life only to become considered dangerous at a later time. There is no doubt that the place of opium in China plays an important role in how the West came to comprehend its supposed effects on individual and society and for the sake of this chapter the way that the supply of opium by the British went from acceptable trading activity to indefensible and immoral conduct. For many at the time the 'Chinese experience' showed that opium could destroy lives, communities and even nations and it also served to demonstrate that there was proper and improper use, manufacture and supply of substances such as opium. The British became tarnished with accusations of indefensible moral conduct in forcing China to open its shores to opium. Supplying opium – other than for medical purposes – became anathema. Medical use (and control of supply) was legitimate whilst non-medical use needed to be controlled to protect the individual and society more broadly. All the while opiates and derivatives such as morphine and heroin, along with cocaine, were not prohibited (or effectively so as in the UK) blame for their supply and 'leakage' for improper use was laid at the door of pharmacists, doctors, and other pedlars acting inappropriately, or at the door of the Chinese in their dens of iniquity. A range of signifiers relating to quackery, pedlars, Jews, deviousness, untrustworthiness, trickery and lack of consideration imbue the image of the dope peddler that became common from the 1920s. These images in turn had built on associations with opium dens and other criminal populations with which drug use and selling had become linked. In the 1980s with the emergence of new drug scares and new drug problems the 'evil' dealer and trafficker took taken centre stage and more than at any time in the past two hundred years (and probably at any time before) became the focus of media, political and public concern.

Current defining aspects of the drug dealer

There are a number of current images of the drug dealer that are, arguably, the linchpins on how the drug market is thought to work, how the drug dealer is believed to operate and as a consequence – because we should be judged by our actions – how drug dealers should be understood. Key, in my opinion, is the belief in dangerous adulteration – the 'cutting' of drugs such as heroin and cocaine with a range of dangerous substances such as strychnine (rat-poison); ground glass; scouring powders and the like to dilute the product and thereby make more profit from each sale. Such substances are used (so it goes) because the dealer will use anything that can be blended in with the drug in question that will go unnoticed by the user at the point of sale and they care little if these substances are dangerous because once the sale is made they are not concerned with any further outcomes. Belief in dangerous adulteration is almost an uncontested truth and as such provides 'proof' that other 'evil' dealer activities are all the more possible – activities such as the provision of free drugs to 'hook' new users, especially children. Children are also thought to be preyed upon by dealers hanging outside school gates or on street corners. It is through such activities that heroin, cocaine and other drug use is thought to be spread across communities. Thus, the 'pusher' – the dealer that seeks to spread drug use indiscriminately – is the worst kind of criminal. The drug markets, within which they operate, are by extension the worst kinds of criminal market, violent and unforgiving and because of the contagious and transforming nature of the drugs they push, increasingly affecting all of our lives. It is these concerns and characterisations that we will now explore.

Footnotes

[1] I am concerned here with the emergence of the particular drug dealer images and associations that came with the modern prohibition of opium and cocaine. There is no doubt that those associated with the illicit sales of prohibited substances, be they tea, coffee, cannabis or tobacco (as well as numerous foods and spices and even games/sports) at other points in the past have met with moral disapproval and were similarly condemned as were the 'bandits' and 'rascals' dealing in opium in Imperial China in 1811 (Fu, Lo-Shu, 1966).

[2] By natural I mean that the cultural norms of the group combined with any obvious environmental conditions that would influence forms of use (e.g. coca or opium chewing in the Andes or areas now demarcated as being in India respectively) as well as the properties of the intoxicant involved.

[3] For a more in-depth exploration of the antecedents and effects of the two wars please refer to Tan Chung, 1978 and Wakeman, 1997.

[4] This is not surprising given that England and the United States had a close relationship and were (as they remain today) cognisant of developments in the medical professions and the workings of their respective governments and trajectory of policy. Similar reforms were also taking place in other European countries but the momentum for national and international reform was largely led by these two world powers.

[5] The 1914 Harrison Act was not thought to be a law of prohibition when initially passed through Congress. It was only intended to be a means of taxing, regulating and controlling aspects of drug marketing and distribution. Its *interpretation* as an act of prohibition by Federal Agents however turned it effectively into an act of prohibition (Brecher, 1972).

[6] As Berridge (1984) notes however the British System was only allowed to exist whilst those being treated and managed to it were not seen as problem drug users. Once a new group of young hedonistic users entered the system in the 1960s the system was revised and tougher measures were imposed.

[7] Indeed perhaps an even clearer entity as the 1960s and other later divisions suggested a clearer distinction between users and dealers than is perhaps reasonably the case – either then or now.

Chapter 2:

Freebies, credit and 'hooking' the young and vulnerable

When the shades of night are falling,
comes a fellow everyone knows.
It's the old dope peddler,
Spreading joy wherever he goes.

Every evening you will find him,
around our neighbourhood.
It's the old dope peddler
doing well by doing good.

He gives the kids free samples,
because he knows full well
that today's young innocent faces
will be tomorrow's clientele.

Here's a cure for all your troubles,
here's an end to all distress.
It's the old dope peddler
with his powdered happiness.

Lyrics[1] to *The Old Dope Peddler* (1953) by Tom Lehrer ©

One prominent belief about the drug dealer is that he preys on the young and innocent in an attempt to expand his customer base: 'Evil Drug Dealers Stalking Every Child in Britain' (*Daily Express*, August 21, 2001, p1). The idea that the evil drug dealer is 'out there' standing on street corners, outside the school gates or leaning from ice-cream vans (using them as a cover and as a means through which to access children) is rarely contested, neither is the idea that they are seeking to 'push' their drugs on to anyone who passes by regardless of age, experience or demeanour. Dealers are said to push (*actively* pursue and entice) their drugs to make money and they care not how they make it nor of the consequences of their actions to those who buy from them.

That beliefs such as this are widely believed and largely uncontested is partly evidenced by a story casually related to me over lunch one day in 2000 by a senior social scientist upon learning of my research interest. Someone, normally of critical faculty, related to me that she knew of an instance involving drug dealing that I might be interested in. Some years ago she told me, when she had been a schoolteacher, a van had been parked in the school playground all morning, each day for a week. Nobody knew what it was there for but it was revealed after it had gone that it had in fact been drug dealers selling drugs to the school children. Amazing huh? The bare faced cheek of it! Now, this story, with suitable moral condemnation, had no doubt been relayed to numerous individuals in social and private gatherings, and had apparently gone unquestioned. For many who listened it probably reinforced existing beliefs and offered yet more 'proof' for those beliefs about evil drug dealers and the lengths they will go to make a sale. What concerned me initially about this story, (which seemed to be proof of such acts given that this was 'first-hand evidence' – my colleague had actually been there) was how the van and its inhabitants avoided questioning by schoolteachers or other staff, and why none of the children had reported this to either their teachers or their parents. After all, even in areas of utmost deprivation and/or high drug use, surely this wouldn't be seen by all schoolchildren as normal and unproblematic? I instantly mused further: why would drug dealers expose themselves in an enclosed space just waiting to be arrested? None of it seemed to make any sense. Moreover, my experience of schools is that any adult 'hanging around' within school grounds for any period of time, never mind actually being in the playground would quickly be intercepted, questioned and assessed as to whether their presence was legitimate or not. If this does not happen very quickly it certainly wouldn't take numerous days. How was it, I asked, that they were not confronted – what kind of a school was this? My colleague (just a little ruffled) wasn't too clear on this as it now emerged that in fact this was a story she had been told about, when at this school by other teachers in the staff room after a discussion about a child in the school who was thought to be 'high' on drugs. Moreover (after further gentle interrogation) it emerged that it may in fact have not been that school but another! The story had gone from apparent first hand evidence of dealers selling to schoolchildren to one of unsubstantiated hearsay of the type found in tabloids in the middle of a drug scare.

My second foray into the minutiae of drug market activities – looking at the provision of free drugs and credit emerged almost naturally from my research on dangerous adulteration and probably from being exposed to stories such as that related above. The adulteration research – as we shall see in the next chapter – had shown that what people thought drug dealers 'did' to the drugs they sold was largely false and this had started me questioning more forcefully other assumed aspects of the drug market. In particular one directly related adulteration 'myth' is that ecstasy is cut with heroin to secretly get ecstasy users hooked on heroin to ensure new and reliable custom. In addition to this, through familiarity with various drug field literatures, I was aware that some of the justifications behind why the provision of free drugs and credit was thought to occur were reliant upon the problematic notion of instant addiction and an illogic of how illicit trade likely occurs. By way of explicating this issue more thoroughly I will outline what is commonly believed about why drug dealers provide free drugs and credit, provide some insight into why this is likely to be a faulty perspective and finally through presentation of the findings of empirical research with drug dealers and drug users from various markets in London and Sydney discuss the real role and rationale of the provision of free drugs and credit – when indeed it does occur.

The notion in a nutshell

The idea that much addictive drug use results from the actions of unscrupulous drug dealers 'pushing' the drugs they sell onto the young, naïve, vulnerable and innocent has been long held and continues to have resonance. Moreover, the accompanying notion that this often involves them giving away free drugs (freebies) to firstly 'hook' (*addict*) the young, naïve, vulnerable and innocent to the drug and secondly, once hooked, to ensnare them as a 'client' encourages a particular view of what the drug problem is and who, in part at least, is to blame for it. Although these notions are not as 'universally' accepted as some beliefs about how dealers operate, such as dangerous adulteration – largely because the drugs field literature does contest that initiation into drugs is usually via friends, family or known acquaintances (McIntosh et al. 2003) – it none-the-less remains as an oft considered route to drug use and addiction by those less acquainted with such literature. In particular and as will be shown later, it is reasonably well ingrained in the popular consciousness as one of the dangers 'out there' that we all need to be so wary of in this age of ubiquitous risk. If it is the case that the 'pushing' of drugs in the manner described above is a real and significant risk then such concern is justified. However, if the belief is either untrue or grossly exaggerated, emphasising danger from 'the pusher' at the expense of those more familiar and trusted by us serves only to distract from where drug initiation is most likely to occur and the aim to prevent drug use will as a consequence, be undermined not reinforced.

Not a new idea

In 1928 one of the most authoritative books on opium and heroin addiction to be published at that time *The Opium Problem* (Terry and Pellens, 1928: 87) referred to the 'drug peddler' whose practice was to give away sufficient amounts of a drug to get the user addicted and then once the user was addicted to charge the user for their drugs with sufficient mark up to cover previous losses. In fact this was put forward as one epidemiological rationale for how opium and heroin addiction was spreading around the US at that time. It is likely that even at this time the idea was fairly well entrenched as a few years earlier *The New York Times* had put a similar spin on how drug use was thought to be spread:

> It is the custom to give away heroin free to the youth until he or she is "hooked." When children are away from home it is a safe practice to accept nothing as a gift to eat, drink or whiff, not even from a supposed friend. When you decline the first offer the boy or girl aiding the peddler will taunt you or challenge you and say "try anything once, you will get a kick out of it"; "watch me"; "come to our 'snow party' and watch the other fellows do it." But once is once too often. The poison is so swift that the poor youth will seek the next party for relief, and the next. A

"snow party" a day for a week will drag a youth into the bondage of addiction worse than death, and from which experience teaches there is no sure escape (*The New York Times,* November 9, 1924).

By the early 1940s, Lindesmith (1941: 204), stating that: 'No evidence has been produced to show that this sort of thing is actually done' was concerned that reports of this kind and such ideas were still being widely propagated. Not only he claimed, was there a lack of evidence to suggest that drug dealers entice the non-drug user with free drugs but there were (and it remains the case) a number of good reasons why such an approach to peddling (pushing) would be actively avoided by the drug dealer. To begin with and perhaps crucially, new users to addictive drugs such as heroin are not addicted particularly quickly. The impression given in *The New York Times* quote above repeats the oft believed but fallacious idea of 'one try and you're hooked'. This is an idea about drugs such as heroin that is not only believed by many lay persons but by many drug users as well. What research that has looked at this issue however (Coomber & Sutton, 2006; Bennett, 1986; Waldorf, 1973) reveals that the process of becoming addicted to heroin by users 'on the street' (as opposed to rats in experiments or therapeutic users given the drug to fight pain) is one that takes on average around six months to one year and for many it is even longer[2]. Thus, as addiction to drugs such as heroin normally takes many months a dealer would not be able to afford to subsidise one, never mind numerous new users in the hope that they would become addicted and then stay with that dealer once addicted for their supplies. Secondly, non-users, particularly children, could not be trusted not to tell others that they were being given free drugs. The risk of exposure, arrest and thus incarceration to the dealer who chooses this route of recruitment would be so high as to make it a highly unlikely activity. Kaplan (1983) and Pearson (1987) are but two researchers that have more recently questioned the wisdom (and the evidence) that drug dealers provide free drugs such as heroin to entice those that are not already users although this is a very under-researched aspect of drug markets.

'Freebies', 'hooking' and adulteration

There are a number of drugs that the idea of giving away free drugs as an attempt to hook the users just cannot be applied to but none-the-less are.

Simply put, drugs such as cannabis, ecstasy, LSD and many of the so-called 'dance' drugs are not addictive drugs in the normative sense[3]. As such, giving free samples of these drugs to new users would be a fruitless and expensive endeavour. Such a fact has not prevented these drugs being represented differently however and in the famous US anti-drug propaganda films *Reefer Madness* (1938), the Anslinger influenced *To the Ends of the Earth* (1948) and *High School Confidential* (1958) cannabis is portrayed in these films as highly addictive and pushed by unscrupulous dealers onto the young. Other drugs such as heroin and cocaine are drugs of addiction but not, as noted above, in a way that is commonly attributed to them. The notion, believed by many users (Forsyth, 1995; McElrath and McEvoy, 2001) that ecstasy is adulterated with heroin is a moderated version of the 'freebies' story. Dealers wanting to secure a reliable clientele cut their ecstasy with heroin to hook the user who will then unknowingly come back to them 'needing' more drugs. One young male user explains it thus: 'Some of them [ecstasy tablets] are different to each other – have different combinations of drugs in them. Such as more heroin and less crack' (Maryland Drug Early Warning System, 2002). The belief is sustained in a number of ways. To begin with it is part and parcel of folklore regarding ecstasy tablets and as such most ecstasy users have heard of the 'existence' of ecstasy laced with heroin: 'Mitsubishi, for example is Ecstasy cut with additional speed which causes increased hyperactivity. Mercedes is Ecstasy cut with heroin' (student ecstasy user reporting to the Daily Trojan, a student paper of the University of Southern California, 2000). Commonly and perhaps somewhat logically, it will be tablets with brown 'speckles' that will gain such a reputation. Secondly, it is common for drug users, even experienced ones, whose 'trip' is in some way different to previous experiences (particularly where there is some unwanted physical consequence; stomach ache; sweating; nausea, etc) not normally experienced, to blame the negative experience on adulterated drugs and in the case of ecstasy, adulteration with heroin. Lastly, the folklore of heroin in ecstasy is perpetuated by reports of it in the media. It is not uncommon for police officers interviewed about the death of a drug user to assert (based on personal assumption and without forensic confirmation) that a dangerous adulterant is the likely reason for the death: 'The pills bought by the deceased were *presumed* to be "ecstasy" or "ecstasy" laced with heroin and/or cocaine' (Florida Department of Law Enforcement, 2000, my emphasis). It is the case that the print and electronic media, usually quoting a police source, regularly report on drug deaths in this way.

Whilst it is the case that 'fakes' or counterfeits of ecstasy and other drugs are sometimes sold to users there are however, no recorded instances of heroin or cocaine being found as adulterants in ecstasy[4] in the many tens of thousands of pills tested worldwide (Coomber, 1997). The idea then that drugs are adulterated with addictive substances designed to hook the unsuspecting into being compulsive drugs users appears to have little credence either in terms of how freebies and credit are actually used in the drugs market place, nor indeed in terms of the pharmacological actions of the drugs and how addiction occurs. A belief in these behaviours however remains strong.

Despite protestations from researchers such as Lindesmith all those years ago, and others more recently, the idea of the pusher at the street corner, at the school gate, leaning out of the ice-cream van (or indeed parked in the playground) has not gone away. In 1996 a New York Professor proselytised:

> The war on drugs creates other casualties beyond those arrested. There are the ones killed in fights over turf; innocents caught in crossfire; citizens terrified of city streets; escalating robberies; *children given free crack to get them addicted and then enlisted as runners and dealers* (Wink, 1996, my emphasis)

and in a similar vein:

> What are we teaching our children? What are we doing to prevent them from using drugs at an age when they are still innocent and vulnerable? Drugs are, I believe, one of the greatest dangers facing us today. Drug dealers roam our schools, offering ten-, twelve-, and fourteen-year-old children free drugs to get them hooked. I cannot tell you how harsh I would be if I were a judge, sentencing these drug dealers, these death merchants (Wiesel, 1997 – 'Ethical Issues for Today'. Carnegie Council on Ethics and International Affairs: Louis Nizer Lectures on Public Policy).

Such ideas however clearly also emanate from supposedly more authoritative sources. Freemantle in *The Fix* (1986) – a book about drug trafficking – uncritically cites firstly Detective Chief John Veitich, Head of Edinburgh's drug squad as bemoaning that:

> The traffickers frequently get new addicts by offering a "loss leader," like supermarkets, giving away as much as thirty-one grains for nothing until their new customer is hooked (p130).

and then (again uncritically) goes on to quote William Skelton, chairman of the Merseyside Drug Council as saying:

> Dealers hang around the roads leading to schools in Liverpool and let the kids have it for nothing until they're hooked...They don't call it heroin, to avoid frightening the kids. they call it happy powder or some other fanciful name. And they say it's not necessary to inject, in case the needle frightens them, too. They teach them how to "Chase the Dragon." After the introduction, of course, the paying starts. And the price goes up, from $6 to $12 a shot (Freemantle, 1986: 133).

In 2002 it was reported that a new law being considered would crack down on those dealers that target schoolchildren:

> Drug dealers who target children at the school gate could face longer jail sentences under a new law being considered by the government. Ministers are discussing a new offence of aggravated drug dealing to tackle those who see children as lucrative customers, said Ivan Lewis, the minister for young people and learning (BBC News, 2002).

It is perhaps easy to see why such a rationale for drug dealing would emerge. Drugs are feared. Drug use by the young is feared in particular. Drug dealers are considered to be less than average in terms of moral standards and the idea of providing enticements is one we are very familiar with in everyday trading transactions. 'Special offers' in many shops provide the buy one get one free approach to selling, or the buy this product and get 20% extra. The intention is to either entice new custom from those who might normally use another brand and/or to cement customer loyalty to existing customers who may have been looking at alternative products.

An idea that permeates our culture?

That the general idea of dealers giving away free drugs permeates our culture in all sorts of ways is visible beyond the type of evangelical posturings of Wink or Wiesal quoted above. All around us are both direct and indirect references to its supposed existence and prevalence. Reference can be found for example in the way that major pharmaceutical companies are often reported as 'pushing' freebies to doctors to get them to prescribe their brand of drugs (*USA Today*, 2006; Irish Parliament Joint Committee on Health and Children, 1998; *Time*, 2005). The analogy is a direct one and a casual exploration on a search engine such as Google (search: 'freebies' drug) will provide the reader with numerous other examples of those being condemned for unscrupulously giving away free goods to entice people to do something the marketers want and it is often with direct reference to how this is the same as that undertaken by drug dealers.

Sometimes the analogy is used merely as a helpful aside with less concentration (and thus more casual acceptance?) on dealing activity:

> Internet affairs are increasingly common, unfortunately. The anonymity is seductive, and given our growing social isolation, it's a tempting way to act out and connect. It often begins innocently enough. But it's like the drug pusher on the corner telling you the first hit is free; after that, be prepared to pay a price for your addiction. That price could be your relationship (Third Age, 2006).

Indirect reference in a similar vein may also be made in the form of common humour. The following joke, which compares computer software developers to drug dealers, again arguably sums up common currency on the way dealers are thought to operate:

Drug Dealers vs. Computers

Drug dealers	Software developers
Refer to their clients as "users".	Refer to their clients as "users".
"The first one's free!"	"Download a free trial version..."
Have important South-East Asian connections (to help move the stuff).	Have important South-East Asian connections (to help debug the code).
Strange jargon: "Stick," "Rock," "Dime bag," "E."	Strange jargon: "SCSI," "RTFM," "Java," "ISDN."
Realize that there's tons of cash in the 14- to 25-year-old market.	Realize that there's tons of cash in the 14- to 25-year-old market.
Job is assisted by the industry's producing newer, more potent mixes.	Job is assisted by the industry's producing newer, faster machines.
Often seen in the company of pimps and hustlers.	Often seen in the company of marketing people and venture capitalists.
Their product causes unhealthy addictions.	DOOM. Quake. SimCity. Duke Nukem

(CyberiaPC.com, 2006)

These analogies are of course drawing attention to the unreasonable and corrupt nature of enticement as entrapment. That such a belief is common currency is arguably further evidenced by the fact that one British primary school (ages 5-11) has gone so far as to update Prokofiev's *Peter and the Wolf* to parody the dangers to children on poor local authority housing estates:

> Her step-father advises Anita not stray to far from the house, especially after dusk, and warns her about the kind of people she might run into. In particular a nasty and highly dangerous drug dealer called Ben Wolf ...in the park they are met by Ben Wolf, *who entices them with offers of free drugs*. Duckie McGowan decides to try it, and for a few moments seems OK. Then suddenly he collapses on the ground and appears to have stopped breathing. (Anita and the wolf, 2002). My emphasis.

There are also numerous popular songs that over the years have also perpetuated a number of drug dealer images including various aspects of 'pushing' such as Steppenwolf's *The Pusher* (1968); Curtis Mayfield's *Freddie's Dead* (1972), Baldwin & Leps The Dealer (1971); or more recently, Didjits *The Man* (1992), Frogs *I've got Drugs out of the Mist* (1989); Boogie Down Productions *Drug Dealer* (1992); Tom Waites re-released *Ice Cream Man* (1991) and DJ Magic Mike's *What I Gotta* (2001). Let's remind ourselves of one of the earlier examples, Tom Lehrer's *The Old Dope Peddler* (1952) which in verse three had this to say:

> He gives the kids free samples,
> Because he knows full well
> That today's young innocent faces
> Will be tomorrow's clientele

If analogy, parody or allegory is lost on some of us there are those that spell it out – as we have seen – in straight and simple language. A Canadian radio talk-show host/counsellor, a supposed authority on drug problems, recently declared without substantiation (because the things we 'know' do not need substantiation? – see Coomber 1997b):

> A pusher will ask: "Are you rolling?" to a raver. If the answer is: "No", then a free sample is offered. Ecstasy is so addictive that even a single use may be enough to start an addiction (Elliot, 2000).

Clearly this 'authority' has a poor understanding not only of pharmacology but also of the nature of addiction but it doesn't stop him from making bold statements to his listening public about either, nor indeed about aspects of how the drug market is assumed to work. Does his audience know (or indeed want to know) any better?

A number of films, such as Spike Lee's *Clockers* (1995); Nicolas Winding Refn's *Pusher* (1996); Danny Boyles *Trainspotting* (1996); BJack Hill's *Coffy* (1973); J. Lee Thompson's *Death Wish 4* (1987); Fernando Meirelles and Katia Lund's *City of God* (2003) amongst many others, have depicted various dealing stereotypes including that of dealers providing free drugs whilst television shows too numerous to mention have done likewise[5].

That the idea of dealers providing free samples to the young, naïve and vulnerable is of common currency we need only refer (as I have in passing above) to the various ways in which it is integrated into cultural representations of the practice and how others who are being maligned can be similarly 'tarred' with one of the most evil of available brushes. Such beliefs also gain currency from other beliefs. As has been argued elsewhere (Coomber, 1997c) each of the various dealer myths serves to support the others. If for example the heinous practice of dangerous adulteration is commonly believed then an equally heinous behaviour of pushing to the young, uninitiated and vulnerable by offering freebies is also easier to believe and vice versa.

No smoke without fire?

Does the provision of free drugs take place? There is almost no research into whether free drugs are provided by drug dealers or indeed under what circumstances they are given if they are. A few pieces of research have referred to it as an aside in relation to other aspects of the research being outlined (Jacobs and Miller, 1998; Jacobs, 1999; Caulkins et al. 1999; Skolnick et al. 1997) but little attempt has been made to understand the nature of 'freebies' in drug market transactions in any detail.

A range of research that has focussed on other aspects of drug market interactions however does provide some fuller insight and further context into the issue. Much of the prominent illicit drug market research literature such as Adler (1985), Adler and Adler (1983; 1994) and Murphy et al. (1990) reporting on the social/business networks of upper-level cocaine and marijuana smugglers and dealers and middle-class dealers respectively, do not at first glance appear to have much resonance with the issue in hand. The provision of freebies, as evidenced by the various quotes and representations above, is really thought to apply to the 'street dealer'. The dealer who preys on the uninitiated or vulnerable looking to 'push' their wares and then hook them as customers. The dealers in Murphy et al.'s (1990) research were considered to be – dealing apart – no different from any other normal law abiding US citizen. Most became dealers through supply to friends and thereafter maintained good networks to maintain and facilitate new clients. Similarly Adler and Adler (1983; 1994) report extensive and varying networks, from closely bonded and friendly ties to those that were either known by reputation and/or occasional business. New business was carefully controlled and tended to involve use of the network, amongst other factors, to maintain security:

> Dealing circles were generally very close, tightly knit groups who were mutually compatible personally, socially, and demographically. They attracted people of roughly the same age, race and ethnic origin who conducted their business along similar standards of security, reliability, involvement and commitment (Adler and Adler, 1994: 311).

These individuals then, working within relatively closed markets[6], were concerned for their own security and for those with whom they worked, and to accrue new business in a way that militates against the kind of practices associated with the giving of free drugs in the public mind. The kind of 'pushing' being explored in this chapter would present unacceptable risks to such individuals and groups. It is the dealers on 'the corner' and on the 'street' who need to be considered. It would be wrong however to simply assume that 'open markets' operate with no informal controls to protect sellers from the buyer who is potentially from a law enforcement agency. A whole range of research, mostly (but not exclusively) from North America, has borne witness to the way that lower-level dealers 'vet' prospective buyers that are unknown to them, looking for any sign that they are not bona-fide drug users (Jacobs, 1999; Knowles, 1999; Jacobs and Miller, 1998; Mieczkowski 1990; Chitwood et al. 1996, Edmunds et al. 1996; Coomber, 2003). Street dealers in open markets also have their 'faces', their regulars and their irregulars. They may operate within a market set-up that provides relatively less security than those operating from closed markets but it is not the case that no security measures are in place or that they care little for them.

The kind of ultra-competitive open markets that operated in New York in the mid-1980s when crack cocaine was fast emerging as one of the most profitable drugs to sell is arguably the kind of drug market that many believe to be typical. In the wake of the decline of organised heroin distribution and the lack of law enforcement attention that accompanied it; the emergence of new independent 'entrepreneurs' and small dealing groups not versed in the 'old ways' (Andrade et al. 1999), and general economic decline all contributed to a high level of market destabilisation. We also need to acknowledge that most new markets do not show the level of openness that accompanied the rise of crack cocaine in the US and indeed the destabilisation experienced in the crack market there, what led Fagan and Chin (1990) to view it as typical of crack markets did not happen in other countries. In fact, the plateauing out of the crack market and then its relative decline (Golub et al. 1994; 1997) in New York has led to a shift of selling from aggressively competitive approaches to a more 'socially bonded' mode of organisation where 'co-operation and inter-reliance' have come to predominate (Curtis and Wendel, 2000; 1999). Other factors such as aggressive or 'zero tolerance' policing of drug markets can also reduce the prevalence of open markets and move dealing 'indoors' and 'off the street' in the sense that sellers become less visible and thus less accessible to law enforcement. A decline in visibility brings with it a concomitant increase in closure or barriers and thus, protection of the seller. Access to a seller needs to be through a known contact and some groups may enhance this by selling/dealing only within their own kinship, ethnic or tightly bonded social groups (Curtis and Wendel, 1999; Edmunds et al. 1996). In the UK, closed markets of lone operators or involving small numbers of closely connected individuals, likely predominate (Dorn et al. 1992; Parker et al. 1998, May et al. 2000) as they may increasingly also do in the US (Andrade et al. 1999; Jacobs, 1999) and other parts of Europe (Paoli, 2001). If this is the case then rather than seeing the unscrupulous pushing of free samples of addictive drugs onto the uninitiated, young and vulnerable we are arguably more likely to have a market situation whereby such individuals are less likely to knowingly come into contact with a dealer than where open markets predominate.

Closed markets are more reliant on the forms of social interaction and networking described by Adler and Adler (1994) than open markets, as an emphasis on maintaining a consistent client base is of greater importance. For Prus (1989a,b) this will motivate those involved, regardless of the licit or illicit nature of the enterprise, to adopt aspects of buying and selling that are generic to all such market activities. This is because all individuals involved in the pursuit of sales will need – if their custom is not to be short lived – to instil trust in their clients and doing this will involve a range of cultivating devices. Jacobs (1999), drawing on Prus (1989a,b) and Bigus (1972) has discussed such issues in relation to crack dealers in the US and specifically refers to the various techniques of 'cultivation' used by dealers to cultivate loyalty and custom in an arena of high competition. Jacobs discusses both the provision of extra 'free' samples and credit in relation to loyalty creating activity and the management of the control over the buyer. Some support for Jacobs' perspective on the meaning of credit was found in the research outlined below but it is important to note that the use of freebies and credit to *existing* drug users is quite distinct from the stereotype outlined previously where such activity is thought to prey on the non-drug or non-addicted user.

It was the specific aim of the research outlined here to provide some empirical basis through which explore these issues further – both from the perspective of the dealer and the buyer. The provision of free drugs has certainly been recorded in other research and is also confirmed by the research presented here. Little evidence (if any) however was found to support the conventional rationale for its existence – the enticement of non-users to an addicted lifestyle for the beneficence of the dealer involved. A second concern of this research was to explore the related, but distinct, practice of the provision of 'credit' to buyers, its prevalence, its rationale and its place in dealing dynamics.

The issue is an important one. As with the common perception of dangerous adulteration the idea of the evil dealer 'pushing' his wares onto to the unsuspecting or merely curious helps produce a relatively dehumanised and homogenous image of what drug dealers are (inhumane/inhuman) and the kind of practices they use to obtain new customers and maximise their profit margins. If however, the belief is for all practical purposes untrue then the image of who and what the drug dealer 'is' is fundamentally undermined as is a particular view of the nature of the drug problem itself. It is fundamentally unhelpful to concentrate public minds and fears on the imagined 'pusher' when survey after survey relates to us that first use, and use thereafter, is in the company of friends, family or acquaintances and that the drugs provided came also from those sources. Sincere warnings about how to avoid initial drug use should focus on where that danger lays not on some likely imagined encounter. The possible consequences for criminal justice and educational policy are thus highly significant.

The real role of freebies and credit in the illicit drug market

The research carried out in London in 2000/1 accessed 21 convicted drug dealers (interviewed in prison) and 60 heroin users from numerous localities around London. The research in Sydney, Australia carried out in 2001/2 focussed on the two most notorious drug markets in that region – Kings Cross and Cabramatta and undertook to interview 'street' heroin dealers only in both locations (n32). The London sample of dealers ranged from a 'front-line' dealer who sold on the streets to passers-by; friend dealers; house dealers; wholesalers and importers to 'couriers'. The sample was not restricted to sellers of one type of drug and 12 had sold 4 or more types of drug with 5 of the sample having sold 6 types of drug or more. The prison was an adult male only institution and as such all interviewees were males over the age of 18 with an average age of 34 years. The Australian dealers were all open market street dealers, 25 were male and 7 were women, and they had an average age of 29 years. The 60 users in the London sample (45 males) had a mean age of 32 years. The mean number of years of heroin use for the users sample was 10.4 years evidencing their obvious experience. For all respondents in all locations questions about the provision of free drugs and credit was immersed within a broader enquiry about being a user or seller of drugs and as such little emphasis was given to these at the time. For more detailed information on both studies see Coomber (2003b) and Coomber & Maher (2006).

'Freebies'

Although some of the dealers said that they did provide free drugs none of the Sydney street dealers reported doing so as a means of soliciting new customers. For these individuals the commonest sale was a single small purchase. Some incentive was available however for the regular buyer:

> Not with like when you're dealing small, you don't give a sample. When you deal small you don't give a sample, only when you deal big ... sometimes I just give them some free one because you know, if they get like four or five times a day I give them a free one
> (28 year-old Asian-Australian male, Cabramatta)

Similarly, thirteen of the London dealers also said that they would provide free drugs but the circumstances within which this happened were, for nearly all of them, tightly circumscribed by existing and trustworthy relationships. None of the dealers said that they would use the promise of free drugs to entice non-users and this was consistent with the fact that it also emerged that nearly all of the dealers were very careful about to whom they sold drugs and how they needed to have some knowledge of an individual before they would start to sell them drugs (e.g. vouched for by existing contact).

Of those that said that they do or would provide free drugs the circumstances reported under which this would tale place were: only to trusted contacts or regular clients and that this would mainly come in the form of 'testers' 'to let them test for strength' and/or in order to allow them to 'see I've got the best'. Others said that it would be only 'friends' that would benefit in this way. It will be the case however that a client base and friend base are often, at least partially, overlapping. One dealer reported having given out free drugs when 'trying to impress a woman' but even then it was only with 'regular clients' and would be restricted to a 'tester'. Two others did state that it was 'standard procedure' to provide free drugs but in one case this actually meant the provision of *extra* drugs when the buyer had bought a certain amount:

> Yes. If someone bought five rocks they'd get one free

Another related a similar approach:

> Yes. Depends on how much you have at any one time, for example if I've got 500 E's (ecstasy tablets) I can afford to give 6 (tablets) instead of 5

The dealer that talked of the provision of free drugs being 'standard procedure' had also clearly stipulated that it 'depends on the buyer' and as such was likely to relate to the provision of testers or extras to regular and reliable clients. Only one 'front-line' dealer, a dealer who operated on the street in the Ladbroke Grove area of North London, stated that he regularly used the enticement of free drugs to get ('touting') new clients (without knowing anything about them). Even here however the individual involved was clear that he could 'tell' a user and that he was essentially looking to draw users away from competition (in a busy open market place) and that the provision of free drugs (a taster) would be so that the user could experience the quality of his samples. In a similar vein he also claimed that he would be forced to give the odd 'freebie' if he knew an existing customer was (or was thinking of) buying elsewhere.

The users' perspectives on, and experience of, the provision of free drugs was supportive of the narratives provided by the sellers. It is worth recollecting that the average length of time that the users that were interviewed had been dependent on heroin and/or other opiates for example was over 10 years. Within this context of extensive experience, 15 of the 60 said that they had never been given any free drugs and of these many of them simply didn't believe it was a true aspect of the drug market. One 40 year old male user with a 15 year habit merely responded to this question:

> No, this is a dream. No money, no give nothing

Of those that said they had been offered free drugs by drug dealers, none reported an offer by a dealer that didn't know that they were already drug users and in fact the vast majority stressed that the provision of free drugs was almost certainly a sign that they were considered to be a good/respected customer – and almost only happened once the customer was well known and trusted by the dealer. There was however far from consistent experience among the user group and differing interpretations as to the reasons why freebies were provided

Tasters, testers and other devices of securing loyalty and custom

Seeking clientele

Whilst most of those who received freebies were well known and had a relative relationship of trust with the dealer involved a small number of respondents did report having been offered free drugs by dealers they were not regular customers of as an enticement to gain their custom:

> Yeah, to get you onto their stuff. When I met new dealers, but the older ones knew me and what I took, but new ones – they'd always offer

And,

> Yes, because of the competition between them [the dealers]

Responses such as this perhaps sum up the way that some users experienced the user/dealer relationship but a number of other respondents reported (as did the 15 who reported never having been offered free drugs) that such a situation was neither routine nor predictable. One user, asked if they had been offered free drugs responded:

> Yeh, ...*but very rare*, and only recently [despite a 17 year habit] – a dealer trying to get me as a customer

Seeking to retain clientele

Whilst the provision of small amounts of free drugs to try to attract new clientele (existing users, not just anyone) was experienced by a number (n11) of the interviewees, others had primarily experienced it in relation to dealers 'keeping them sweet' to retain their custom. The supply of 'tasters' and 'testers', allowing the client to taste or test the drug on offer before buying and for free was mentioned by a further 11 interviewees. Some interpreted this as reflecting their status as a valued customer:

> Yes [I have been offered freebies] but 'cos I was worth a lot to them

or,

> Yeah, a bloke who supplies us sometimes give us a free £10 bag for being a good customer. But I've never been given them to get me on stuff, just 'cos we're good customers

The suggestion made by a number of these respondents is that once a dealer has built up a relationship of relative trust with his/her client they may be willing, for good (reliable) customers, to give 'a little extra', supplemental to what is being bought. This may be done ''up-front' as with the last quotation or in the slightly more surreptitious manner of offering tasters or pretending they want the client to 'test' the drugs for them. That this is also not to be seen as routine, predictable or even consistent behaviour amongst dealers is borne out by those never offered freebies and by some of those that had been:

> Yeah, testers – it's quite rare really

Drugs for services but not money

Clearly, how a user interprets what constitutes a freebie is sometimes ambiguous. One of those that answered that they had not been offered freebies declared:

> No. I mean, I'd buy my whack and they wanted me to do them a favour and that was kudos – I wasn't going to do them a favour for nothing – they'd actually give to me to check it out

This user clearly felt that he was being asked to check the quality of the heroin as a kind of favour to the dealer and that this reflected some kind of status he held as an experienced addict. Whilst that may or may not have been the case it did reflect another aspect of 'free' drug provision – drugs for services rendered – in this case 'helping the dealer test the quality of the sample. Other respondents that had answered that they had received free drugs reported driving dealers around, running errands or 'weighing-up' samples as examples of the 'favours' that they had done to obtain their freebies. The free drugs were not in this sense completely free as they involved a certain amount of expended labour ultimately remunerated by the provision of heroin or other drugs.

As regards how drug markets can be gendered in relation to women numerous pieces of research have reported on the way that sex can be implicated in drug transactions (Maher 1996; 1997; Maher and Daley, 1996; Denton and O'Malley, 1999; Dunlap and Johnson, 1996; Taylor, 1993; Goldstein et al. 1992; Sommers et al. 1996). The extent to which women resort to providing sex for drugs is contentious, probably overstated in the research literature (Denton and O'Malley, 2001) and may indeed be more prevalent in some geographical areas and amongst some groups of women than others (see May et al. 1999). In relation to this research none of the 25 women users mentioned having been asked to provide sexual favours by dealers. It may be of course that this was something that they did not wish to reveal to the researcher. However, although sexual favours/victimisation undoubtedly plays a part for many women in drug transactions it is worth noting that this is distinct from the issue being explored here. Not only are women who 'pay' for drugs with sex already existing addicted drug users they could also, as suggested above in relation to other services for drugs, hardly be considered to be receiving something for nothing. 'Payment' is either being solicited, or taken from them.

Did all of those that reported being offered free drugs really get offered them?

There is a certain amount of disparity between the experiences of the users in regard to having been offered free drugs. Fifteen of the 60 said that they hadn't been offered free drugs. Other buyers' interpretation of 'free' actually related to services rendered. Some of the respondents were clear that they had been offered drugs for being good customers but the impression given generally was that this wasn't a regular occurrence. A small number however reported an experience that was generally out of synch with the rest of those interviewed and gave the impression that 'it happens all the time', that 'they [the dealers] just want to get you as a customer'. These respondents, rather than reporting faithfully on their actual experience may in fact be relaying their general belief about what dealers do and why – a kind of 'I know it's true'. The idea that drug dealers regularly try to entice people by providing free drugs is as discussed above a well-rehearsed narrative and commonly relayed. These respondents may thus be either exaggerating their experience of being offered free drugs or it may in fact be the case that they have not been offered free drugs but, in the context of an interview would perhaps feel in some way 'less' for having not been offered, that they were not as immersed in the drugs scene as they would like (the researcher and themselves?) to believe.

Giving credit – the cultivation of a secure, reliable client base

The provision of credit was relatively widespread. Nearly all of the dealers had provided some kind of credit at some time but once again this was fairly tightly circumscribed and not encouraged. Credit was permitted almost exclusively to those that each dealer in various ways described as either 'regular trusted customers', 'people I know', 'friends' or people who are 'safe'. When asked if he offered credit to his clients one 'street' dealer explained:

> Yes, to regular customers. If they let me down they won't get it again. A lot is based on credit and trust

Similar sentiments were outlined by dealer who described himself as operating at the wholesale level:

> Yes, originally I did but people still owe me. When I sold H it was cash or nothing

Two of the dealers were specific about heroin and crack cocaine not being available for credit. The inference here was that users of these two drugs were inherently less reliable than users of other drugs. The other dealers did not discriminate in this way and controlled the management of credit by being selective to whom (which individuals as opposed to what kind of drug user) it was given.

Another, who described himself as being in-between a street dealer and a wholesaler stated:

> Seldom. To people who are safe, that can afford to. Some people spending £200 a day

One mid-level wholesaler for instance who largely dealt with other lower level dealers explained the process slightly higher up:

> Yes, when dealing with large sums of money you're giving people bail – sale or return. Also, you might negotiate if the last batch was no good

Despite providing credit this dealer was one of those who never provided free drugs.

As for the users nearly all (n52) said that they had been permitted or offered credit. For six of these however this was specified as a 'rare' occurrence.

Consistent with the dealer reports however the overriding structural relationship that was evident for nearly all of those that were offered or provided credit was that the dealer was able to trust them due to an existing relationship that had 'proven' itself. The buyers consistently related that credit was given to them either because they were a 'good customer', were a 'regular buyer' and/or were a 'known' quantity. A few reasoned that the dealer provided credit to retain customers.

Five of those that had been offered either hadn't accepted it or had done so only reluctantly due to a concern about being indebted:

> Yeah, but I never used to like taking credit 'cos it's a downward track and you think oh, I'm not paying for it, I've still got x amount but I can get some more ...so I never really liked getting credit

Another respondent however saw the offer of credit more positively, seeing it as helpful as opposed to problematic:

> Yes. A regular customer. It's good as you can't always pay at the time

Other contexts where 'pushers' may operate unsolicited

Both the London and Sydney research suggests that the archetypal pusher who indiscriminately looks to sell 'his' wares to any passer by, to children and the otherwise vulnerable is an unhelpful way of understanding drug transaction activity. The 'rave' and similar 'dance' events however do present a different context for drug sales and users do report being approached by dealers although they themselves have not sought the dealer out. The dealer on the dance floor however has very little incentive to provide *free* drugs or credit to individuals that they do not know. If they know the individual in question then the relationships outlined above are likely to apply. It may be the case that a dance hall based dealer will seek to sell fake or counterfeit drugs as something else (e.g. MDA as MDMA) if they are short of the drug required as they do not expect to see the user again – but this will only apply if the dealer does not frequent a particular venue as the 'comeback' would likely be feared (see Coomber, 1997b for more on this). It is also the case that the underlying rationale for seeing freebies as enticing new users is related to the idea that the users will be 'hooked' once they have tried the drug. Dance hall drugs do not tend to be of the normatively addictive type and even if they were unless the user was taking them daily for a period of time they would not get addicted and therefore have no need to return to the dealer. Giving drugs to a passing stranger in the hope that they would come back for more would be simply throwing drugs (and therefore money) away. Finally, it is also the case that the vast majority of those who attend 'raves' and dance clubs and events are existing drug users (Winstock et al. 2001; Lenton et al. 1997). The pusher in the dance hall, whilst reprehensible is not the pusher at the street corner whispering to anyone who comes along.

The provision of credit from the perspective of the dealers appears to be distinct from their perception of how freebies are utilised in drug market transactions. Whereas freebies are a way of garnering loyalty, making it worthwhile for the user to come to the dealer they tend also to be used to entice existing users away from other dealers and or to keep existing users 'sweet'. The 'tasting' or testing of samples is also for some common practice to enable the buyer to be reassured on the quality of the potential buy whilst for others it appears to be a way of making their customers feel a little privileged. Credit however tends to operate slightly differently to this. Although the provision of credit does help cement relationships and clearly it does tie the buyer to the dealer to a point, credit only tends to be given to those already considered trustworthy where a relationship (considered reliable) has already been established. Whilst the provision of credit for most of the dealers is standard practice with those they feel they can trust it is not the preferred way of conducting business. As we shall see (below) it is also the case that not all *users* want to resort to credit in their transactions with drug dealers whereas users-dealers use it as a means to manage their drug buying and selling.

Managing a relationship

That not all dealers consider the provision of free drugs as standard procedure is fairly clear. What dealers are trying to do is manage a relationship. One dealer cognisant of this stated:

> Yes, [he gives freebies] but not too often...can get into trouble because they might get to expect it

Whilst it's clear that 'what drug dealers do' is rarely the consistent and coherent behaviour that would be suggested by politicians and the media it is, as above worth noting the consistency of structure that often bounds the differences of approach to the provision of 'freebies'. So although there is a range of practices freebies are predominately offered to help bind existing relationships. They are rarely given to those unknown and/or not 'trusted' by the dealer although clearly the concept of trust being used here is a fluid one.

We shouldn't forget that some differentiation of practice will also result from what the dealer believes they should be doing as a dealer. There is no 'school' for dealers and initiation into dealing is diverse and relatively unstructured both in terms of practice and knowledge. In Coomber (1997a) one relatively inexperienced dealer interviewed in relation to the cutting of the cocaine reported using amphetamine as a cutting agent. Amphetamine is almost never found in the forensic analysis of street cocaine yet it is widely believed by users that it is a common cutting agent (Cohen, 1989; Coomber, 1997b; Decorte, 2001). It was speculated that this novice dealer was cutting the cocaine he sold with amphetamine due to his existing belief that that is what he was supposed to do. In the research being reported on here one of the dealers alluded to such a possibility when he stated:

> Up and coming [dealers] who don't know what the game's about will give freebies to encourage clients – just want to get rich quickly – don't really care who they sell to

This position is also in contradiction to the commonly assumed rationale for the cutting of drugs that asserts that dealers are always trying to fiddle or short-change their customers. In Coomber (1997a) it was reported that, rather than always looking to cut the drugs they sell to such an extent that customers are being fiddled, in fact dealers are often concerned to get a 'rep' (reputation) for quality drugs and with this in mind often think that the drugs they intend to sell on have already been cut prior to reaching them and as such they are wary of cutting them further. Importantly, and in in opposition to the conventional image of the dealer being the feared character in drug selling, it was found that dealers often cited a fear of potential reprisal from those they sell to as another reason not to cut their drugs or provide poor quality.

Cheap drugs as a 'marketing tool' and evidence of dealer slyness

Reference by the police or the media sometimes refers to instances where drugs are being given away much more cheaply by some dealers than others: 'CRACK DOWN – One hit of killer drug drops to less than price of a pint – Evil pushers offer addicts 'buy 3 get 2 free' deals for Xmas' (*Sunday Mirror*, December 26, 2004). Depending on how you present such an activity you can either make this sound akin to the idea that dealers entice new users with free drugs or suggest that it is nothing special unusual nor particularly bad at all. There is nothing neither surprising nor heinous about dealers who have managed to obtain new cheap supplies to set their prices lower than previously. This is just an effect of market opportunism. Likewise, as already discussed above, if a dealer 'gives away' an extra 20 tablets of ecstasy with every 20 bought this has nothing in fact to do with 'free' drugs at all. In both cases the drugs dispensed are being dispensed at the market level for that dealer. If other dealers are not providing 40 tablets for the price of 20 this is because they either didn't obtain them for a similarly low price (and thus the price has in effect halved rather than any being given away for free) or they are unwilling to make a lesser profit.

Discussion

The idea that heroin and other addictive drug use is partly spread through the activities of evil drug dealers enticing the uninitiated and otherwise vulnerable through the provision of free drugs remains unproven. It is certainly highly questionable that it is an activity that defines any significant part of drug market activity. As has been discussed there are good reasons why such a marketing strategy would be logically and practicably flawed. Moreover, the research outlined suggests that the provision of free drugs to opiate users in London and Sydney, whilst not uncommon, is tightly circumscribed by particular rationales and structures. In opposition to the rational of the archetypal 'freebie' it appears that free drugs are provided to existing users already known to the dealer and are intended to bolster the existing or potential buyer/seller relationship. Although the provision of credit in drug transactions is also used to buoy such a relationship it is more likely to be provided by sellers to those considered sufficiently trustworthy and usually to those with whom a relationship has been established. Together, the two modes of operation represent a means to the seller to try to enhance their management of the dealing relationship by rewarding good expenditure and/or engaging new, recent or occasional users in such a relationship (freebies), or simply retaining and managing trusted clientele who cannot or would prefer not to pay up front (credit). It could be argued that the provision of free drugs to clients is a way of cultivating business, either in the sense of enticing users away from other dealers by allowing the tasting or testing of the quality of their wares, and the bolstering of existing business by making the buyer feel special or that they are getting a good deal. It could however be argued that the provision of credit is normatively used not as a means to cultivate in quite the same way but is more a means to cement and acknowledge a relationship already cultivated. This differs marginally from Jacobs (1999) position in his observation and analysis of crack buyers/dealers in that he sees both activities as more closely related and as cultivation devices. There is however a danger of overstating the use of both freebies and credit – although extent of use may differ between the crack cocaine market in St Louis and heroin markets[7] in London and Sydney. The provision of both in these samples however is by no means universal consistent or even predictable. Whilst users are keen to get any 'extras' they can it is clear that these are provided under particular circumstances. Primarily, the provision of free drugs would be to reward those who buy in sufficient quantity to be rewarded. It is unlikely that clients buying for sole use on a daily basis would be worthy of any extras and this may explain how twenty-five percent of the user sample had never been offered free drugs whilst nearly all had been offered credit at some time. Other reasons to provide free drugs would be for services rendered – however moderate (although to classify this as free is stretching a point), or to persuade a new contact to test a dealers product in the hope of gaining a new customer. This latter reason however is widely assumed by the users but rarely mentioned by the dealers (in fact by only one 'front-line' dealer) who effectively suggest that their client base tends to seek them out and transactions are only made when satisfied by the contacts credentials – e.g. vouched for by another client. The provision of free drugs, according to the samples accessed and reported on here, is therefore a relatively rare occurrence with dealers using it selectively but wary of buyers expecting such provision on a regular basis. Likewise, the provision of credit may have benefits and disbenefits. From a dealers perspective it can demonstrate loyalty to existing and trusted clients but poorly managed may also result in unwanted debt and severance from the client. In relation to other dealers or user dealers below the seller (e.g. a wholesaler providing drugs to a house dealer or friend dealer) the provision of credit, once trust has been established, is less problematic. The dealer expects the buyer to pay for the drugs once they have sold them on. A relationship like this starts with small amounts until the buyer has proven himself or herself trustful and builds to larger amounts over time. Friends and trusted clients apart, significant credit will normally be extended only to other sellers, a point also made by Jacobs (1999) and Skolnick et al. (1997). From a users perspective, as some of this sample suggested, the provision of credit may be problematic as it can lead to escalating debt and other problems as a consequence whilst for others it helps them to manage their use when funds are not available.

Overall then we can see that one of the key defining activities of the contemporary drug dealer – indiscriminate 'pushing' employing the enticement of free addictive drugs is undermined by both the evidence that is available and by a number of false assumptions about the way in which addiction to such drugs works and how drug markets operate. in the next chapter we will closely consider a related activity – the adulteration of street drugs with dangerous substances.

Footnotes

[1] On this ditty Lehrer has said that it "... was just intended as a takeoff on a certain genre of sentimental songs, like 'The Old Lamplighter' and 'The Umbrella Man,' which no one remembers any more. The idea was, it was only going to be funny if I took the most repulsive, antisocial character to write the song about. I thought about doing 'The Abortionist,' but at that time you couldn't even say that. The dope peddler was the second choice, so there it was". http://www. rhino.com/features/liners/72776lin.lasso [Accessed: 17.6.2001]

[2] Under normal circumstances this is clearly the case and numerous studies report that the route to addictive use is much longer than often supposed. However, some individuals can become 'hooked' almost immediately but in these instances it is usually to do with something akin to a 'will to addiction'. In Coomber and Sutton (2006) for example a number of respondents reported moving to daily use straight away as they had wanted to assume an addicted lifestyle or had felt it inevitable and chose not to control their intake or resist the onset of addiction. It is highly unlikely that an unwitting child or individual would succumb in such a way.

[3] It is possible that almost any substance could be considered addictive in the sense that some individuals appear capable of problematic and compulsive use of even those drugs that for the vast majority do not result in dependence. Tolerance to LSD builds up so quickly that daily use would soon result in no effect being experienced whilst drugs such as cannabis and ecstasy tend not to produce addictive outcomes and if they do this would be unpredictable and over a long period of time whilst drugs such as cannabis and ecstasy tend not to produce addictive outcomes and if they do this would be unpredictable and over a long period of time.

[4] In 2001 the Dutch police did send out a memorandum to other police forces warning that a single ecstasy tablet containing heroin had been found and that a 'rogue batch' was circulating. No new tablets were found and consequent speculation suggested that this tablet may well have been a hoax taking advantage of existing belief systems about ecstasy adulteration.

[5] But UK produced programmes such as *The Bill, Liverpool1, Eastenders; Grange Hill and Brookside* to name but a few have all had storylines depicting a range of stereotypical dealer activities including dangerous adulteration and dealers pushing free drugs.

[6] Edmunds et al. (1996) describe closed markets as those where the buying of illicit drugs is not straight forward, where the buyer needs to be a 'known' quantity and/or has to traverse a number of barriers to protect the sellers. An open market is described as one where those barriers are significantly less, sometimes nominal and where drugs can be sought without being known.

[7] The dealers in this survey however mostly had experience of selling heroin and crack cocaine as well as experience earlier in their careers of selling drugs such as cannabis and amphetamine.

Chapter 3:

Dangerous adulteration[1] – what dealers do to the drugs they sell and why

Happy addicts come back, unhappy ones buy elsewhere, dead ones can't buy anything

I guess I am not that kind of person; what I would call 'evil'

(Dealers interviewed in Coomber, 1997d)

As we saw in the previous chapter there are a number of common assumptions about what drugs dealers do and how they operate despite there being little or no evidence to support such assumptions. In this chapter we will be looking a lot closer at one of those areas only briefly touched upon – that of dangerous adulteration – but one that is, in my opinion, the lynch-pin for the continuation of many other assumptions and propagated images that surround both illicit drugs and those that sell them. We shall see that the common notion of dangerous adulteration has little, if indeed any credence and also – perhaps more surprisingly – that the cutting of street drugs per se (either with or without 'dangerous' substances) itself tends to be neither routine nor predictable.

In presenting this part of my research into drug dealers and drug markets I could pretend that I had been wiser than others, that I had suspected the fallacy of much that is frequently reported about the risks relating to

62

dangerous adulteration but the very fact that I wasn't 'wise before the event' is itself partly indicative of the extent to which this idea was (and remains) relatively uncontested. The origins of this research rest in one specific event and can be traced very precisely in time. On November 12, 1995 Leah Betts, a teenager from Essex in England, was admitted to hospital after collapsing at her eighteenth birthday party – held at her home. After it had emerged that earlier that evening Leah had taken an ecstasy tablet her parents took the decision to allow the local and national media to take graphic pictures of the dying teenager 'hooked' up to intravenous drips and monitoring equipment. The following morning Leah's picture was plastered over the front pages of nearly all of the national tabloids and her tragic experience became the dominant news item for a number of days and a recurrent one thereafter. That there was an intention to shock is unarguable and the success of the coverage in this respect was far-reaching[2]. The rationale for Leah's parents allowing the cameras 'in' and their daughter's plight to be so extensively exposed was to warn others of the dangers of drugs. To warn others what might happen to them if they too, like Leah, took substances that they couldn't know what they contained. Indeed it was this very line of argumentation that had been put forward as the likely culprit of Leah's predicament – that the ecstasy she took had been cut with some dangerous substance that had poisoned her. *The Guardian* (November 14, 1995) for example reported that, 'Police said a binding agent such as bicarbonate of soda or scouring powder could have been responsible for the contamination'.

This initial speculation fuelled by police officers at the scene and reported by the media proved to be false. Forensic tests showed the tablet that Leah had used was in fact 100% MDMA, or 'ecstasy', with no adulterants or diluents of any kind present. Although the papers reported that this was the case the 'retractions', as ever, were small and easy to miss. It was at this point that I began to wonder about dangerous drug adulteration itself. I didn't question its existence or the practice but I knew from a number of years of researching in the 'drugs field' that most publicised drug related risks were exaggerated and that the number of fatalities from heroin in the UK for example were much lower than most people would suspect when reading and listening to comments about heroin from politicians, the police and other authoritative sources. In fact the number of fatalities from heroin was fairly small (two or three hundred a year at that time) compared to the number of users (one hundred and twenty thousand plus addicted users, plus many more non-addicted users). Moreover, most of these users were using several times a day (or week) and given that heroin was considered the 'dirtiest drug' if dangerous adulteration was as common as suggested, where, I wondered, were all the bodies? Perhaps, I considered, rather than dangerous adulteration resulting in overdose or death, as portrayed by television dramas and by police officers after a drug fatality, it has other health consequences that have been as yet relatively neglected by research. Intrigued I started to acquire as much information about dangerous adulteration as I could and it soon became evident to me that much that was assumed about the practices of drug dealers, particularly in relation to the cutting of drugs, was largely unsubstantiated and highly problematic.

To begin with I found that there had been almost no research conducted on and around the adulteration of illicit drugs beyond the narrow and limited focus of the forensic science community. In that literature there was some sparse reporting on the kinds of adulterants and diluents found in (usually) heroin and certain other illicit substances over the years. As much concern, if not more however, centred on the analytical methods and technology (e.g. gas chromatography, mass spectrometry, or NMR spectroscopic) used to extract the data and its relative efficacy in doing so – as is the wont of forensic science. Almost no comment was made on what was found or the ramifications it had for our understanding of cutting practices. Moreover, the reporting of what was found, as we shall see, was (and it remains the case) sufficiently flawed as to unintentionally provide a picture of the 'impurity' of street drugs, which was in fact quite different to the reality.

What is believed about dangerous adulteration?

The notion that illicit street drugs, particularly heroin (and currently 'ecstasy') are full of dangerous impurities likely to lead to serious harm or death is a common one. It is a common notion because there is hardly a source of authoritative or public information that does not subscribe to it and/or propagate it. Even within the drugs field references to adulteration, failing to go into any great substantiating or contextual detail, provides throw away statements like: 'The adulterants that dealers use to cut heroin or cocaine may be anything from quinine to rat poison and can kill naive users who unwittingly inject contaminated substances' (Zackon, 1988: 62), or, 'street heroin may be adulterated with substances such as lactose, glucose, chalk dust, caffeine, boric acid or talcum powder and may be as little as 25% pure heroin' (NCIS, 1993: 13) or, 'but then milk powder and brick dust are not the best things to put into people's veins' (Fazey, 1991: 19). More often, even where the source may demonstrate a more considered approach, there is a tendency to attach the issue of adulteration onto other problems associated with drug purity without care to delineate levels of importance between them and their respective dangers:

> Users' ignorance about the identity, purity and potency of street drugs leads to greater and more frequent health related problems than can be attributed to the pharmacological actions and effects of the drugs themselves (Coc et al. 1987: 46).

Drug field workers are another common source of information about drugs and drug markets. The assumption made is that because drug field workers are 'close' to the users, that they therefore have access to privileged information. Unfortunately, this is often not the case. Drug field workers are not necessarily well versed in much of the drugs literature particularly that of drug markets. Users moreover are notoriously uninformed about a whole range of aspects of drugs, the hazards of their use, addiction (Davies, 1993) or those that use drugs different to them. Users however tend to think of themselves as knowledgeable and in turn many drug field workers will believe they have access to good street knowledge. *The Observer* (September 26, 1999) provides one such example in relation to cutting:

> The economics of heroin dealing were explained by a drugs counsellor, Michael Czerkas, who works 300 miles away on the Knowle West council estate in Bristol. 'The wholesale price of an ounce of pureish heroin is around £800. Dealers never sell pure heroin. They cut it, say, five times. So for an outlay of £800, the dealer sells 500 small bags at a tenner a bag: £5,000. He's making a profit of £4,200 on every ounce of smack.

An attempt to clarify with Michael Czerkas how he came about his information was unfortunately met with no reply. Users meanwhile regularly attribute 'bad hits', an illness after drug use, or just an unusual/unexpected 'hit' to dangerous adulteration (McElrath and McEvoy, 2002; Forsyth, 1995; Cohen, 1989; CESAR, 2001). Examples of media (particularly television and film) representations of impurities being responsible for drug deaths are common as are statements by members of the criminal justice and drug treatment systems.

The police, as referred to in relation to the Leah Betts tragedy above, often provide statements to the media that (uninformed, i.e. prior to any analysis) make assumptions about the cause of a drug death as likely fact. When nineteen year old student Lorna Spinks, perhaps the second most infamous ecstasy related UK death, died in 2001 no specific substances were mentioned but the much relied upon 'rogue batch' was surmised by police to be responsible. However, Lorna Spinks death, along with each of the other eight deaths that were attributed to rogue ecstasy in 2001 were consequently proven not to have been related to either 'super-strength' tablets or tablets that were in any way 'rogue'. Another similar example shows that little has been learned by the police and that assumption and extant beliefs often obviate the need for evidence:

> Police have not yet confirmed the exact cause of death of the two men, but they know both had taken ecstasy – a "bad batch" of the drug appeared to be to blame, they said, mixed with a contaminant that may have been the rat poison strychnine (*The Guardian*, June 28, 2001).

Once again, as with the drugs that Leah Betts and Lorna Spinks had taken, no evidence of dangerous adulterants was found. A journalist with a least some taste for checking his sources in this case also interviewed a toxicology expert who admitted to being confused as to why the police would say such a thing as no such contaminants had ever been found in ecstasy.

Health Authorities and health workers/practitioners also provide written and online materials that provide insight into the general line of understanding:

> Currently in Toronto there is a report of crack tainted with cyanide... and Cheryl Littleton, nurse practitioner at the Hospital for Sick

Children's adolescent unit, has heard of teens buying heroin and Ecstasy combinations (Dubey, 1996).

If drug field researchers and workers, the police and the media warn of dangerous adulteration, what are the views of the general public? It was only later in the sequence of this research that I undertook a survey of public beliefs about drug adulteration but its results are worth reporting here. Prior to undertaking this particular research I had been reasonably content to assume that, as information about drug adulteration was only really available from the media, often via politicians or police, and that as we have seen these sources regularly cite dangerous adulteration as both widespread and to be the common cause of drug fatalities, that the publics' beliefs would echo those positions. The research (Coomber, 1999) very much suggested that this was the case with over 90% of the 248 students[3] that were interviewed believing that street drugs were adulterated with dangerous substances such as rat-poison, domestic scouring powders, brick dust, chalk and/or other dangerous drugs (e.g. heroin or ground glass in ecstasy). Not only did this group strongly believe in the use of dangerous adulteration as a practice they also had some confidence in why their beliefs were reliable. Forty-three percent understood the practice to be so well known that it was simply 'common knowledge'. That is, it is considered to be a type of knowledge that needs little reflection and on which the basic and essential aspects of the issue are understood. It could be argued that for these respondents this is not an issue that is deemed to be contentious in any serious sense but one that is relatively straightforward. Many others stated that in conjunction with it being 'common knowledge' or in exclusion to it that their beliefs were informed by 'sources such as the media' (47%) or that they had had drug education that had informed them on the issue (24%). Importantly, twenty-two percent of the respondents also stated that they believed what they did because they had 'first hand knowledge' of what cutting agents were used. This invariably meant that they felt themselves to have some kind of privileged or 'insider' knowledge to what street drugs were cut with. Although this kind of 'I know it happens' responding proved problematic in a number of important ways it mirrored in some respects the reporting of drug dealers interviewed in an earlier study where, as we shall see, the majority reported strong beliefs that dangerous adulteration was a common practice but then failed to substantiate those claims.

A political convenience for all?

The idea that drugs have harmful adulterants in them has also proved useful as a political football for pretty much anyone concerned with the 'drug problem' – regardless of perspective. Not surprisingly, those that call for total prohibition on drugs and take what would be seen as a hard-line or zero-tolerance stance on drug use often refer to the dangers inherent in drug use only made more serious by the dangerous cutting agents to be found in them. Perhaps more surprisingly, but in an equally uncritical and unquestioning manner we find that both those from a harm-reduction perspective and the legalisation perspective also refer to the existence of dangerous adulteration as respective reasons for the provision of substitute prescribing and/or the availability of pharmaceutically pure drugs over the counter. This is the view of one proponent of legalisation on the problem:

> Heroin, so benign in the hands of doctors, becomes highly dangerous when it is cut by black-market dealers – with paracetamol, drain cleaner, sand, sugar, starch, powdered milk, talcum powder, coffee, brick dust, cement dust, gravy powder, face powder or curry powder. None of these adulterants was ever intended to be injected into human veins. Some of them, such as drain cleaner, are simply toxic and poison their users. Others – sand or brick dust – are carried into tiny capillaries and digital blood vessels where they form clots, cutting off the supply of blood to fingers or toes. Very rapidly, venous gangrene sets in, the tissue starts to die, the fingers or toes go black and then have only one destiny: amputation. Needless suffering – inflicted not by heroin, but by its black-market adulterants (Davies, 2001).

What we find then is that impure drugs with dangerous contaminants are commonly conceived of as widespread by drug field experts and workers, by the police, politicians, the media, the general public, drug users and most damningly of all as we shall see, for those that question the assumption – the drug dealers themselves. Moreover it is a convenient idea for almost everyone. Even drug users can blame it for the unwanted side-effects they sometimes experience (Forsyth, 1995; McElrath and McEvoy, 2001) rather than blaming the drugs themselves or their inappropriate or excessive use of them and drug dealers can – by dealing good drugs – use it as a reference point as to why *their* drugs are good and they should be trusted.

In many respects, because of this and as I have already mentioned, the idea of dangerous adulteration has pretty much attained the status of an unquestioned 'truth' in Western society[4]. It has been accepted by just about everyone and questioned by few. In the drugs field especially, where many assumptions are critically questioned all the time this is rarity.

Little serious debate

Unsurprisingly, because of its status as a relatively unquestioned truth little serious debate has taken place as to the nature of dangerous adulteration or of the dangers posed by the particular impurities considered to be the problem. This is somewhat surprising given the nature of those substances commonly perceived to be involved: Vim, Ajax, ground light-bulb glass, brick-dust, talcum powder, rat-poison (strychnine). The list is longer than that stated but the general drift I am sure is encapsulated in these examples. These are perceived as dangerous, health/life threatening substances. 'Vim in the veins' is in fact a common saying and clearly alludes to the belief that messing with street drugs means a serious gamble is being played every time they are used:

> The ingestion of ecstasy, as with most illicit drugs, essentially reduces to a game of Russian roulette because the contents of the tablets are unknown and unregulated and the dealers and suppliers are concealed and unaccountable (Weir, 2000: 4).

and,

> While a Raver may take a tablet containing 25 milligram of their drug of choice, the very next tablet may not contain the drug, may have twice the drug or even contain rat poison. They can be playing a pharmaceutical version of Russian roulette (Cox, 2001.)

As reported in the previous chapter, it is also often believed that drugs such as ecstasy and amphetamine are 'laced' with drugs such as heroin. The dual rationales given for this adulteration are (mimicking fears around the adulteration of heroin) that illegal drugs per se are necessarily laced with dangerous substances, and/or that pernicious dealers adulterate with substances like heroin in order to 'hook' unsuspecting users of 'soft' non-addictive drugs onto the more addictive heroin and thus secure a regular client base, or just because they are 'evil'. The belief that adulterants present a real and common risk to the drug taker and that they are particularly pernicious in nature is thus a prevalent position taken by many. Are these perceptions useful? What do we know about adulteration and drug impurities?

What was known and what I found out

At the beginning of the chapter I referred to the fact that when embarking on this research, all I wanted to do was get a better, more informed idea, about what actual harms were resulting from the adulteration of street drugs. I soon found out that, sparse forensic research and unsubstantiated hearsay apart, almost nothing had been written on the topic and what had been written was narrow and un-contextualised. Smelling a research opportunity but not realising where it would lead me I started to collect data that would eventually lead me to review the available forensic literature, produce some new secondary readings of US Drug Enforcement Administration data and even to be instrumental in producing new important forensic data on the topic itself. Moreover, as a compliment to this forensic data I sought to understand better the motivations for the cutting of street drugs and undertook a number of surveys of drug dealers – some in prison and convicted for drug dealing, some in local drug markets in London, some in 'hyper-space' and eventually in two open street drug markets in Sydney, Australia. The results were surprising and as each piece of the jigsaw came together it was clear that the results were mutually supportive.

From reading the largely minimalist coverage from reports and papers of 'what is in street drugs' – of what substances were present in samples of heroin, cocaine and other illicit drugs – it very quickly became apparent that the 'dangerous' substances so commonly assumed were just not being found. What follows is a fairly detailed and lengthy outline of that evidence but I make no apologies for this as detailed analysis of drug market activity is few and far between and to some extent what allows stereotype to prevail. Space does however limit what it is possible to relay on the topic and for those wishing to delve more deeply into the issues raised – and in particular the methods employed – I refer you to (Coomber. 1997a,b,c,d; 1999; Coomber & Maher, 2006).

Low purity doesn't necessarily mean high levels of cutting

One of the first surprising bits of information to emerge from my foray into the forensic literature was the fact that the way purity levels are reported in the media and even in 'briefing' documents circulated to criminal justice authorities and government departments is highly misleading. Usually such reporting refers to two basic bits of information – the average level of purity of heroin for example, for any given time period, and the adulterants and diluents found. This immediately gives the impression that a heroin sample of say 60% purity is made up of 40% 'impurities'. Whilst, in a literal (forensic) sense this is the case, it is far from the case that impurity = cutting agent/s. A significant proportion of what makes up the other 40% may well be other opium alkaloids that are created during the inefficient synthesising of the heroin and/or during degradation over time – for example if stored or transported poorly. It will not *all* be adulterants, and sometimes no adulterants will be present at all. Gough (1991: 527) for example reported on a 30 kg seizure divided into 30 packages which consisted of an average diamorphine (heroin) content of 76%; accompanied by acetylcodeine at 6.4%; 6-acetylmorphine at 2.1%. Other opiate alkaloids, noscapine and papaverine also accounted for 17.6% and 6% of the samples on average. Thus we can see that a sample where the purity of heroin is formally recorded as being around 70%, the other 30% could be almost exclusively made up other opiates and by-products from the production process but that common reporting approaches that show only purity levels give an impression that the other 30% was simply 'something else'. This is often – as we shall see- not the case. It is worth noting that this (important?) piece of contextual information is, in my experience, never added to reports on drug seizure purities. This omission perhaps tells us a couple of things. Firstly that although Forensic Scientists know this kind of information they haven't found it important enough to emphasise (even as a footnote) and this may be because they either do not recognise its significance or do not tend to report beyond basic technical or method issues (e.g. see Zhang et al. 2004). Secondly, it appears that the fact that 'impurity is not equal to cutting agents' may be poorly understood even within the ranks of forensic scientists for, to my surprise when collating this data in the mid-1990s, the then Head of the UK Forensic Science Service told me that this was something that he even had to remind his own staff about.

The forensic evidence: heroin, cocaine, amphetamines and ecstasy

Forensic analysis of drug samples over a number of decades, in different countries, locations within countries and of different drugs do help us to understand more about adulteration patterns and about impurity/purity levels. The first point to make is that the vast majority of substances found in drugs which have been put there after the production of the drug, that is, with the specific desire to adulterate or dilute the drug are comparatively harmless[5]. The second point to make is that many of the substances found are in fact purposively added during production or manufacture as a specific product – rather than a result of hap-hazard cutting – and that the particular mixes involved may even change over time according to customer preference – of which more later.

Heroin

In the UK the 'other substances' found in heroin generally consist of paracetamol, caffeine, sugars and other opiate alkaloids (acetylcodeine, papaverine, noscapine), and have done so since the early 1990s (FIB, 2005; NCIS, 1994; Kaa, 1994; ISDD, 1994). Occasionally, but not normally, other substances such as diazepam, methaqualone or phenobarbitonel are also found (FIB, 2003; Coomber, 1997a) although these substances may well have been more popular in earlier periods. Although the purity levels vary (and thus the percentage of a sample which is impure) – since 1987 the average purity of street heroin in the UK has been around the 38% mark. Elsewhere a similar picture is evident in terms of adulterants and diluents[6]. Relatively comprehensive analysis of heroin samples by the US Drug Enforcement Administration (DEA) since 1990 reveals numerous sugars, prescription drugs (primarily paracetamol), opium alkaloids and occasionally salts but none of the 'dangerous' adulterants/diluents commonly asserted or feared (Coomber, 1999). Similarly, the German Federal Criminal Police Office (Bundeskriminalamt, BKA) which undertook a twelve year 'comprehensive characterization' of heroin found caffeine to be the most frequently detected adulterant along with phenobarbital and paracetamol (called acetaminophen in the US and in the DEA reports) and other (largely prescription) drugs. No 'unusual' substances were reported (Neumann, 1994). In Sydney Australia, in the one project that has really considered these issues, heroin was found to be of a relatively high purity and to contain 'normal' adulterants and diluents (Maher, Swift and Dawson, 2001). In the UK in 1993 paracetamol was found in 41% of cases where any adulterant was found, and caffeine in 33% of the cases tested by The Home Office's Forensic Science Service (Drug Abuse Trends, 1993: 19). Twelve years later these two substances remain the commonest adulterants (FIB, 2005).

The common cutting agents found in street heroin are comparatively benign in health terms[7] to the user and are there for the explicit purpose of 'bulking' the drug out, and sometimes even to 'improve' it, sometimes both. Caffeine, for example, apart from increasing the quantity of 'heroin' through dilution, also improves the percentage uptake of the heroin (as do phenobarbital and methaqualone) to the user (Huizer, 1987: 209). The existence of caffeine (cut 1 to 1 with heroin) for example in heroin (base) which is to be smoked or 'chased' has been shown to enable a higher amount of the heroin (around 76%) to be recovered (i.e. the amount of heroin left available in the 'smoke' which is inhaled), after volatiazation (the heating, melting and then vaporization of the drug for inhalation or 'chasing') than when compared to pure heroin alone. Recovery after volatization for heroin alone was around 60% (Huizer, 1987: 209). Paracetamol is also useful for such adulteration because it has approximately the same melting point as heroin and has analgesic properties. Other adulterants also function with dual purposes. Quinine, for example, is thought to 'heighten[s] the sensation of the rush' (Preble and Casey, 1969), and dilutes, and because of its bitter taste is well hidden in the bitter tasting heroin. Customer preference also affects adulteration/dilution practices and Strang (1990) some time ago urged us 'to realise that contaminants in samples of heroin or cocaine are not all contaminants – many of them are active ingredients which may contribute to (rather than detract from) the overall effect. Thus the percentage purity of a heroin sample is not a complete indication of its perceived psychoactive effect or even its appeal to the discerning heroin user and thus its 'quality'. This is no doubt one of the reasons why Chinese white heroin is much revered by aficionado heroin addicts (as reflected by its higher market price) even though the brown heroin from South West Asia may have higher actual heroin content. It may well be that these changes in the quality of the experience resulting from other opiate and non-opiate active 'contaminants', may well be similar to the difference between a fine claret or a malt whisky, when compared with equivalent solutions of ethanol' (Strang, 1990: 203). In terms of understanding what is *in* street heroin we have to acknowledge that much of the 'contaminants' are the result of the (in)efficiency of the processes of manufacture and/or storage/transportation and/or the production of an initial *product* for market, not simply dilution for profit. This is even likely the case where the dreaded 'rat poison' raises its ugly head.

Strychnine as an adulterant – where the idea of rat poison (likely) originates

Strychnine *has* been found in heroin. Strychnine is also used as a rat poison. The two together however do not add up to 'drug dealers cut their drugs with anything even rat poison'. To begin with strychnine has not been found in just any old heroin, it is found in Heroin No.3 a particular form of heroin that is produced for 'Chasing the Dragon', a form of administration whereby the user 'burns' the heroin on a piece of foil and then 'chases' the fumes and inhales them. Heroin No.3 is not (without further preparation) amenable to injection. Heroin No.3 is but one variant of smoking heroin and is relatively rare in many drug markets including those of the UK and the US. It is however found in numerous other drug markets around the world (UNODC, 2005). The exact aetiology as to how strychnine came to be in this variant of heroin will be forever lost to history (as will the precise reason for so many other adulterants) but its use in Heroin No.3 (not all Heroin No.3 has strychnine in it – the variable ingredients appear to be strychnine hydrochloride or quinine hydrochloride) makes some sense. Firstly, like quinine it has a bitter taste and as such is 'hidden' in the bitter tasting heroin. However, strychnine tends not to appear in amounts sufficient for it to be seen as a significant diluting agent. We do not see heroin made up of 50-60% strychnine. At the levels found strychnine is neither a particularly risky additive nor is it being used to dilute. In Eskes and Brown's (1975) analyses the average content of strychnine was 2% of the sample with a range of 0.5 to 4.8 per cent. Although this heroin was being injected they suggested that because only around 5mg of strychnine would have been present in each injection: 'The amount of strychnine in the strychnine-containing heroin samples is probably insufficient to be a threat to life' (p68). In fact the liver copes comfortably with such quantities of strychnine (Henry, 1995). Some suggest that strychnine hydrochloride is used to provide a distinctive taste – to make it an aficionado's heroin but there are likely to be a number of reasons for its presence. Strychnine has, as already mentioned, stimulant properties and there are historical examples of it being used to enhance performance in Roman Gladiators in 600 B.C. (Wadler, 1999) as well as provide four times World Champion cyclist Victor Linart an end of race 'boost' in the 1920s. It was also used medicinally for many years to increase muscle stimulation and even to counteract depression or drug and alcohol poisoning. Given the lethargy inducing properties of the opiates it may be reasonable to suggest that strychnine was long ago found in small doses to counteract some of the perceived negative 'side-effects' of opiate consumption – an ancient variant of contemporary co-use of heroin and cocaine. It would likely have developed side by side with medicinal use but perhaps also as antidote for overdose. The inclusion of small amounts of strychnine in opium as a means to protect against overdose would have thus made intuitive sense. It is but a small step from here for the practice to also migrate into smoking opium when and where this became popular. When this did happen (almost by accident and for – ironically – 'protective' reasons) a new benefit would likely have been discovered.

As well as caffeine, Huizer (1987) also found strychnine to be an effective substance through which to *increase* the amount of heroin retrievable through 'chasing' (inhaling) in Heroin No.3. In other words, for those experienced in smoking opium without strychnine present it is likely that early inclusion would have provided a notable increase in the amount of opiate available to the user. The process would be more efficient and the user would prefer that variant to the one without. On a similar – albeit contemporised line of thought – Eskes and Brown (1975: 68), after finding 57% (28) of 49 seizures contained a heroin, caffeine, strychnine mix concluded that the strychnine was present due to the intended manufacture of heroin prepared not for injecting but for smoking and that its presence was not related to dilution for profit (i.e. as a 'cutting' agent). Strychnine then, rather than understood as being present in heroin due to the deranged, immoral and uncaring nature of the drug dealer has a much more reasoned explanation for its presence. It does not appear in heroin everywhere and where it does appear there is no published evidence that it contributes to overdose deaths (or poisonings) to a greater degree than where it is absent. We can none-the-less see how even the mention of strychnine being found in forensic samples would lead to the 'drug dealers use rat poison' kind of position.

Cocaine powder and crack cocaine

Strangely enough, cocaine is not a drug which has overly concerned too many commentators regarding its adulteration. This may be for a number of reasons. Likely explanations would be that the dangerousness in cocaine is seen to be in itself (its supposed ability to bring on sudden heart-attacks – even in moderate doses – although even this has been subject to some telling criticism (cf. Alexander & Wong, 1990)), the fact that too many people are known to use cocaine experimentally and recreationally without too many health related complications (WHO/UNICRI, 1995), and, especially in relation to 'crack' cocaine the (mistaken) belief that this is a 'pure' form of the drug. Cocaine powder, in the UK, is, in general. adulterated to a greater extent than heroin and this has been true for the last ten years or so. Even so the rate of cutting is not particularly severe. In fact the extent to which cocaine is cut (on average) has decreased in recent years. So, whereas the average purity of cocaine in 1991 was 81% at importation and 44% on the street (NCIS, 1994) more recently (2001 – 2005) Customs seizures have recorded an average cocaine purity of around 70% whilst police seizures have commonly been between 40% – 55% (FIB, 2005). In the US cocaine levels are now typically high (around 60-80%) with adulteration/dilution no longer being the norm (Caulkins et al. 2004). The common adulterants in cocaine are phenacetin[8]; lignocaine, benzocaine, caffeine, paracetamol and procaine (FIB, 2005) – nearly all substances that have analgesic and/or stimulant properties showing once again the purposive nature of such cutting. Common diluents are glucose, mannitol and lactose – sugars that cause few if any health problems as additives. Ampehtamines, are a substance that users may expect to be a common adulterant of cocaine (given the similarity of effect and of appearance, and that it is comparatively cheaper) but forensic analysis does not tend to report amphetamine as an adulterant of cocaine. In this vein, Cohen (1989) in his study of Cocaine Use in Amsterdam found, despite the belief of 87% (160) of his cocaine using research subjects of the common existence of amphetamine (and the perceived negative effects of it), the samples he bought from them and tested did not reveal any of the substance.

Crack cocaine, indicated by Customs seizures is not commonly imported directly into the UK. It is therefore after importation that the cocaine powder is converted into crack. The purity of police crack seizures in between 2001 and 2005 averaged around 70% (FIB, 2005). Although not adulterated/ diluted for street sales crack cocaine is essentially 'the converted base form of salt (cocaine powder) created by using an alkali. The active part of the drug remains unchanged. All the properties and the impurities in cocaine will therefore remain in crack, the only difference between crack and cocaine is the delivering system' (Bean, 1993: 3). Thus the difference in crack and cocaine is not that all the impurities are 'burnt away' (although some are) leaving 'pure' cocaine as is commonly asserted. The marginal 'increase' in purity between imported cocaine (which is in hydrocloride form – 'salt') and that of crack stems from the hydrocloride residue being burnt away in the conversion process (King, 1995).

Amphetamines

Arguably, heroin is the drug around which fears of adulterants have surfaced most often, and from which our view of other drugs have then been partially coloured. In recent years this general fear around adulterants has been particularly acute with regard to amphetamines and other 'dance drugs' such as Ecstasy. One Consultant Psychiatrist, generally well informed about amphetamines and even practising (relatively radically) substitute prescribing of pharmaceutically prepared amphetamine for street amphetamine (to apparently positive effect), has stated in relation to the injecting of street amphetamine that '95% is not amphetamine, its something else – talcum powder or something' (Myles, 1995). Amphetamine is thus the ultimate 'dirty drug'. It has historically been a relatively impure street drug but in recent years it has been even more so. In 1984 the average purity in the UK was around 20%, in the mid 1990s it dropped to an average low of around 5% (HOSB, 1993) but has recovered somewhat in the last five years (2001-2005) to around 10%. But to state that 'that 95%' something else is a harmful or dangerous additive like talcum powder, is unhelpful. Amphetamine is implicated in relatively few deaths in the UK and yet, after cannabis, it had (until recently) long been easily the most used illicit drug and even now remains roughly on a par with cocaine and ecstasy – both of which have seen recent increases (HOSB, 1993; Condon and Smith, 2003). If the problem was in the adulterants, health problems (unrelated to the primary drug) would be greater. Once again, analysis of cutting agents reveals that the commonest cutting agent is caffeine (a white granular powder with stimulant properties) with lactose, glucose and lignocaine being found frequently and substances such as ketamine, MDMA, ephedrine, phenacetin and even cocaine having been found (DAT, 2004; FIB, 2005). Each either merely 'bulks' the sample or 'enhances' it. The presence of cocaine however should read as a warning in how to interpret forensic data. It is unlikely that cocaine (relatively more expensive) is ever used as a cutting agent for the cheaper amphetamine. It is more likely that the amphetamine was 'contaminated' by being cut up on the same surface that had also had some cocaine on it previously. This would also probably explain the occurrence of the phenacetin which as a common cutting agent of cocaine would also have been present earlier. Inorganic substances reported to be found in amphetamine (of the limited analysis which has been carried out) rather than finding brick-dust or glass have only found trace elements of substances such as antimony, barium, strontium, zinc and copper (Marumo et al. 1994) which would be found as trace elements in many substances, including food anyway. Although amphetamine is the most adulterated and diluted of common street drugs it too doesn't appear to conform, as we shall see, to the 'cut at every stage' model commonly believed and it is probable most amphetamine is cut once, high up the chain of distribution. This again would tend to militate against 'unusual' adulteration.

Ecstasy

One famous story from 1993, encapsulating stories of heroin laced Ecstasy and deaths at raves caused by unknown contaminants, was titled: 'Bitter pills' and appeared in the widely read weekly London 'events' guide *Time Out*. This story claimed that, 'Ecstasy has turned to agony for thousands of E users as dealers spike tablets and capsules with heroin, LSD, rat poison and crushed glass', and that, 'Organised crime gangs, lured by the promise of vast profits, are widely thought to be behind the trend' (Flanagan 1993: 12-13). The story is perhaps typical of adulteration scares and an example of how the media need little evidence to produce sensationalised and fear invoking material. It was a relatively easy story to write as it was able to exploit both what is commonly thought to be present in street drugs such as heroin and because ecstasy related deaths have attained a high profile in the media. Evidence in the research literature however suggests these deaths bear no relation to adulterants but to the context in which they are taken (cf. Henry, 1992). Detection work however found the story to have 'no supporting evidence such as lab tests or reports from doctors who had treated drug users'. Moreover the source of the story proved to be anecdotal and unreliable (Saunders, 1994).

Despite such stories early analysis of ecstasy (3,4-methylenedioxymeth-amphetamine or MDMA) in the mid 1990s found little by way of problem cutting agents. In essence the same is true today (FIB, 2005). Although users believe that heroin may be found in ecstasy Forsyth (1995: 201) for example found that 37 of 319 'ecstasy' samples previously taken were believed by the users to have contained heroin it has not been found in any of the hundreds of thousands of analysed tablets between then and now. Analysis by the UK's Forensic Science Service, by the Dutch Drug Advice Bureau and by 'independent' drug analysis laboratories such as Dancesafe and the Drug Detection Lab tends to show that ecstasy tablets are usually just that – ecstasy tablets. Of the 570,683 'ecstasy' analysed tablets (i.e. tablets submitted for testing that were unknown until testing was complete) in the second quarter of 2005 by the Forensic Science Service for example 'the majority contained MDMA as the main drug with only 153 containing MDEA as the main drug. No tablets were reported with MDA as the main drug' (FIB, 2005).

The issues around 'dance drugs' however are slightly broader than they are most other illicit drugs – particularly in regard to being sold 'fake' or alternative drugs. Because the 'club' or 'dance' drug scene is a varied one and because there are numerous 'dance' drugs being sold (many with similar effects but some with quite distinct effects from MDMA) it is not uncommon for individuals to buy fake drugs (often over-the counter drugs such as caffeine tablets or aspirin) to alternative drugs such as ketamine. In the case of the latter an individual expecting an MDMA 'high' may well experience a traumatic event on ketamine.

We can see then that with heroin, cocaine, and amphetamine the common substances other than the primary drug (drug as sold) are usually intended to dilute the substance and/or do so by detracting as little as possible from the drug itself, possibly enhancing it. In relation to drugs sold as ecstasy, substitutes may be encountered but these in the main attempt to mimic the drug (e.g. LSD + amphetamine; MDA). Thus the existence of other substances than the primary drug often has a distinct and purposeful rationale which goes beyond the simple desire to increase the quantity by bulking the drugs out (like adding water to whisky). It is more involved than that.

Less adulteration than commonly assumed?

In addition to raising significant doubts about dangerous adulteration research also suggested that, in the UK at least, there was far less adulteration taking place than might be expected. Less adulteration that is, both in terms of the amounts of adulterants/diluents put in to many street drugs and the number of times adulteration/dilution was taking place down through the chain of distribution. Information on purity of heroin at point of importation showed that there was often far less difference in the purity levels of those drugs seized by Customs (i.e. before they reach whatever level of distribution) and those seized even at street level (drugs at the end of the distribution channel – the final product) than conventional perspectives on cutting would suggest should be the case. In 1991, 1992 and 1993 for example, purity of heroin seizures at importation were 52.5%, 59.3% and 55% (HM Customs and Excise, 1995 personal communication). Corresponding average purities at street level were 45%, 46% and 39.25% respectively (NCIS, 1994). In other words average purity levels between imported seizures and street level seizures differed by only about 8-14% in these years. Lewis et al. (1985: 175-6) had also found in their study of the heroin market in London in the mid-1980s that 'The average level of dilution evident from fieldwork data, was not as great as might have been expected', and that 'On average, purity on point of import into Britain is in the region of 70 per cent and retail purity in the region of 45-55 per cent'. My later research on the US forensic data (Coomber, 1999a) also confirmed that much less cutting was also taking place there than had previously been suspected and this finding was consistent with my earlier survey of US drug dealers who, in opposition to much of the literature, had said that they didn't routinely cut the powdered drugs that they sold (Coomber, 1997e). It was this earlier survey which had led me to undertake the secondary analysis of the forensic data to see what, if anything was different about the US. I in fact found similarity (as I was later to also do in Australia) rather than difference. Although such analysis at the time was rare, a similar picture had also been found elsewhere. Kaa (1994: 171) for example had found that in Denmark, over the twelve year period covered, although there was a consistently wide range of purity found in any one year: 'The average purity of wholesale samples (45%) was only slightly higher than the purity of retail samples (36%)'.

Even in relation to amphetamine, where purity at importation may be around 60% as it was in the early 1990s and has been for the last couple of years (HM Customs and Excise, 1995; FIB, 2005), the adulteration down to the current average of around 8% at the retail (street) level is likely to be the product of a single ('high level' i.e. the importer) 'cut'. There is a simple reason as to why this appears to be the case. Analysis of post-importation seizures only tends to reveal samples which have a purity of around 5-8%. This is regardless of the weight of samples seized. If there was cutting all down the line of distribution (from e.g. 1kg seizures all the way down to 10g) then progressively weaker samples might be expected to be seized and a range of purities found by forensic labs (individual samples obviously show a wider range but on average the above statement holds). In other words, whatever point in the chain of distribution the seizure is made, the purity tends to always be roughly that found at the street level, indicating that once the initial dilution has been made down to around 8% that further cutting is probably negligible. A further complication to this picture emerges when we consider that amphetamine reported to be, say 70% pure is in fact by another definition 100% amphetamine. This is because a sample containing 70% base amphetamine (isolated amphetamine is in fact liquid in form) will necessarily have been converted into a salt (the drug which appears on the street) through the use of sulphuric acid producing the commonly known amphetamine sulphate. The 'other 27%' is residual sulphate. Thus a 70% purity rating does not necessarily indicate any adulteration/dilution at all.

The final piece of the forensic jigsaw regarding the extent of cutting in the UK was completed by some specially arranged forensic analysis of street heroin (Coomber, 1997d). In collaboration with the Forensic Science Service each of the 228 'street' heroin seizures analysed in 1995/96 were re-analysed to see how many of the samples contained *no adulterants at all* – a form of analysis not normally recorded.

The findings were, in some respects astounding: in 44% (100) of the samples no adulterants were found at all. Now we already know from Customs and

Excise analysis that many source countries do adulterate/dilute prior to exporting – even if it is often fairly minimal in terms of bulk (Coomber, 1997d). This means that we would expect to see a certain amount of adulteration prior to importation anyway. This finding however, where nearly half of the 228 random street seizures of heroin analysed had neither paracetamol nor caffeine (the predominating adulterants of heroin) or any other such agent present suggested that far less cutting was taking place than had to this point been realised. Nearly half of the samples seized, from around the country, had managed to – post-importation – get all the way down to street level without having been cut even once! Although the other 56% of the 228 samples did contain cutting agents it was impossible to tell what proportion of these had had their adulterants added post-importation? The probability then, given that purity levels of seizures at the borders and on the streets do not differ fantastically, is that very little actual cutting takes place once heroin is in the UK[9].

What the dealers said they did to the drugs they sold and why.

The forensic research however only revealed so much. Indeed earlier in the research, before the forensic evidence became even weightier and more convincing, I decided that too little was known about what drug sellers actually do to the drugs they sell. In part this was because the evidence was suggesting that they didn't routinely and predictably do much of what everyone seemed to believe that they did do and also because there was a paucity of research evidence on such activity. What was known appeared to be outdated and reliant on older research. The 'classical' model of drug distribution and the practice of 'cutting' as elaborated by Preble and Casey (1969) had long influenced thinking about what drug dealers do to the drugs they sell – and arguably still does to some degree. In the US of the 1960s they found that the highly structured and multi-layered chain of distribution involving organised crime syndicates in the heroin market created an ongoing process of adulteration/dilution all the way down to the street. This would often involve one to one cuts of the samples passed down the chain until the resulting purity was perhaps a tenth of its original imported strength. Even here however, samples would be tested for quality throughout the chain leaving little or no room for adulteration with obviously harmful substances:

The kilo connection pays $20,000 for the original kilogram (kilo, kee), and gives it a one and one cut (known as hitting it), that is, he makes two kilos out of one by adding the common adulterants of milk sugar, mannite [mannitol] (a product from the ash tree used as a mild laxative) and quinine (Preble and Casey, 1969: 9).

Preble and Casey describe each level (of which there were at least six) in similar terms, significant (one and one, two and one) cuts made all the way down the chain. At this time and until the late 1980s the average purity of street heroin in the US remained relatively low (around 3-5%) broadly supporting the kind of model outlined by Preble and Casey. However, although Preble and Casey's research no doubt adequately represented what was taking place in New York and in numerous other drug markets at that time, from the forensic evidence that was emerging it no longer seemed applicable to London (or the US as revealed later by the DEA data sets) if it ever was.

Who was spoken to and surveyed

Initially, 31 (mostly heroin) male drug dealers from London and the South East of England, 13 of whom were serving prison sentences as convicted drug dealers, were interviewed about dealing in general – issues about cutting were embedded in the broader focus of the interview to avoid it being given special consideration. This is a separate sample to those interviewed in prison in the last chapter and was distinct research that preceded it. The dealers ranged from street dealers, to wholesale suppliers and importers. The results of that research encouraged me to survey 80 ('powder') dealers from 14 countries and 4 continents using (at the time) highly innovative survey methods via the internet[10], to review 'restricted' US data and finally to interview male and female heroin street dealers (in open markets) in Sydney Australia – research that ultimately derived from and then fed back in to much of what appears in this book. Throughout the various stages of the research the cumulative findings, from different locations, populations and data sets, supported and mutually reinforced those that had already emerged.

Cutting with dangerous substances – the mythical 'other'

Of those interviewed and surveyed, none (unsurprisingly) of the dealers admitted to cutting the drugs they sold with dangerous substances but nearly all believed that the cutting of heroin with dangerous substances was a common occurrence[11]. This initially produced an interesting finding – after all who should know better than the actual dealers themselves – as it conflicted with the forensic evidence. As a researcher I hadn't expected any of the dealers to own up to such a heinous act if they had actually carried it out but interviews were constructed in such a way that the dealers were asked not only if they believed in dangerous cutting but if they had any first-hand knowledge of it to substantiate their belief – and if so what it was. The dealers were thus given the opportunity (if they had done such a thing themselves) to substantiate their belief and show the researcher that they knew what they were talking about by projecting the act onto some mythical other. In the London research only three claimed to have such first-hand knowledge and further 'interrogation' by the researcher on this first-hand knowledge suggested that all three claims were highly suspect with at least two reduced to hearsay of the kind whereby they 'know it happens'. One, a prison inmate (cocaine and heroin addict/dealer) who initially and with great confidence stated that he believed brick-dust, talcum powder, Ajax, Vim, strychnine and other dangerous substances were adulterants/diluents in drugs sold on the street and in prison. When encouraged to provide more detail his proof became far less coherent and then contradictory. New (weak) inmates to prison he assured me, 'still clucking' (withdrawing) would be given 'dust off the floor mixed with a little bit of heroin' by the unscrupulous prison dealers. When we returned to the topic later on he said that this weak heroin was in fact probably cut with Anadin or paracetamol (neither of which were easily available). Finally, he acknowledged that the adulteration/dilution of the drug was probably all done 'outside' by the suppliers to those selling inside (and would thus be unlikely to be any different to that found outside). Another reported that they had known someone who had boasted that they had used brick-dust in place of heroin but on closer examination were unsure as to whether this person had in fact been lying or not 'because he was an idiot'. The third respondent who stated that 'Ajax was substituted for smack [heroin]' (and had no knowledge of anything else) was quite clear that this had taken place as a narrowly targeted 'revenge' hit on one individual (however, as we shall see later in this chapter I argue that such an action is not consistent with an understanding of normative cutting practices and that there is every chance that this act of targeting specific individuals with spiked drugs is extremely rare if it actually happens because of the relatively inefficient nature of the approach). Of the internet sample only four reported 'first-hand knowledge' of cutting with talcum powder, a substance not[12] generally found in forensic samples and which as an *occasional* diluent is unlikely to be a significant health risk whereas a fifth claimed to have used 'A very small amount of strychnine to teach a guy not to bull-shit to us'. None of the Sydney dealers claimed any first-hand knowledge of the use of dangerous cutting agents.

Mixing knowledge and beliefs with myth?

A few of the dealers interviewed, although clearly knowledgeable about *their* involvement in drug supply and adulteration/dilution, appeared to perpetuate particularly detailed ideas on adulteration which had greater levels of inconsistency and apparent willingness to refer to common mythologies than their other responses when it came to more speculative knowledge. One cocaine dealer (who saw himself as a 'cocaine dealer' although he also supplied amphetamine, LSD, and ecstasy) for example, had much to say about the adulteration/dilution of cocaine (mainly with the sugar mannitol at the higher level) but also with glucose, caffeine, or any white crushable Over The Counter (OTC) drug. However, when it came to heroin and heroin dealers these were considered types that you do not mix with. He had an image of heroin as a 'dirty' drug (whereas cocaine was a 'clean' non-problematic drug) and of heroin users/dealers as desperate and dirty. In fact it was this desperation which meant that these individuals were the ones who used Vim and Ajax – because of the desperate state they had been reduced to. Ironically, he readily dismissed the idea of dangerous adulterants in cocaine as unlikely due to the supposed discerning nature of the user, 'word of mouth' being very effective in highlighting a dealer who was selling poor quality drugs, and, that such rumours were in reality unreliable, often started by rival 'firms' seeking to undermine competition. He furthermore subscribed to the unsubstantiated myth of heroin dealers enticing school kids by mixing amphetamine with heroin to get them hooked, another clear sign that some of his beliefs about adulteration/dilution and heroin were based on the type of prejudice and relative ignorance found in and perpetuated by the tabloid press (cf. Lindesmith 1941, Kaplan, 1983, Coomber, 1995a,b). The theme of desperation in fact was a common link to each of those who believed dangerous adulteration to take place. A second cocaine and amphetamine supplier who was also on occasion an importer whilst claiming not to have ever adulterated/diluted these drugs himself, again did believe it happened but only by the 'desperate'. These desperados he believed used talc and amphetamine in cocaine, and, brick-dust in heroin. Yet another 'importer' (mainly of cannabis, but occasionally of cocaine and amphetamine) whilst showing enough knowledge to suggest that he knew what he should, when asked to elaborate on the likely adulteration/dilution of amphetamine down through the chain of distribution he suggested that it would always be 'stepped on' (adulterated/diluted) at each level. Again, as we have already seen, this is wholly inconsistent with findings from forensic analysis on amphetamine sulphate which tends to show that a very large single 'cut' is made at the stage of importation and that purity then differs little regardless of the weight seized – differing weight i.e. Kilos, half-kilos, ounces etc normally indicates differing levels of distribution (Coomber, 1997b).

How much cutting did they do?

The extent of cutting varied between individuals. Overall however in each of the research samples the vast majority 'never' cut the drugs they sold (approx 70%) or did so only sometimes or rarely. Only 1 of the London sample, 4 of the Internet sample and 3 of the Sydney dealers reported 'always' cutting the drugs that they sold. Of those that had done so in the past these were reported as having been fairly rare occurrences and many reported no longer doing it. A number of these individuals had been selling drugs for a long time and as such may have picked up the practice from an earlier era when cutting was more prevalent. The one London dealer who claimed to always cut the 4 to 5 ounces of heroin he sold a month reported that he always used glucose and that this would be by around 10-20% depending on the initial strength. He can be usefully compared however to a dealer of 15 years who described himself as being at the 'bottom' of the drug distribution hierarchy. He reported selling a roughly comparable 1 kilogramme monthly but had never adulterated/diluted at any time.

Why they said they didn't cut the drugs they sold

There were a number of meaningful reasons reported by the dealers who did not cut the drugs they sold as to why they would not or did not.

Profit is primarily made in other ways

As we have seen the primary rationale given for why drug dealers cut the drugs they sell is dilution – so that more profit can be realised from any one batch. However such an approach appears to have been overtaken by far simpler methods that enable dealers to retain as much quality as possible. The primary method cited involves the 'bagging' or 'wrapping' of the initial bought weight, for example, 2 ounces of cocaine into 60, single gramme 'bags' or 'wraps' (there are approximately 28-30 grammes to an ounce) and charging a slightly higher price for a gramme or half-gramme of cocaine than is equal to one thirtieth of an ounce (in the last quarter of 1993 the average wrap size for heroin was 200mg (a fifth of a gramme), for cocaine 375mg, for amphetamine 600mg, and for crack 200mg). In other words selling small amounts at an price which is more than the initially divided worth. All street dealers that intend to gain from the enterprise of selling drugs increase the aggregate worth of their supply in this way as a matter of course. Profit is therefore inherent in the sale of drugs down the chain of supply simply by splitting larger sales into smaller ones.

The second method cited as a means to realising a profit is through 'short counts' or by skimming a small amount off of the individual sample. It was evident from the interviews that some take more care over this than others. One long term drug dealer (10 years) who had earned all of his income from selling drugs since leaving school was clear that he received most of his profit from the mark-up on small sales not from 'stepping on it' (dilution – although he would *sometimes* do this to amphetamine). Moreover he suggested he was lazy when it came to wrapping it up and often did not bother with short counts and when he did, the amount of skimming was arbitrary and negligible, except with ecstasy where he would skim a few tablets off the top of a 'parcel' of 200-300 for personal use. Otherwise, an ounce of whatever drug was being divided up would be split into the approximate weights by eye, for example, 56 roughly equal bags for half gramme deals and then wrapped. Selling short on weight was not commonly mentioned by the respondents. The impression gained overall was that profit was *primarily* gleaned from selling in smaller weights at proportionately higher prices, and secondly by dilution which is another way of producing an effective short count but providing the expected weight.

Dangerous cutting – 'It's just daft': the humanist and rational calculative response

Asked why they did not cut their drugs with substances such as Vim, Ajax, brick-dust and the like, the responses tended to fall into two essential categories: first, the humanitarian, that it 'wouldn't be ethical ... seems ridiculous', 'because you would have to be crazy', 'because it is dangerous', 'I don't want to kill anybody' type of response and second, the rational calculative, 'the comeback', 'would be sussed' [found out], 'bad for business' type of response. Often, some combination of both forms of response would be reported. Two of the Australian dealers provided typical responses:

> [referring to dangerous adulteration] Um, I don't think tha t anybody can be that evil, know what I mean?

> It's dangerous as it is already and you could kill people. You will lose your customer.

One response from the London sample combined the humanitarian with the ruthlessness of doing business to those he did not fear reprisal from 'I sold 16 year olds aspirin and they believed it was 'E'. It didn't hurt me or them. I'd never use worming tablets – that's evil'. Many were also concerned to stress that they believed they had a good name on the street for quality drugs and suggested they took great pride in preserving this status.

The overwhelming nature of the responses does not sit easily with the common stereotype of the drug dealer and why they would cut the drugs they sell. It does however make good logical sense if you do not start with a simplistic and demonised perspective on 'who' and 'what' they are. Simply put they do not put – and have no rationale for doing so – dangerous substances into the drugs they sell. There are many reasons for this but the most prosaic of these is that, psychopaths apart, nobody would. Other reasons that also conflict with simple images of the dealer are that in many cases they are actually afraid of their customers and the potential 'pay-back' for dealing dangerous or even just very poor quality drugs. This clearly goes against the image of the vicious and feared dealer but as we shall see in chapter six dealers come in all shapes, sizes and personality types. They are men, women, working class, middle class, skinny, large, cowardly and mean – in short many are very ordinary and as such – dealing apart – have similar morals and fears as those in the non-dealing population. The rationale for not cutting at all – but also with unsafe substances – usually revolved around wanting to be known for good quality supply and having a level of pride in the drugs they sold. Some as we shall see in the next section even sought to minimize the harm from drugs for their customers. For some others they simply reported either not knowing what to do (to cut the drugs e.g. what with, how to mix it, to what extent) and/or not wishing to dilute what they believed to be an already heavily 'stepped on' product.

What those that did cut their drugs used as cutting agents

Those that did cut the drugs they sold (and consistent with that found and reported by forensic analysis), said that they mainly used sugars such as lactose and glucose, Over The Counter (OTC) drugs such as paracetamol, and substances such as caffeine and bicarbonate of soda.

Accessing the 'truth' about things from those 'in the know' – an important methodological issue

What emerged from the interviews and survey in methodological terms was important both for the research specifically but also generally as regards any research where access to so called 'key informants' is considered central to the research. Some key informants are clearly more 'key' than others. In research on criminal populations a key informant may be a police officer or, as previously stated, a drugs field worker. Either of these will of course have a greater or lesser knowledge of what is being researched depending on the topic. When it comes to drug markets however their knowledge is usually based on assumption rather than empirical evidence (cf Coomber, 2004) and is therefore only more or less reliable. Other types of key informant though may be given greater weighting to their knowledge. Drug dealers we might suspect would know about the drug market and an issue such as dangerous adulteration. As such they would be as 'key' as it is possible to get. However, as this research demonstrated, drug dealers can hold beliefs about the drug market that are consistent with those not involved with drug selling – even though the belief has not been supported by their own experience – and seek to perpetuate a picture of drug dealers as commonly cutting the drugs they sell with dangerous substances. The fact that nearly all of dealers believed in dangerous adulteration but few put forward any reliable substantiation of it this proved to be a key moment in the research and impacts importantly on our understanding of the extent to which the practice of dangerous adulteration is simply accepted – by everyone.

Belief in harmful adulteration – logical problems

Apart from the forensic and other evidence outlined above there are a number of coherent reasons why we might doubt the basis of most fears about adulterated drugs and the particular form (brick-dust; Vim etc) they take. Primarily, the activity of drug selling is just that, the selling of a product. Whether the product has to go down a pyramid or not, the seller for the most part, does not want ill health or death to befall their clients[13]. If they are regularly involved in the trade of drugs then they have no motive to use substances other than those outlined previously such as caffeine, glucose, lactose, and other useful pharmacological compounds. As stated above there may be a direct 'benefit' to the distributor in using these substances. Often they may 'enhance' a product by mimicking and even extending the effects of the primary drug (e.g. amphetamine in cocaine[14]), by increasing the amount of drug available to the user (e.g. caffeine, paracetamol in heroin), or simply by improving (subjectively so), through drug combination, the effects of the drug taking experience (Strang, 1990). Another logistical issue relates to the fact that most of the adulterants/diluents used are both readily available and even cheap. The financial incentive, even for the mythical[15] desperate junkie prepared to do anything to get their next hit, is negligible. In any case, resorting to the grinding down of a light-bulb or a brick does not strike me as very likely. It is easier to grab a bottle containing paracetamol or vitamins or even to use glucose or milk powder from the kitchen cabinet. Following this logic we would have to ask when would obviously dangerous substances, likely to cause real harm be used. Arguably, such action may occur. But, statistics on drug fatalities, especially around drugs like amphetamine

(95% impure) are very low (less than 10 a year (HOSB 1993) given the very high levels of use in the UK. Clearly such adulteration is not normal or even commonplace, or if it does take place not highly dangerous. For someone to knowingly mix a dangerous substance in a drug sample with the express intention to sell it on knowing it would cause harm is likely to happen for one of two reasons, both of which, I would argue represent a qualitatively different activity to what we would normally understand as drug adulteration/dilution. The first scenario is that the person cutting the drugs is psychopathic. This could also be the case of your local baker, brewer or fishmonger. It would be a chance relationship which produced a psychotic drug dealer who was at one and the same time willing to undermine his/her income by killing off their clients (and putting off future ones). He/she would have to be stupid as well as mad. The second scenario has more logic to it but is perhaps more reliant on particular structural situations to be more likely – revenge. It is not uncommon to hear anecdotes relating to revenge or grudge killings within the drugs underworld through the adulteration of drugs with poisons. The reporting of drug related deaths in the UK where poisons have been recorded in addition to the primary drug are however virtually non-existent. One recorded example of strychnine poisoning in Dublin in the early 1980s cites how 'Eight young adults sniffed quantities of strychnine in the mistaken belief that it was cocaine ...[and that] It is not known how these patients acquired the strychnine, which was apparently inhaled by mistake for cocaine at a party' (O'Callaghan et al. 1982: 478). A fatal (uninformed) mistake (one of the eight died) is as likely a cause here as is the supposition of attempted murder. There may be a number of reasons why we might suppose this. Often, drug related killings are intended to be much more visible. Those doing the killing will want to use the visibility of the killing as a symbolic warning to others. Also, the adulteration of drugs even with poisons such as strychnine is an extremely imprecise and sloppy method through which to cause harm or commit murder. Only one of the eight died, seven survived. The one who died may not have been a target at all. A drug user may share their drugs or even sell them on. They may also discover the adulteration, become aware of who is attempting to cause them harm and as a consequence perhaps effectively endanger the person who originally tried to hurt them. If such a method is used to deal with unwanted members of the drug world then it is perhaps more likely to happen in the organised crime infiltrated structures of drug distribution in the US but my suspicion is that it is in fact another part of drug mythology. Overall, the point to be made, whether or not this does or does not happen, is that it is a very rare event. It is not the result of normal drug adulteration/dilution practices and is unlikely to touch users on the street as such poisoning would be a targeted event. It is qualitatively distinct from an understanding of adulteration practices where the danger is thought to come from day to day methods of distribution because it needs to be understood as a direct attempt to do harm to specific individuals. If a car is used to murder somebody it would hardly be reasonable to understand the incident as an accident or even within the normal understanding of what dangers cars on the roads constitute to pedestrians.

Another, but perhaps even more unlikely scenario is where extreme ignorance on the part of the person cutting the drugs led to them using dangerous adulterants. There was a case in the last century in Bradford for example where the intended diluent of Plaster of Paris in peppermint lozenges was accidently substituted with arsenic by a new apprentice and resulted in 30 deaths (Postgate, 1990). In a more contemporary vein it is possible that an occasional, ignorant, street level dealer may use talcum powder as a diluent instead of paracetamol, glucose or some other commonly used substance. This would possibly explain the rare occurrence of pulmonary granulomas in the lungs of drug users, consistent with exposure to starch or talc) who inhale their drugs (c.f. Johnson & Petru, 1991; Marschke et al. 1975). It is likely however that unless susceptibility exists occasional exposure to talc would not result in such problems. The fact that such cases are not widespread would suggest that talc[16] – which tends not to appear in quantities consistent with being a cutting agent[17] – is not, in general a risk in this sense.

The point to be made is that of the above scenarios none of them happen often enough or constitute a way of behaving able to usefully contribute to an understanding of *normal* adulteration practices, adulterants or the dangers in them.

Dangerous adulteration – a total myth?

A form of dangerous drug adulteration – albeit differently to how it is portrayed or generally understood – does sometimes happen. That is, there are occasions when new variations on street heroin appear and contribute to increased mortality figures. The introduction to some US cities heroin adulterated with scopolamine in the mid-1990s was initially widely reported as having caused numerous overdoses and a number of deaths through 'poisoning' (Furst, 2000). In the final analysis no fatalities were reported as having resulted from the 241 heroin users admitted to hospital with varying forms of anticholinergic toxicity (Hamilton et al. 2000; Perrone, Shaw and De Roos, 1999). Many, none-the-less, did need extensive medical assistance. Although, as seems likely, scopolamine was purposively added to street heroin to enhance it, and that this was an error of judgement by those that did it, the *intent* was not to poison. Episodes such as this and those resulting from degradation, or contamination, however remain rare and given the clandestine and relatively non-hygienic production conditions of illicit drugs this may be surprising. It demonstrates however the vagaries of the illicit drugs market and that risks such as these are real. It does not however demonstrate the activity of purposive dangerous adulteration.

All in all then, the forensic evidence coupled with various other empirical and logistical evidence into the day-to-day practices of drug dealers, suggests quite strongly that the purposive cutting of street drugs with obviously *dangerous* or poisonous substances is highly improbable (if not mythical) and at the very least it is unsubstantiated. In fact the amount of cutting that takes place in the drug distribution system per se is, in comparison to common perception, quite minimal and it appears that it is often the case that street drugs can travel down through the drug distribution chain without being cut with any substance at all. Where it does occur – again in direct opposition to common perception – it is often with substances that (e.g. paracetamol, caffeine) that are not simply diluting the product but can 'add' to it. They are certainly not – as a rule of thumb – not hap-hazard or indiscriminate 'cuts'.

In the next chapter we look at a 'drug hoax' that has assimilated a number of the drug dealer 'myths' covered so far and become one of the most pervasive of urban legends – the Blue Star LSD Hoax. Unfortunately, as we shall see, this is no ordinary urban legend and its ongoing presence is rarely treated as a hoax.

Footnotes

[1] Note on terminology: The term adulterant is used in this paper to refer to substances added to illicit drugs in the process of selling and distribution. Adulterants proper are in fact other psychoactive drugs (like caffeine, or paracetamol) which are much cheaper than the main substance, have a similar or complimentary effect when mixed with it, and therefore help hide the fact that the substance has been diluted. Substances which are not psychoactive, such as glucose and lactose, are more formally known as 'diluents'. These are added to a drug to increase the amount of drug available to be sold. It should be noted however that some substances which are found in street drugs will be the result of the particular manufacturing process used to make the drug. In this sense those substances might be more properly referred to as 'impurities'. 'Excipients' found in drugs (primarily pills/tablets) are the products used to bind the drug together. Common excipients are starch, gelatin or other gums (ISDD, 1994).

[2] A picture of Leah, unconscious in hospital and attached to various life-saving/preserving technologies was used in a drug prevention campaign and placed on large advertising billboards around the country.

[3] A convenience sample of 248 university students was used in this research. It was not a representative sample of the British public but it is argued that given that students are more likely to be drug users and comparatively more experienced of the 'drug scene' than would be a representative sample and as such more knowledgeable about, or perhaps reflective upon, what 'really happens' then it is possible that with a representative sample an even greater percentage than 90% would have believed in dangerous adulteration. A fuller discussion of these issues is undertaken in the paper itself.

[4] Clearly, since I undertook this research and published a sequence of academic and other papers on my findings there has been some impact on the unquestioning stance of some towards the issue. In general however I would suggest that little change has taken place either in terms of general assumptions or presentations about dangerous adulteration.

[5] Certainly in comparison to the level of harms (either in degree or prevalence) often attributed to them

[6] See note 1, this chapter, for an explanation of adulterants and diluents.

[7] Obviously, paracetamol is not a harmless substance per se but given the amounts found in heroin and the corresponding dose this would deliver, it is relatively benign when the risks it presents in this way are considered.

[8] Phenacetin has been cited as a possible carcinogen in humans and is no longer legally available in numerous countries. It is suspected that the Phenacetin found in cocaine is diverted stock from those areas where it is still available legally (personal communication, 2005).

[9] My later secondary re-analysis of the US DEA data likewise found that certain cities in the US consistently, year after year, provided heroin samples for analysis where no cutting agents were found to be present. Again, this was a finding either not noticed or simply ignored by the forensic scientists involved or those that presented the analytic data.

[10] Such research is highly dependent on appropriate methodology and sample – great care was taken to assess the reliability of the findings – for more information on this see Coomber 1997c and 1997d.

[11] Apart from the 'Asian' street dealers in Cabramatta, Sydney. These individuals were less aware of rumours or beliefs in dangerous cutting and none claimed any first-hand knowledge of such activity.

[12] As stated earlier 'talc' is an excipient of numerous over-the-counter drugs is found in small amounts but this is not the same as perfumed talcum powder bought in shops.

[13] This is, in a sense, largely a logistical position (apart from the forensic evidence which so far has failed to show the existence of the type of adulterant/diluents commonly feared). Statements of commercial intent and quality assurance are obviously less explicit and liable to less formal sanction in the black market of drugs. 'Proof' of the absence of malevolent

behaviour is difficult to obtain. Ongoing research by the author whereby drug dealers have been interviewed about their adulteration/dilution practices however is showing that dealers actively avoid using dangerous adulterants/diluents not just for commercial but also for humane reasons. One dealer, not untypical of the responses, for example, stated when asked as to why they had not used certain adulterants/diluents 'Didn't want to harm anybody', another that it is 'too dangerous' and yet another that it was 'not good business practice'. Others demonstrated their less than malicious approach by using vitamin C and even a homeopathic nasal remedy.

14. Although research has suggested that amphetamine is not commonly used as an adulterant/diluent in cocaine (Cohen, 1989; Drug Abuse Trends, 1993) interviews by the author have revealed that at least one London based cocaine dealer regularly adulterates cocaine with amphetamine. Thus, whilst this practice is believed to be widespread (cf Cohen 1989) by users of cocaine there is insufficient evidence to suggest that it is more than an isolated practice, perhaps one that occasional user/dealers on the 'fringe' employ, for being essentially users, they like many other users, believe it commonplace and thus suitable?

15 One cocaine dealer recently interviewed by the author felt that it was only heroin 'junkies' who got desperate enough to use Vim or such substances. The scenario he gave as likely however demonstrated a lack of knowledge of both heroin users and its use. What his strongly held opinion more readily indicated was that dealers of certain drugs like cocaine may see themselves as dealing with a relatively 'clean' and non-problematic drug whilst retaining typical prejudices and stereotypes of heroin and heroin addicts.

16 Talc – also used as a bulking agent in over the counter drugs such as paracetamol is not the same thing as perfumed talcum powder.

17 Rather, it probably appears because talc is a common diluent used in paracetamol and its presence in a substance that *is* used for adulteration means that it is a happenstance of that process.

Chapter 4:

The Myth of the Blue Star LSD Tattoo

'It's coming to a town near you – soon'.

Drug dealers are luring youngsters by selling cut-price LSD with pictures of comic characters such as Dennis the Menace drawn on the hallucinogenic tabs, West Midland police say (*The Times*, August 18, 1993).

One of the most pervasive of drug stories and one that manages to encapsulate nearly all the drug dealer images mentioned so far, as well as a number of misleading drug effect images, is that of the Blue Star LSD tattoo. Reports of Blue Star Tattoos laced with killer LSD have been circulating on and off in towns and cities in countries all around the world for at least the last twenty-five years. In 2001 for example, both London and Sydney experienced their latest Blue Star scares and in the time since so have many other locations around the world. Despite the fact that the Blue Star LSD tattoo has been acknowledged as a hoax by enforcement authorities such as the US Drug Enforcement Administration; London's Metropolitan Police; and many other authorities, it continues almost unabated in one form or another to permeate and worry communities and to gain serious media attention. It also perpetuates, and thus reinforces, unhelpful drug and drug dealer images and, as we shall see, there is good reason to suspect that it is likely to continue to do so.

Over the years a typical 'Blue Star' LSD tattoo scare has been started by the 'posting' of a flyer or information sheet in a public space. The flyer may be posted on a street side telegraph pole, sent to a school, a community centre, local media or even a local police station. More recent developments have seen warnings posted on websites, or more commonly, passed on in emails. Although generally known as the Blue Star Tattoo there have been a number of decorative variants: early examples referred to tattoos hosting pictures of Superman and Mickey Mouse whilst later ones have referred to postage stamp sized transfers with Bart Simpson, clowns and other contemporary cartoon favourites. Another famous version that – stylistically at least – like the Blue Star is a little prosaic when compared to cartoon representations and the idea of engaging children, is that of the Red Pyramid Tattoo. Regardless of the decoration or cartoon character however the information sheets all provide the same essential warning: that drug dealers in the given locality are unscrupulously enticing children to buy LSD soaked transfers or tattoos by decorating them with popular cartoon characters. Impregnated with LSD, the stamps are said to be particularly dangerous because 'the drug can be absorbed through the skin'[1] simply by handling them and that because 'some are laced with strychnine' the 'trip' could be fatal. The flyers usually claim the stamps to be a 'new way of selling acid (LSD) by appealing to young children' and on some versions there are claims that many children have already died. They always advise the holder to pass the information sheet onto appropriate authorities such as schools, day care centres, friends and neighbours and the trustworthiness of the information is usually given credence by being on the headed notepaper of a hospital. a health authority, a police force or some other 'authority'. In some cases further credibility is suggested through the presence of a signature of an individual in authority such as a doctor. On occasion the stated individuals do exist but they have never been the originators of the warnings. Nearly all schools now of course have their own websites and following the 2001 scare in London I found numerous examples where the received warning was then posted to the school page warning parents of the new danger and to be especially vigilant. Despite the fact that flyers are often not very professionally or even particularly well produced, as might be expected of a flyer coming from some authority or another, their impact does not appear to be lessened. In fact the willingness of people to accept the flyers at face value has much to do with their continued success.

WE HAVE been informed that a very dangerous drug is being circulated illegally in some parts of New England. You should be aware of its presence in the area and its severe danger to all who might come in contact with the substance. Please caution your children to be on the alert for any materials that fall into the category described and to make note of the individual who might want to pass it on to them.

MICKEY MOUSE ACID (L.S.D.) has been circulated widely throughout some parts of New England as a part of or in the form of a "sticker" or label. It may be available to school age children (See picture).

DO NOT HANDLE!!! CONTACT WITH MOISTURE AND SKIN COULD CAUSE THE SAME EFFECT AS TAKING A DOSE OF ACID ORALLY!!! The picture is Mickey Mouse in the Walt Disney Movie -- "The Sorcerer's Apprentice" from "Fantasia". The actual size is ½" square. Mickey Mouse is wearing a red gown, blue hat, yellow shoes and has the appearance of a "lick and stick tatoo". All Disney Cartoon characters have been used in the distribution of this LSD

If you have seen the substance, know the whereabouts of its, or have any information regarding it, please call your local Police Department at once.

Top: an early example of a 'Blue Star' flyer. Below left : An example of an actual Sorcerer's Apprentice Mickey Mouse LSD blotter tab from which the flyer derived its main image. Below right: A single 'Snoopy' LSD tab. Mickey Mouse and Snoopy images reproduced with kind permission from the Blotter Barn project all © 2006 Blotter Barn. 'Tab' images have been enlarged for the purpose of illustration.

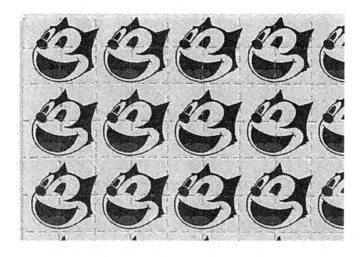

Further examples of LSD 'blotter art' - 'Felix' and Tin Tin. Such images on street LSD appear to have promoted the view that such art was designed to seduce the interest of children. Reproduced with kind permission from the Blotter Barn project all © 2006 Blotter Barn.

CIBA-GEIGY's Health Care Management Program

HEALTH ADVISORY - "DRUG WATCH"

Attached Public Service Announcement From
The Leaguers, Incorporated
Early Childhood Development Center

A form of tatoo called "Blue Star" is being sold to school children. It is a small sheet of white paper containing a blue star, the size of a pencil eraser. Each star is soaked with LSD.

Each star can be removed and placed in the mouth. THE LSD CAN ALSO BE ABSORBED THROUGH THE SKIN BY HANDLING THE PAPER.

There is also brightly colored tabs resembling postage stamps that have pictures of superman butterflies, clowns, Mickey Mouse and other Disney characters on them. These stamps are packed in a red cardboard box wrapped in foil. This is a new way of selling ACID by appealing to young children.

A young child could happen upon these and have a fatal "trip". It is also learned that little children could be given a free "tatoo" by other children who want to have some fun, or by other cultivating new customers.

A red stamp called "RED PYRAMID" is also being distributed along with "MICRO DOT" in various colors and another kind "WINDOW PANE", which has a grid that can be cut out.

THESE ARE ALL LACED WITH DRUGS ..... PLEASE advise your community and your children about these drugs. If you or your child see any of the above, DO NOT HANDLE!!! THESE DRUGS ARE KNOWN TO REACT VERY QUICKLY and some are laced with Strychnine.

Symptoms are: hallucinations, severe vomiting, uncontrolled laughter, mood change and change in body temperature. Go to the hospital as soon as possible and call the police.

Please feel free to reproduce this article and distribute it within your communities.

FOR THOSE OF YOU WITH SMALL CHILDREN, THIS IS VERY SCARY INFORMATION; BUT IMPORTANT FOR YOU TO KNOW.

An 1990 Blue Star example 'from' Ciba Geigy's Health Care Management Programme.

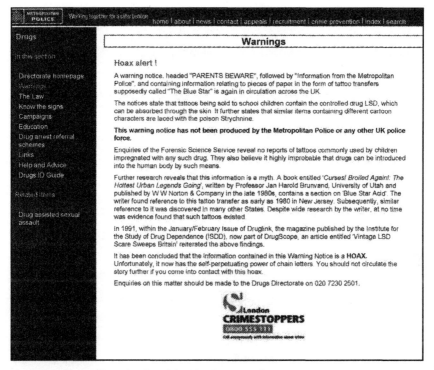

Warnings

Hoax alert !

A warning notice. headed "PARENTS BEWARE", followed by "Information from the Metropolitan Police". and containing information relating to pieces of paper in the form of tattoo transfers supposedly called "The Blue Star" is again in circulation across the UK

The notices state that tattoos being sold to school children contain the controlled drug LSD, which can be absorbed through the skin It further states that similar items containing different cartoon characters are laced with the poison Strychnine.

This warning notice has not been produced by the Metropolitan Police or any other UK police force.

Enquiries of the Forensic Science Service reveal no reports of tattoos commonly used by children impregnated with any such drug. They also believe it highly improbable that drugs can be introduced into the human body by such means.

Further research reveals that this information is a myth. A book entitled *Curses! Broiled Again!: The Hottest Urban Legends Going'*, written by Professor Jan Harold Brunvand, University of Utah and published by W W Norton & Company in the late 1980s, contains a section on 'Blue Star Acid'. The writer found reference to this tattoo transfer as early as 1980 in New Jersey. Subsequently, similar reference to it was discovered in many other States. Despite wide research by the writer, at no time was evidence found that such tattoos existed

In 1991, within the January/February Issue of Druglink, the magazine published by the Institute for the Study of Drug Dependence (ISDD), now part of DrugScope, an article entitled 'Vintage LSD Scare Sweeps Britain' reiterated the above findings.

It has been concluded that the information contained in this Warning Notice is a **HOAX**. Unfortunately, it now has the self-perpetuating power of chain letters You should not circulate the story further if you come into contact with this hoax.

Enquiries on this matter should be made to the Drugs Directorate on 020 7230 2501.

CRIMESTOPPERS

The Metropolitan Police refutation of the Blue Star Tattoo hoax.

For illustrative purposes – I could have used numerous others – let's look briefly at three recent case studies, one from London, England in 2001 one from Ireland in 2002 and one from South Africa in 2003/4.

Case Study 1: London, England 2001

The "Blue Star" hoax that hit England in 2001 is indicative of both how the scare works and also of why it will likely continue. In August of that year a flyer was circulated around the country that followed the pattern outlined above. It was sent to schools, the local media, to police stations and to community groups. The flyer, claimed to originate from the Metropolitan Police and local newspapers all over the country, from Somerset to Wigan and Manchester, Staines to Darlington, and East-Grinstead to Harrow, ran headlines or stories reporting dangers relating to LSD and strychnine soaked transfers aimed at children. One local newspaper in Croydon, South London was even made aware of the story by the local police station's press liaison officer who was blissfully unaware (I contacted him personally) that either the story or the flyer were false. At least three schools placed warnings on their school web sites.

My reporting of this particular scare in 2001 is not the stuff of sustained research, more of interested observance and as such is far from exhaustive. I'm sure that many more local schools, television and radio media transmitted warnings than I found out about and warnings proliferated thereon. What can not be easily measured is the worry and fear that parents and others responsible for children feel in the wake of seemingly real communications about a seemingly real and believable threat emanating (falsely) from a trusted authority such as the Metropolitan Police. What is perhaps even more surprising about this particular scare is that the Metropolitan Police had been used as a 'source' by Blue Star circulators previously in 1992 and that the Metropolitan Police have ever since maintained a web page dedicated to warning people not to be taken in by what is an unsubstantiated myth. This, as already stated, did not prevent a police officer whose job it is to liaise with the media to take the flyer as genuine and to help propagate the myth. Part of the problem that the Metropolitan Police (and indeed all police forces) have in regard to the Blue Star LSD Tattoo myth is that personnel change. Personnel also change in the media, in schools and in all other information giving institutions. Recurrent events are thus not always picked up by those not in post the last time it circulated. It is also the case that the myth is more believable to many than it is suspect because it reinforces a range of drug and drug dealer images that are considered completely reasonable by what is a relatively uninformed public and police force when it comes to the way that drugs and drug markets work. It is this reason that this particular scare will periodically continue to surface and successfully spread – even within the area bounded by the Metropolitan Police.

In the box we can see a typical example of how well-meaning authorities and local media can be easily swept along on a tide of concern. This warning in the *Bucks Free Press*, (July 23, 2001) a local 'free to door' and online newspaper includes reference to specific police officers and to the aforementioned [fake] Metropolitan Police circular. We can also see that specific officers are named (true in this case) who have passed the warning on to the media and that despite not being aware of any incidents Detective Sergeant Daniel felt propelled to make the warning public because: " ...we want to make sure it doesn't start happening here."

Parents warned about drug-laced stick-on tattoos

By Syreeta Lund

POLICE are warning the public about cartoon transfers laced with the hallucinogenic drug LSD after fears they could be offered to children. Characters such as Bart Simpson and Mickey Mouse appear on the stick-on tattoos, which are the size of a postage stamp. High Wycombe police, who were warned about the harmless-looking transfers by the Metropolitan Police, say the drug can be soaked into the skin just by handling them.

Detective Sergeant Gareth Daniel, of High Wycombe CID, has already sent out a warning to Neighbourhood Watch coordinators around the area. He said: "We thought it only fair to warn people in case it happens here. The transfers are laced with LSD and the most important thing to get across is that transfers should not be bought anywhere other than a shop. "If you do come across them you should only pick them up with gloves because the LSD can be absorbed through the skin." A circular from the Metropolitan Police, following reports in London, said that the transfers initially contained a picture of a small blue star but now they contain a selection of popular cartoon characters. Superman, Bart Simpson, Mickey Mouse and images of clowns and butterflies are along the pictures on the drug-laden transfers. Det Sgt Daniel said: "Kids are attracted by the pictures. Initially the transfers had a small blue star on them but now they have Bart Simpson and other Disney characters." He said they do not know how widespread the transfers are but they have not had any reports in the area yet. He said: "But we want to make sure it doesn't start happening here."

If anyone has any information about the transfers or sees anyone selling the transfers call High Wycombe police on 01494 465888.

2:06pm Monday 23rd July 2001

Case Study 2: Carlow, Ireland, 2002

On April 8, 2002 *The Nationalist* reported that two separate school principals in Carlow; South East Ireland submitted copies of a Blue Star warning that they had been given to the Carlow Garda (police) Station. The police however, were unable to confirm whether the warnings were credible or if the tattoos were available in Carlow itself. Parents, the paper reported, had already been sent copies of the warning by one of the principals – a local Bishop – who whilst admitting being unaware of the origins of the warning felt that it was in parents' best interest to be informed and that having been made aware of the threat that it would have been wrong to not to have done anything about it. No rebuttal or follow-up was printed by the paper.

Case Study 3: Pretoria, South Africa, 2003/4

More recently in 2003 hundreds of schoolchildren from schools in Pretoria, South Africa were issued with warning letters to take home from their schools. The warnings were on Tshwane Metropolitan Police letterhead paper but did not originate from that source. The warnings themselves followed the standard structure seen so many times elsewhere and finally, after receiving national news prominence prompted the intervention of the Organised Crime Unit to deny the credibility of the warnings. This was followed by a statement from the Department of the Minister of Education promising to investigate the claims (*The Mercury*, 2004, September 22). In September 2005, Curro Private School in Durbanville, South Africa placed a Blue Star warning on its public web pages.

What we see with each of these examples is the ease with which the scares can gain ground. People in authority, faced with making a decision about the safety of local children, disseminate the warning. Dissemination is undertaken for the best of motives. For many the information is highly credible (at the 'that's what happens' level) whilst for others who may be more circumspect the risk of not passing on the information – if it proves to be correct – presents a risk too great to chance not passing on the information.

No smoke without fire: how do we know that it is a hoax?

Despite its prevalence and unlike many other 'drug myths' that usually have some kind of event or example to give some credence to their continued existence there are no known occurrences of an LSD laced tattoo of this nature recorded by any police authority anywhere. Indeed the US Drug Enforcement Agency (not a body known for a 'soft' stance on drugs or indeed on drug dealers) for many years[2] also published a Web page dedicated to informing the public of this very fact. The DEA declared there to be no evidence that cartoon adorned LSD blotters – which are none-the-less common, along with a great variety of other 'art-work'– have been used by dealers to target children and that 'no evidence of a child being injured by touching an LSD-laden "tattoo" has been recorded, though hundreds of incidents of the "Blue Star Hoax" itself have been documented'. Beyond this however and once we look at the detail of the flyers there are a number of other reasons to evidence that not only that this is indeed a hoax but that it is in fact a poor one.

Inaccuracies

The hoax relies on a number of inaccuracies relating to the way that LSD and drug markets work. To begin with it is highly unlikely that LSD can be absorbed into the skin simply by touching it, particularly from paper[4], and strychnine would not be able to do so in a way that is harmful in the amounts that would be present. The Blue Star Hoax also, as stated at the head of this chapter relies on a number of other commonly held drug and drug dealer myths to substantiate it in the eyes of a fearsome public. As we saw in the last chapter the supposed presence of strychnine in numerous drugs is a common piece of drug folklore and the police it is true, often claim, following a drug death, that a drug (read heroin, ecstasy, cocaine) contaminated with some poison or another to be the likely cause. As we saw however, reports following analysis almost never claim this to be the case and usually confirm the drug not to have had any poisonous substances present[5]. The supposed presence of strychnine in LSD however has a slightly different history with LSD user folklore commonly regarding the various physical 'side-effects' that users sometimes experience after use, particularly stomach aches or related problems, to the presence of strychnine or some other naturally occurring 'poison' present in the ergot fungus from which LSD is derived (Coomber, 1997a; Shulgin, 1996). Strychnine however is totally unrelated to ergot, is not a by-product of the synthesis of LSD and is not found in street samples[6]. There are numerous possible reasons for stomach cramps, both pharmaco-logical and biosocial[7].

We have also seen (chapter two) that the idea that drug dealers try to hook (addict) children or recreational drug users with the twin approaches of either providing free (addictive) drugs or by offering them drugs (e.g. ecstasy laced with heroin) secretly cut with an addictive drug is unfounded. Both are reliant upon a false notion of how quickly and easily an addiction forms as well as a poor understanding of drug market mechanisms. The point however is that these ideas are reasonably prevalent amongst members of the criminal justice system, the lay public and drug users as well. It is also the case that such activities are considered to be completely within the behavioural remit of drug dealers who, being morally decrepit, will stoop to any level. As such it is by drawing on these commonly assumed drug market activities and drug properties that a specific hybrid, the Blue Star Hoax probably originated and from where its credibility as a believable phenomenon comes from. It is however, when looked at closely, even weaker than the more conventional variants on this theme like those that deal with drugs such as heroin or cocaine.

In the case of the Blue Star Tattoo this whole scenario is made even more unlikely because LSD is not an addictive drug[8] and unknown use of it would not be likely to lead to a pleasant experience and thus a wish to take it again, either through compulsion (instant addiction) or through reward. Indeed, use of hallucinogens by unsuspecting individuals is likely to be highly traumatic. The rationale for drug dealers targeting children with LSD soaked transfers – especially those also containing strychnine – thus has little by way of reason attached to it unless you assume that the dealers in question are so depraved that they are seeking to do purposive harm to children for the sake (or fun) of it. However, without the general ignorance of drug effects and drug market activities, without the existence of a number of common notions relating to addiction, the power of 'drugs' and what drug dealers do to the drugs they sell, and without the defining characteristics of *what* drug dealers are, the Hoax would die out.

It is almost certain that the Blue Star Tattoo in one variant or another will continue to emerge around the country and around the world. It is only when the public and the police become more informed about drug issues and rely less on common assumption based around fear and anxiety – however understandable – that we will see its demise.

How did it start?

Understanding how myths such as this get started is important. Such knowledge may reveal to us not only how and why a certain set of beliefs emerged and were perpetuated but also provide further evidence as to their problematic nature. According to urban legend specialist Jan Harold Brunvand (1986) the Blue Star tattoo hoax appears to have actually started life as the 'Mickey Mouse Acid' scare, with that particular character emphasised (see page 98) in the summer of 1981.

Although rumours of 'Mickey Mouse Acid' did exist before this it seems that a Superintendent Jack McCormick of the Ohio Bureau of Criminal Investigation became 'the "unwilling father" of the story in his own and nearby states' (Brunvand, 1986: 167) unintentionally giving the rumours more of a factual basis than they had hitherto possessed. Wanting confirmation of the Mickey Mouse Acid rumour that was spreading journalists pressed McCormick for details. At this time we might assume that the very existence of LSD tabs baring the picture of a cartoon character would raise suspicion in the public mind of dealers targeting children in order to get them 'hooked' on the drug. McCormick told them what he knew – that neither he or any officers in his jurisdiction had come across any 'lick and stick' LSD transfers or tattoos but that he was aware of rumours in other states of their existence. All he knew about, he declared, was the traditional LSD 'blotter' acid that was common everywhere. When a dealer was later arrested with five thousand LSD tabs each with a little blue star on them McCormick did his best to allay concerns that this proved the existence of such marketing by dealers. Moreover, none of the stars for example contained LSD and were not of the lick and stick variety. After persistent questioning McCormick reportedly became impatient and along with some 'technical stuff' he admittedly made up some of the information as he went along. Whilst Brunvand doesn't relay exactly what McCormick 'made up' and perhaps even McCormick was unable to recall (or more likely too embarrassed to do so publicly) it is likely that he fanned the flames of publicity by asserting the *possibility* of much of what the rumours contained. Whatever the content, the result after a little 'embroidering' by the media, was as Brunvand puts it to give 'the legend a new lease of life'.

A conflation of events

Whilst Brunvand appears to have located the specific time, place and action that gave impetus and some substantiation to what at this point was a burgeoning rumour this only tells part of the story. The origins of rumours, myths and urban legends no doubt have diffuse beginnings. Prior to the mid-1970s LSD was primarily available as tablets (pills) or powder. Blotter tabs along with gel-tabs afforded more consistency in purity and potency and thus became the established norm after 1976 (Stafford, 1992). The emergence of this rumour only became possible once LSD became commonly available in blotter paper form and then decorated in some way that adults and law enforcement bodies could interpret as likely to interest children. The emergence of decorated or illustrated blotter tabs can be traced back to the late 1960s but the use of cartoon characters doesn't appear to have emerged until the late 1970s and early 1980s (Shapiro, 2001 personal communication). Until these events, the possibility that LSD dealers were overtly targeting children by using drugs decorated with images they would find attractive could not be demonstrated. At this particular point in time heroin in New York City was being sold by brand name. This was a new marketing phenomenon in the illegal drugs market and related to that particular drug in that location (Wendel & Curtis, 2000). It is possible however that the Mickey Mouse Acid rumour is a simple conflation of these two new phenomena that more or less coincided: decorated LSD blotter tabs and brand marketing of heroin (but in the popular mind 'drugs') in New York. It is a short step from here to integrate such paraphernalia to what people assumed drug dealers already did – 'pushed' their drugs to children to get them hooked to secure a new client. This was simply a more effective tool through which to achieve that objective. In fact Brunvand points to the existence of a bulletin issued in 1980 by the New Jersey State Police Narcotic Bureau that has pictures of various LSD tabs with cartoon characters on accompanied by a warning stating 'Children may be susceptible to this type of cartoon stamp believing it to be a tattoo transfer' (Brunvand, 1986: 167). There is no suggestion that children are being targeted but a suggestion that children may confuse it with a tattoo transfer. We can see perhaps how such information sheets could provide a source of concern. We don't know of course whether the bulletin is a result of the rumours or the rumours partly derived from such bulletins. What we can reasonably assume however is that once such bulletins started to be produced (and they continue to this day) by authorities such as the police then the rumour is given credence, authority and its life guaranteed for just a little longer. We might also surmise that once such bulletins and statements were being circulated that then, as today, the rumour/hoax is mainly circulated by well meaning and very concerned individuals and community groups looking to protect their children and communities. Given this, in many senses, and as others have suggested this isn't a hoax in the proper sense of the word. The aim isn't to deceive, trick or play a practical joke but is, for the most part, a concerned and concerted effort to help others be aware of a (perceived) real and present danger. In reality it is therefore probably closer to what has been called a contamination legend[9].

It is possible that the Mickey Mouse Acid rumour may partly have roots in an even older apocryphal story that itself circulates, evolves and re-emerges. Brunvand citing the work of folklorists Opie and Opie relates a folktale that emerged on the introduction of the world's first postage stamp the Penny Black in 1840. They record that at that time rumours circulated that 'the glue used was poisonous, that the most vile ingredients were employed in its manufacture, that human material was not excluded, and that those so rash as to lick the Queen's head were in danger of contacting cholera' (Opie and Opie, cited in Brunvand, 1986: 168). If this story, or variants of it, have become part of the public (or some parts of the public) psyche then the rumour of the LSD 'stamps' laced with poison perhaps had less work to do to be believable than if it was absent. Further to this, concerns around drink and food being adulterated with poison (to kill) or a sleeping draught (to e.g. kidnap – or shanghai – men to force them to become sailors) has long been a concern to people over time as has the distrust of most black market products (Coomber, 1997c). It is in this sense that Brunvand refers to the probability that most (apparently contemporary) urban legends have a plot or theme that is much older, often from previous centuries and part of the older tradition of oral folklore. A deconstruction of this early rumour would probably need to understand the fears and distrust attached to the emergence of a new technology (often feared and resented) that asks the public to take the glue into their own bodies (glue has long associations with dead bodies – both animal and human) and fear of diseases like cholera and ignorance of how it is contracted would be high. At the very least is shows how rumours of the Mickey Mouse Acid variety existed long ago.

It is therefore the underlying context, the existing belief systems about what drugs do to people about the activities of drug dealers and the fear of them preying on children that enabled the scare to manifest itself in the way it did. The unfortunate statements by Superintendent McCormick probably only fanned a slumbering fire. It is moreover this underlying context of (uninformed) beliefs that provides the seedbed for its continuing success.

Why so successful?

The initial Mickey Mouse Acid rumours and latterly the Blue Star LSD Tattoo hoax have been successful because, as stated above, it is able to exploit people's ignorance, feed their worst fears and obtain their ready deference to authority and information providers. Stories about drugs, drug users and drug dealers however are a special case in the sense that they feed fear more readily than some other topics.

There are some important parallels regarding the success of the Blue Star hoax from the field of media effects. Although it has proven notoriously difficult to show the effects of the media on behaviour (McQuail, 1987) – for example how violent media portrayals lead to increases in violence by those that are exposed to them – in terms of acting as an information source the effects are sometimes less difficult to demonstrate. The key issues with information reception are those relating to what is considered to be a relevant 'authority' and the pre-existing lack of prior knowledge about a particular phenomenon (Morely, 1992). Research suggests that individuals' receive and accept information from the media in different ways depending on who they are (in terms of class, ethnicity, gender etc). The authority or rather the acceptability and credibility of the information source or disseminator is of importance here. The more credible the source in the eyes of those receiving the information, the more credence is given to the information. At its simplest most of us would probably give Jim, (a postal worker) who, over a pint in the pub chooses to pass comment on how refugees are affecting employment opportunities less credibility than a number of people whose job it is to research and analyse such phenomena. This is an easy example but the transmission of different types of information is received in a complex ad-mixture of ways and authority is not always so easy to distinguish between. A Bishop is a source of authority for some but not for others and even this may depend on the topic – for example, church derived information on the amount of poverty in any one society may receive little challenge whereas other data about levels of church related corruption or immorality may be questioned as to its reliability. It is also the case that authorities such as governments, doctors and even teachers have in recent times had the reliability of their information and practice increasingly questioned (Feldman, 1997).

More pointedly, if we look to the field of drugs education we see some important parallels. We know for example that educating schoolchildren on drug prevention issues tends to be less successful if the information provider (such as police officer or teacher who is seen as a bit 'stuffy') is seen to lack credibility and some improved success has been achieved by using peers or individuals with credible experience (Parkin and McKeganey, 2000). In relation to illicit drugs the primary source of information about illicit drugs, drug users, drug dealers and drug markets comes from the media – this is even true for most drug users and drug dealers. Moreover the general level of knowledge about drugs is weak, even by those disseminating the information – the media, where the relatively homogenised coverage has a tendency towards scare stories and stereotyped images (Reinarman and Duskin, 1992; Ben-Yehuda, 1994; Coomber et al. 2000). In general this means that the level of knowledge about drugs in society is small, tends to be compartmental-ised in a variety of stereotypical ways and new information is mostly only available from the news media. The general public therefore is almost totally reliant on the news media to 'inform' them about drug issues and although few people fully trust the news media to 'tell the truth' there is evidence that much of what is produced about drugs in that media conforms to popular stereotypes of drugs, drug users and drug markets.

An example of how fact and fiction can become blurred, melded and then feared comes from a different drug related rumour, this time about ecstasy:

> I'd like to go over some popular myths associated with MDMA now. Ecstasy drains your spinal fluid. This one always kind of tickles me. Nothing can drain your spinal fluid but a needle inserted in your back. Unfortunately, this is exactly what happened to MDMA users in the 1980's, because MDMA researchers were examining samples of spinal fluid looking for abnormalities. I think this is how the rumour got

generated. The drug itself will not drain your spinal fluid, nor will it cause Parkinson's disease, and I am asked this all the time. There is a drug called MPTP, which causes Parkinsonism. In 1985, this was hitting the media, with scary pictures of heroin users who had mistakenly injected MPTP and were frozen stiff or shaking, and it made a big impact on television shows, and it was the same time as the first big media wave about MDMA, and people got confused (Holland, 2000).

For Brunvand (CNN, 1999), there are some key structural aspects for the success of urban legends in general that also help us to understand the success of Blue Star LSD legend: they often have some basis (or apparent basis) in truth (e.g. LSD *is* produced on 'tabs' or stamps of attractive design); they evolve to remain contemporary (witness the shift from Mickey Mouse to Bart Simpson) and they prey on popular fear and ignorance. In fact the Blue Star LSD legend, for these very reasons, has been cited by Brunvand (CNN, 1999) as the urban legend that has proved most difficult to debunk of all. As discussed above we might add that it helps if the topic is one of current concern (when are illicit drugs not?), if the source is given credibility or authority and if the general level of knowledge about it is weak or absent as this facilitates greater deference to the authorities who (apparently) spread the rumour or hoax.

The actual spreading of the Blue Star hoax is of course what gives it its power. This happens on a number of levels. Sometimes it is national television news media that provides the outlet (as in Australia in 2001) but more commonly it has worked in the age-old fashion that supported traditional folklaw, hearsay or ancient rumour – word of mouth and the passing on of the warning to those who then disseminate it further. The last way that it works is simply by becoming so ubiquitous (or sufficiently so) that it becomes passed on in general cultural forms such as music or literature – similar to how the idea of the dealer giving away free drugs is culturally entrenched as we saw in chapter two. In Sheila Quigley's best-selling (2004) novel *Run for Home* the following paragraph alludes to the Blue Star rumour:

'Taking a key from a chain around her neck, she opened the roll-top lid. Inside was a large brown envelope. Carefully she shook the contents on to the palm of her left hand, and with her fingernail she moved the brightly coloured tattoos around. Bart Simpson grinned up at her. Tweety Pie smiled shyly, and Sylvester licked his lips. These were only a few of the kids' favourite characters portrayed on the tattoos, which when applied to the skin in the traditional way, sent a dose of LSD right into the blood stream.'

Although Quigley is happy to acknowledge that: 'It's what you pick up. It's all pure fiction and what you pick up here, there, television etc.' she is none-the-less happy to accept much of what she writes as reasonable: 'But the drugs I have seen it around the estates and its horrendous. It really is. I hear some of the words used and I know for a fact that they do use each others' urine for drug testing.' (*Shotsmag*, 2005). Quigley is really just demonstrating how ('on the estates') the generally accepted existence of particular phenomena can then be effortlessly transported into other forms of everyday communication – in this case the fictional novel. Those that read it will barely notice the paragraph but the extent that it will confirm an existing belief or sow the seed of a new one is difficult to estimate.

Why is the hoax damaging and should we care?

The problem with these widespread reports is that they are helping to perpetuate a recurring and widespread set of beliefs that helps create and recreate images of drug dangers that are false and of drug dealer activity that is misinformed. Many of the images already encountered in this book are all wrapped up together in this widely circulated and recurring hoax. Almost single handed the Blue Star LSD hoax is able to confirm to many that all that is suspected about drug dealers and drug related dangers is evidently true. The hoax often goes unquestioned. Even where rebuttals do take place these are unlikely to reach the same population that was made aware of the supposed menace in the first place as retractions of headlines and reporting on hoaxes are rarely given as much print space or media time as is evidence of a frightening menace threatening our children.

For some, folktales, rumour, urban legends and hoax's of the Blue Star kind betray a deeper societal meaning, are symbolic of how we should be constantly wary in dangerous world or remind us of what is, or should be considered good and appropriate behaviour and how to interpret that which is bad. This book is as much about myths, misconceptions and beliefs as it about trying to reposition our understanding of drugs, drug dealers and drug markets but one of the principal stalling points in analysis of myth has always been its difficulty in demonstrating effect. On the one hand we can attribute myth with deeper symbolic meaning (that it is supposed to provide society and the individual with a framework – through story – within which to learn and be guided) but on the other hand – especially in contemporary society – we struggle to see its effects. This is patently not the case in relation to modern rumours such as the Blue Star – the effects are direct and real. So, whilst some of the theoretical positioning on myth, meme and rumour also betray varying levels of determinism this is not however necessary for understanding one essential facet of some of these phenomena – that they can be highly powerful mediums that impact significantly on individuals and communities.

The last three chapters have discussed specific activities that drug dealers are supposed to carry out. Belief in the activities described also has knock-on effects for how the drug market itself is thought to operate and how it can be usefully characterised. As we shall see in the following chapter – particularly in relation to drug market violence – the form or forms the drug market takes and the character of those markets often fails to conform to common understanding of them.

Footnotes

[1] Text taken from an August 2001 version claiming to have come from the Metropolitan Police.

[2] For some reason, after numerous years of hosting it, the DEA took down this web page around 2003. It may be that the page was removed because sightings in the US have decreased in recent years (although as we have seen, the warnings recur) and/or the page itself may not have received sufficient hits for it to be worth a continued presence.

3 http://www.met.police.uk/drugs/warnings.htm

[4] It is hypothetically possible for LSD to be absorbed through the skin but not very likely. This is also true for strychnine. It is clear however that the warnings suggest to be both easy and likely.

[5] Indeed after researching this area for over ten years I am yet to come across an example in the UK whereby the suspicion of dangerous contaminants by police has on analysis been found to be correct.

[6] Alexander Shulgin has reported the existence of strychnine in 'legal' samples 'The few times that I have indeed found it present, have been in legal exhibits where it usually occurred in admixture with brucine (also from the plant Strychnos nux-vomica) in criminal cases involving attempted or successful poisoning' (Shulgin, 1993). As stated in Coomber (1997a) purposive use of poisons to attempt to do harm to others is qualitatively different to how dangerous adulteration – as an indiscriminate, common or even routine practice – is presented. Moreover the sample that Shulgin was referring to were white powder samples, common in the 1960s and 1970s but not since (personal communication 2002)

[7] For example Stafford (1992) has suggested that variations in LSD synthesis mean that different versions may react differently with human physiology and/or some people may have a greater susceptibility under all or certain circumstances to such reactions. It is also possible that LSD experienced under varying environmental circumstances – as is common with other drugs – produces a varying psychological and physiological outcome, or may even be psycho-somatic as suggested by Leary et al. (1995) and Lilly (1987). Also degradation of some of the materials used in synthesis may cause problems. Given all of this it is perhaps instructive for this chapter that people still choose to blame such effects on a substance not found in the analysis of street blotter LSD.

[8] LSD is generally not considered an addictive drug because tolerance to LSD builds very quickly and attempts to take the drug too regularly will result in no effect being experienced.

[9] For more information of contamination legends see Brunvand (1986) or Seal (2001).

Chapter 5:

Re-assessing drug market violence

The murder rate in Columbia's second largest city, Medellin, is six a day ...bodies are often dismembered or tortured. It is quite common for the nose or the ears, the tongue or the penis, to be cut off before death (Freemantle, *The Fix*, 1986: 211).

Smithy rang me up and told me that some cunt was throwing my name around down the street, so I had to go and find out who it was and sort him out didn't I? ... When I saw the little cunt...I went over to him and grabbed him by the throat. I pushed him over the fence. I warned him to be careful, as next time I'd do something else, fix him properly (quoted in Denton, *Dealing: Women in the Drug Economy*, 2001: 85).

This chapter is primarily concerned with discussing and contextualising the nature of violence *within* drug markets in the West as opposed to producer countries such as Columbia and Brazil where completely different economic, political and social conditions prevail. The levels of violence in some producer countries, as evidenced by the quote at the head of this chapter, are often beyond our normal comprehension. In such contexts however, the production of such extreme and consistent violence is about far more than the drug trade alone and often relates to significant levels of long term political and social destabilisation (Kirk, 2003). In the West there is a focussed concern around the evil nature of drugs, the nature of drug dealer activities and the dynamics of the market in *our* midst and one of the key issues is the way that violence is thought to permeate such markets from the bottom to the top.

Arguably, current archetypal images of drug markets and the drug dealers that populate them are epitomised by media reports from 1970s/80s New York City in the US and Toxteth in Liverpool, Brixton in London and St Pauls in Bristol, in the UK. These present us variously, with images of the Mafia, of the Triads, of 'Yardies', of gangs or units of organised crime and violent individuals. The images are of turf wars, guns, and a market driven by large sums of money and managed by increasingly unrestrained violence that is spreading further and further into 'normal' society as innocent bystanders get caught in the cross-fire. Alternatively, when the 'order' of organised crime is taken out of the equation we are often presented with images of relative chaos on the streets or housing estates where individual dealers, work partners or small outfits are constantly fighting the competition to keep their clients and the 'corner' that they operate. Moreover, because for those involved in drug markets there is no recourse to the forms of marketplace regulation enjoyed by legal traders (laws and law enforcement) to protect them against fraud, robbery and the like it is generally accepted that this too leads to greater levels of violence. This occurs because dealers and users are both more vulnerable to predatory crime because they cannot go to the police to complain and because retaliation often has to then take the form of physical violence. It is the contention of this chapter however that although excessive violent activity is part and parcel of much of the drug market and is of course elevated beyond that of licit markets it probably isn't the general experience of most of the dealers (even 'street' dealers) and users that participate in it beyond the level of their extant cultural milieu. In part this is because not all drug markets are the same and thus present the same circumstances and risks but also because not all dealers conform to the retaliatory model as shall be discussed further below. As such, it is argued that the extent of violence that is directly related to *the* drug market is often greatly overstated. That it cannot be applied consistently to many drug market contexts and that there has been an accumulation of research that has (perhaps unintentionally) emphasised the violent nature of drug markets as opposed to recognising the consistent levels of routine and mundane activity in most markets that are not particularly violent in essence. Lastly, it is suggested that much of what passes for drug market violence is in fact often the 'culture of violence' that many of those involved in drug trade live by anyway. That such cultures of violence, and their absence, contribute greatly to the levels of violence experienced within any particular context along with a range of other aspects of the 'risk environment' such as the way that the market is organised and forced to operate – for example by policing activity.

Crack markets in other parts of the US and the World have not produced the violence associated with the emergence of that market in 1980s New York. Many drug markets (often depending on whether they are highly fragmented; highly organised; burgeoning, mature, or fading out; open or closed; rural or urban) will have vastly different levels of associated violence. Likewise different levels of violence are associated with different drugs, the gender of the sellers and the cultural background and even the class of the sellers. This chapter will argue that such huge differentiation within the drug market makes it facile to attribute menacing levels of violence with *the* drug market when there are many drug markets populated by many types of operators. This will be done using a reflective re-reading of the current literature and recent empirical research from street markets in London, Sydney (undertaken by this author), and New York.

Drug markets and images of violence

I have already described in previous chapters some of the constituent activities that are thought to 'make up' the drug market. To some degree the assumed behaviours dealt with there: enticement of the young with addictive drugs; dangerous adulteration, and the selling (cheap) of LSD stamps laced with poisons are all part and parcel of the danger and violence that is supposedly inherent to the drugs trade. These activities, which are seen as routine and common, refer to indiscriminate, uncaring and even pathological violence against others. In this sense they help to provide part of a patchwork of understanding that links to other themes of violent behaviour within drug markets, such as that related to the ways in which market competition is said to be played out, but at the same time helps to make them more credible.

A more generalised imagery of drug market and drug dealer violence also can not be divorced from the long history that has associated – often absurdly – illicit drugs with causing violence through pharmacological means. This most simplistic of associations – what Goldstein (1985) characterised as the psychopharmacological model – refers to the way that drugs are thought to increase the volatility of drug market relationships because those involved are under the influence of violence causing substances. This is in fact a longstanding notion that at least in part, has its historical origins outside of bio-pharmacology and is perhaps better understood as emanating from ignorance, prejudice, fear and racism.

Drugs cause violence...

We saw in chapter one that negative images of drug users and drug suppliers were often suffused in racial overtones that combined with understanding of drugs such as opium, cocaine and cannabis as producing individuals bereft of morality. The outcome, it was feared and reported, was the marauding drug user capable of and likely to perpetrate all manner of violent acts. Not just any drug user however, for a particular theme which proved to be important to the development of drug controls from the second half of the nineteenth century was the association of such drugs with specific minority groups and violent and criminal behaviours. In the United States, fears at this time particularly centred on black men, Chinese immigrants, and Chicanos (Musto, 1987). The following testimony given before a committee of the US House of Representatives in 1910 is indicative of this type of thinking and carries in it almost every white stereotype of black men of the period:

> The coloured people seem to have a weakness for it [cocaine]. It is a very seductive drug, and it produces extreme exhilaration. Persons under the influence on it believe they are millionaires. They have an exaggerated ego. They imagine they can lift this building, if they want to, or can do anything they want to. They have no regard for right or wrong. It produces a kind of temporary insanity. They would just as leave rape a women as anything else and a great many of the southern rape cases have been traced to cocaine (Quoted in Inciardi, 1986: 72).

Likewise, Courtwright (1995: 210) refers to a municipal court judge in Mississippi who stated that:

> ...anyone who deliberately put cocaine into a Negro was more dangerous than a person who would inoculate a dog with rabies.

Interestingly, although many middle-class white people used cocaine it was not considered to be particularly problematic for them or associated with them. 'Cocainism' was associated with and understood as problematic among prostitutes, gamblers and other 'dope-fiends' in the US criminal underworld (Courtwright, 1995). Along with opium (Harding, 1998) cocaine was also considered to have significant transformative powers as Courtwright has pointed out:

> Cocaine was said to destroy the moral senses, turning women into prostitutes, boys into thieves and men into hardened killers (p210).

Musto (1987: 7) notes how:

> ...anecdotes often told of superhuman strength, of unnatural cunning and how cocaine was thought to actually improve pistol marksmanship. Others told how blacks were unaffected by .32 calibre bullets and this belief is said to have caused southern police departments to switch to .38 calibre revolvers.' These fantasies Musto argues 'characterised white fear, not the reality of cocaine's effects, and gave one more reason for the repression of blacks.

In the 1930s Harry Anslinger attributed Mexican derived (and 'pushed') cannabis with the power to undermine morality and subvert a user's behaviour so entirely that for him cannabis not heroin or cocaine was the most dangerous of drugs. Some of these images clearly no longer have *direct* resonance in the sense that drugs are not thought to discriminate between non-white and white populations when making people violent. It was important however to relate some of the history that contributes to thinking about the ways that drugs have been thought to make people violent. It has a history. Initially the idea was inextricably linked to fear of others and 'what would make them even more fearsome'. So whilst we no longer see certain groups as *more* susceptible violence *caused* by drugs, the legacy remains in terms of *how* notions of drug related violence are primarily located within the substance.

There is insufficient space here to consider this issue fully but suffice it to say that whilst the use of various substances such as alcohol and a number of illicit drugs is strongly correlated with violent outcomes it is far from proven that such substances are the cause of that violence (Chaiken and Chaiken, 1994; Collins, 1994; Parker, 1993; NIDA, 1990). Cannabis use, by and large, is no longer associated with violent outcomes. Some studies have shown heroin users (in particular contexts) to be less likely to commit violent crime than even non-drug users and numerous studies have suggested that drug related violence is often carried out by persons that had a pre-drug use record of violence. Moreover, once the cross-cultural evidence is brought to bear the picture is clouded even further. There are numerous examples of drugs commonly associated with violence (e.g. alcohol[1] and PCP) being used in contexts where violent outcomes are *not* associated with use of the drug and in some cases where the association is inversely related (cf. Heath, 2004; Falk, 1994; McAndrew and Edgerton, 1963). Despite this however it remains a commonly believed notion that alcohol and various drugs *make* otherwise non violent people violent as opposed to the belief systems that predominate around the drugs in question.

It is not a leap of faith to suggest that the commonly accepted position that drugs cause violence will also heavily inculcate how people view how the drug market is likely to operate: drug dealers are usually drug users and they are involved in a dangerous business; drugs make people violent – two and two makes four.

Goldstein (1985 and Goldstein et al. 1997) has shown that pharmacology is of less significance for understanding drug market violence than what he termed 'systemic' or structural relationships found in the drug market itself. However we might none-the-less hypothesise that the *belief,* by various authorities, that drugs are a significant cause of such violence and that they are also portrayed that way by the media impacts upon how drug markets are generally perceived; that the problems within them again relate back simply to the problems that drugs, not people or systems, are thought to cause. In this sense one consequence of understanding the pharmacological powers of drugs as significantly contributing to drug market violence is that it almost precludes any possibility of separating out the concept of any drug market interaction as not likely to involve violent outcomes. As such it provides limits on our imagination of what drug markets *can* look like and how they might otherwise function. A further consequence is that it obscures more meaningful understanding of the great variations of drug market violence that does occur, such as those situated in cultural norms and not specifically in the drug trade nor in the consumption of drugs – of which more later.

Specific drug market imagery

'"First they were selling pot, then cocaine, then crack," he said. "Then they started going for the children." Children as young as 7 years old were approached with pills, and a small boy had to roll under a car to avoid a gun battle, he said (*New York Times*, May 25, 1986).

If anybody was surprised that Camden was recently ranked America's most dangerous city, it wasn't the people who live here...In the past 12 months, there have been 53 homicides, including a 12-year-old shot to death on his porch for his radio, more than 800 aggravated assaults, including a toddler shot in the back of the head, at least 750 robberies and 150 acts of arson, more than 10,000 arrests ...And so Camden's latest explosion of violence, which defies most national trends, is, for all its tragic aspects, also miserably timed. The city's dream of renaissance is being interrupted by a brutal reality, and at the cusp of a supposed economic recovery, the most thriving trade remains crack cocaine (*New York Times*, December 29, 2004).

If these quotes provide a flavour of the reportage surrounding drug markets then the 10 page headline story printed in *U.S. News & World Report* (August 19, 1991) systematically encapsulated all of the images commonly associated with them. The stories of top-down and gang controlled drug markets across America portrayed excessive violence as at the hub of drug market activity and as Brownstein (1999) notes the clear analogy drawn (with a photograph) was with that of the lawlessness and ruthlessness of Al Capone and colleagues/ rivals of the prohibition era. News media stories such as those above are also reflected in the broader fictional cinematic and written media. Although there are a number of films that show drug use and even some dealers in a fairly normalised light (*Human Traffic; Blow*) most depict individuals in circumstances where violence is the consequence of their actions or part and parcel of them (*Trainspotting; Narc; Spun*). Likewise, depictions of dealers in written fiction such as Ed McBain's *The Pusher*, Donald Goines' *Dopefiend* and the Yardie trilogy of Victor Headley present us with images of dealers that are either grotesque, violent and morally decrepit (Goines), just plain nasty (McBain) or the sympathetic but none-the-less ruthless (Headley). When we have so many sources delivering up particular drug market images we should not be surprised that we find it hard to imagine outside of those sources. Harking back to chapter three we can remind ourselves that drug dealers who were not cutting the drugs they sold and who had no first hand knowledge that it took place none-the-less commonly believed that cutting was routine and dangerous adulteration to be common. The strength of the pervasive and largely uncontested image is thus clear.

Fictional media often also stakes some kind of spurious claim to the credibility of its representations – both of drug use and users as well as of drug dealers and drug markets – through the background of the author. Credibility to story lines and the authenticity of character behaviour are routinely attributed to those writers that had formally been (or still are) drug users; police officers; those working with drug users; those that simply had good contacts with authorities such as the police, or perhaps even just showed awareness of 'the street'. In most cases however these individuals (looking to make money from the sales of their wares) titillate their audience with stereotyped views of drug users and drug dealers and add little to general knowledge on these issues beyond reinforcing the stereotypes of the most visible sections of the populations they are depicting. Mostly, their representations are overly simple and undermined by research on the areas covered.

The images in fiction by and large reflect the images of drug users, drug dealers and drug markets that we are familiar with and indeed these images are the same ones that the news media, politicians and enforcement agencies tend to replicate. In terms of market organisation two primary images predominate: the low level dealer providing to users (and as we have already seen, also often perceived as the archetypal pusher of street drugs) and the 'pyramid' of organised traffickers that sit on top of the low level dealer controlled by one or more 'Mr Big'. In the latter case this means individuals or syndicates that control the upper echelons of a highly controlled and largely centralised drug market. That there is a common belief in Mr Big (or Mr Bigs) and a (relatively) centralised drugs market can be seen by the historical focus of much enforcement activity (Dorn et al. 1992; Kleiman, 1998) and by the pronouncements of MPs such as Dr Brian Iddon:

> Drug selling is the biggest pyramid selling racket in the world. Reference was made to the fact that someone can be taken out of the pyramid and another person pops in. That is the nature of pyramid selling—the profits in the pyramid are so great that it never collapses. Even Mr. Big at the top stays, and if he is taken out, another Mr. Big goes into the same pyramid, whether it is the Italian mafia or another organisation that trades drugs, such as the IRA. In my estimation, the only way to collapse the global drugs trade is to collapse those pyramids. Economically, the only way to collapse a global pyramid that is making fantastic profits is to collapse the profits, which can only be done by taking out the risk and all the enforcement action throughout the world (Dr Brian Iddon speaking in the House of Commons, January 18, 2005).

The US Drug Enforcement Administration for example maintains that Columbian and Mexican cartels control importation and mid-level distribution into numerous US cities and maintain 'operational headquarters' in many of those cities (USSC, 1995). Not too dissimilarly the United Nations Office of Drug Control in its 1997 *World Drug* Report (p123) has stated that:

> The most prominent trafficking organizations appear to be characterized by highly centralized management control at the upper echelons, with compartmentalization of functions and task specialization at the lower levels... Another common feature – especially of the cocaine industry – is vertical integration, that is, some, or all of the stages along which the drug passes from source to consumer are controlled by the same network.

These highly controlled and organised structures are also considered to be part and parcel of why the drug trade is considered to be so violent. Such individuals and organisations are thought to run the drug trade with gloves of iron. Those that run foul of the organisation are dealt with severely and (relatively) publicly. Controlling the drug trade is a violent business run by ruthless people (Reuter, 1983). Goode (1997) has stated that such views are common amongst his students (and by implication the general public) and indeed we can even see that such images are reinforced even by everyday items such as video games. *Narc*, is a successful video game where the object is to outwit and ultimately beat 'the evil drug lord Mr Big' who is seeking to unleash a new drug on an unsuspecting city.

The question however, is to what extent this vision of the drug trade – particularly post-importation, the drug trade within our borders – really fits this picture? It would be facile to suggest that such a position has no substance. Such images are reminiscent of the New York heroin market of the late 1960s and early 1970s that Johnson et al. (2000b) have described as being run by a few key players – such as Nicky Barnes organisation's control of Harlem – and how this controlled access to drugs – either for purchase or for selling. It is also consistent with, and has taken a great deal of credence from, traditional criminological views on organised crime (Reuter, 1983). The image however is one that has probably only ever applied to particular points in time and to particular geographical locations – particularly in the West. The centralised control of the drug market over areas of New York by organisations such as Nicky Barnes in the 1960s gave way in the 1970s and 1980s, as Johnson et al. (2000b) go on to point out to greater level of competition and finally in the late 1980s and early 1990s to a market that was essentially fragmented, decentralised and much more chaotic in nature than that that had preceded it. Mieczkowski (1990) has shown how the crack market in Detroit in the 1980s shifted between freelance operators to small group networks and back again to a preponderance of freelancers whilst Reuter et al. (1990) estimated that in the District of Columbia around 45% of cocaine sellers worked alone as freelance operators. Some markets in the US show significant levels of gang control (but in practice co-existing with freelance operators but the major drug markets have now for some time been highly competitive rather than monopoly or even oligopoly controlled. This is perhaps best summed up by a 1995 report to Congress on *Cocaine and Federal Sentencing Policy* where (citing the work of Johnson et al. 1991) it is acknowledged:

Despite a systematic effort to locate vertically-organized crack distribution groups in which one or two persons control the activities and gain the returns from labor of 15 or more persons, no such groups have been located, and no distributors report knowing of such groups. Instead, freelance crack selling dominates most drug street scenes (USSC, 1995: 66).

In the UK, until the 1960s, illicit drug markets had been of nominal size and had not been characterised by the same kinds of structures seen in parts of the US such as high levels of violence, the involvement of organised crime or street gangs. It is perhaps of little surprise then that when drug field researchers did start to look at the structure of the drug market in the UK in the 1970s and 1980s that it didn't conform to the rigid hierarchically controlled image that UK policing strategies were founded upon. Indeed, Lewis et al. (1985: 288) referring to their research into drug markets in London between 1980-1983 concluded that:

> The dispersed and fragmentary nature of the retail heroin market is such that it is unlikely that any single group or cartel could ever dominate the domestic delivery system from top to bottom.

Lewis et al. (1985) argued that Moore's (1977) model of 'vertical disintegration' – where the market becomes increasingly diverse and dispersed as the drugs work their way down through the chain of distribution was more apposite to the market they had observed. Further research with a wider geographical ambit some years later found a similar picture. Dorn, Murji and South (1992: x) in their investigation into the working of the drug market in the UK found little by way of large trafficking organisations and state: 'At the end it [the research] no longer seemed remarkable: no cartels; no mafia; no drug barons; and correspondingly, relatively little corruption.' In the UK therefore, we find that closed markets of lone operators or involving small numbers of closely connected individuals likely predominate (Dorn et al. 1992; 1993; Parker et al. 1998, May et al. 2000; Lupton et al. 2002) as they also appear to in other parts of Europe (Paoli et al. 2001). Ruggiero and South (1995) for example looking at a range of European (East and West) countries suggest overall that there is an absence of monopoly control and that there is an absence of top-down control by organised crime – even in the North East of Italy where such structures have been almost unthinkingly assumed. Organised crime does integrate with a broader often ephemeral network of small to medium sized firms (in Turin for example) but doesn't tend to 'control the markets'. These co-exist – especially when 'soft drugs' are concerned – with even greater fragmentation and flux in a context of competition where individual dealers also operate. Further, Paoli (2002: 145) argues – again following the lead of earlier research by Roger Lewis (1994) – that for the markets in Frankfurt and Milan the vast majority of drug deals that take place are characterised by 'numerous, relatively small, and often ephemeral enterprises' and that 'flexible hierarchies and dynamic disorder...*dominate the trading and distribution of the major illicit drugs in local (and probably not only local) Western European contexts*' (my emphasis)..

This is not to deny however that 'organised crime' of differing levels is, to varying degrees, integrated into drug market structures in certain locations/ nations but to push the image of mob or kingpin controlled markets is wide of the mark (see Becchi, 1996). Moreover, this is not to deny in some locales that gangs (e.g. US); kin-groups; ethnic groupings or even distinct crime families don't significantly control or predominate in certain pockets of 'turf' (UK, much of Europe) but that for the most part this happens in tandem with and within a broader market and varies over time. So, whilst it is the case that drug markets in some geographical areas show greater or lesser levels of organisation at different points in the chain of distribution the evidence – in the West at least – increasingly points to largely disorganised, fragmented markets populated by many individual. small and medium sized operators. Moreover, these operators – be they lone (user-dealers, entrepreneurs, opportunists, criminal diversifiers) or part of a kin-group or other mutual set up are as easily defined by their differences as by their similarities (supposedly imposed on them by the structural conditions of being a drug seller).

Dorn et al. (1992) amongst others (Ruggiero and South, 1994; Adler, 1985; Murphy et al. 1990; Pearson and Hobbs, 2001; Curtis & Wendel, 2000) have sought to describe the various personnel in the drug trade but regardless of what typology is used (of which more in chapter six) the upshot is that we find a description of a variety of individuals whose entry into the drugs field, their rationales for selling drugs, their experience of the drug trade, their personalities, their backgrounds and even their everyday values are diverse. A consequence of this is that the selling of drugs will have different meanings to different people involved in the drug trade and this will impact on the ways they react and act within and to the trade itself. Again even these can differ over time, may depend on the drug being sold, the culture of the location and the culture/s of selling adopted, among other factors. Thus there is a tension between trying to understand the drug market as *essentially* characterised in one way or another and that which suggests that drug markets, and those that populate them, can differ significantly.

Drug markets – the forms they take and their relationship to violence

Beyond the popular imagery of drug markets outlined above there are also market specific characterisations that the research literature points towards as an explanation for drug market violence. In what has been considered a seminal paper on the subject Goldstein (1985) argued that the primary factor involved in most drug related violence is actually 'systemic' in nature rather than produced directly by the drug (psychopharmacologically) or through the need to rob to get money for drugs (economic compulsive) – both common conceptions. Simply put, systemic violence results from the structural conditions created by drug sellers working in a competitive and illegal environment (regardless of the structure in place – monopoly, oligopoly, gang-controlled or freelance). Systemic violence is the outcome of a range of pressures in an illicit market and examples of these pressures in a system where recourse to normal legal sanctions are absent were given as follows:

> 1. disputes over territory between rival drug dealers. 2. assaults and homicides committed within dealing hierarchies as a means of enforcing normative codes. 3. robberies of drug dealers and the usually violent retaliation by the dealer or his/her bosses. 4. elimination of informers. 5. punishment for selling adulterated or phony drugs. 6. punishment for failing to pay one's debts. 7. disputes over drugs or drug paraphernalia. 8. robbery violence related to the social ecology of copping areas. Substantial numbers of users of any drug become involved in drug distribution as their drug-using careers progress and, hence, increase their risk of becoming a victim or perpetrator of systemic violence (Goldstein, 1985: 347).

In support of this and in relation to the drug often considered to be most closely linked with psychopharmacological violence – crack cocaine – both Goldstein et al. (1992) and Brownstein et al. (1992) later valuably demonstrated crack related homicides in New York to be primarily the result of context and system rather than being the result of psychopharmacology[2]. The focus had started to shift – at least in academic circles – from an emphasis on violent drug crazed individuals to that of the dynamics and circumstances produced by involvement in illicit drug markets. Numerous others have expanded at length on the various violent contexts that involvement in the illicit drug trade brings with it. Jacobs (2000: 1) in *Robbing Drug Dealers* has written on the 'taken for granted' features of the drug dealing scene in St. Louis, Missouri where 'Burns and rip-offs...in a context systematically organized around mutual predation' is inherent. Bourgois' (1995) ethnography of crack selling in Harlem is as much about the culture/s of street life and exclusion as it is about drug dealing but the over-riding sense that the reader is given however is how violence permeates every facet of the drug trade at street level. Topalli et al. (2002: 337) again referring to St. Louis relate how 'direct retaliation is the *preferred response* [to being robbed] because it serves three important aims: reputation maintenance, loss recovery and vengeance' [my emphasis]. Brownstein (1999) outlines various facets of the drug market 'system' that produce violent outcomes such as battling over market share and managing and retaining the reputation of a seller and a seller's product/s. Brownstein, as have numerous others before him, also provides graphic tales and case studies of extreme dealer violence. Bean (2002: 125) less specifically and referring to 'drug markets generally' suggests that in regard to those who default on credit – regardless of context or individual – that there is a standard drug dealer response when he states, 'However, the demand for repayment does not vary, and nor do the punishments for those who default' (Bean 2002: 125). To some large degree this idea of systemic violence which is generalisable – and which is no doubt an improvement on that which refers simply to bio-chemical causality – is strongly bound to the notion of system that Goldstein first produced, that of an over-riding *economic system* that has its own consequences. Brownstein (1999: 48) outlines this way of thinking neatly:

Whatever drug is being bought and sold, a drug market is an economic market. There are differences in terms of things such as the characteristics of sellers and buyers, the level of demand for the product, the organization of the business, and the size of and frequency of purchases. But *the underlying dynamic of any drug market is economic*. There are buyers and sellers, supply and demand, and competition (my emphasis).

The weakness to this explanatory model – as I hope will become clearer – is that it has a tendency to ignore where other influences such as class, gender or culture, may predominate when it comes to the issue of the prevalence and causality of violence in drug markets. In doing so it arguably over generalises the likely systemic outcomes of market structures vis-à-vis drug market violence and ignores when and why such pressures can be militated against and to what extent.

In addition, although the various pieces of drug market research that focus (either theoretically or descriptively) on systemic pressures add valuably to our understanding of drug markets the very fact that nearly all of the research cited is based on New York or other relatively violent inner city North American drug markets is problematic. In the main this is because not all drug markets resemble the conditions in North America (even all of those in North America) which at various points in the last 30 years have been at the extreme end of the violence spectrum. In addition to the fact that a great deal of research has been on cities such as New York a great deal of research on drug markets has focussed – either intentionally or unintentionally – on the violence to be seen within it. In and of themselves neither of these situations is surprising. Growth in drug related violence will attract community disquiet, media interest, political and law enforcement concern as well as academic researcher interest and (sometimes more importantly) the attraction of research funding. A consequence of this is that research, although interested in the distinct machinations of drug market activity may focus on the violence within it because it is 'in your face' and highly visible, lends towards the fascinating for those otherwise outside of the culture and/ or is easier to describe than is the relative absence of something. In illicit drug market research the tendency is not to report on the mundane and what is similar to non-drug market activity but to try to explicate that which is feared and poorly understood.

The overly homogenised image of the drug market

The stereotyped images so far alluded to have one important thing in common – they suggest (either explicitly or by weight of focus on particular types of market in particular types of geographical area) that there is 'a' drug market model that we can and should understand drug markets through, and broad behavioural characteristics inherent within those markets (such as the extreme levels of violence) that tell us how drug markets work. It is however – as already suggested – the *differences* that are key to a better understanding of drug market (and drug related) violence.

The effect of fragmented and differentiated markets on violence and other behaviours

Simply put, fragmented and highly differentiated markets composed of different individuals with different backgrounds operating at different levels of the drug market will produce different levels of corresponding behaviour. This will be the case even if the drug market has various systemic pressures that make certain behaviours or outcomes – such as the use of violence – more likely. A few comparative examples may help here by way of illustration:

1. John is a 'friend dealer' who has only ever sold cannabis to his friends. He has been selling for 10 years since he left school. He used to buy the drugs he sold from a friend of his brothers that he knew from school and he makes enough money to pay for his own use plus a little bit extra. He has never been arrested and only sells to people he knows quite well. He is a little bit of an advocate for cannabis believing that it is a positive life-enhancer. He now grows his own supply and doesn't really consider himself a 'dealer'. Not only has he never experienced violence connected to his selling of cannabis but he has never experienced any significant violence amongst his peer group or in his day to day life.

2. Aimee is a long-time heroin addict. She sells heroin on the street in an open market. The street market she sells on is highly visible and contains numerous other (mainly) user/dealers. Although the *threat* of violence irregularly occurs Aimee has never been beaten or experienced physical violence connected with her trade. She feels

it is usually possible to 'walk away' from the violent threat (which often relates to 'stroppy' other users). She has previously been robbed of her drugs but this rarely happens and she finds that she has no need to seek retribution nor to resist. As such she doesn't experience her activity as particularly violent or problematic.

3. Jack is a crack addict and he sells crack. He grew up on a local authority housing estate with a long-term reputation for high levels of criminality and deprivation. Jack 'drifted' into criminality, drug use and dealing almost naturally – many of those around him were involved in all of these activities and Jack was part and parcel of that culture. This culture also has many traditional male macho values and attitudes and varying levels of violence are routinely used as a means to resolve domestic and social conflicts. A lifestyle where violence had long been integrated into Jack's personal and 'business' dealings was for Jack the norm and more or less a daily occurrence. Jack sold on an open street market and when Jack had been robbed of his drugs he retaliated with violence on his perpetrator. Jack regularly used the threat of violence and maintained a 'violent disposition' in his dealings with buyers and other sellers. Such a disposition was as much about saving/ maintaining 'face' in his living/working environment in a way that was essentially a cultural norm than it was about drug market risks and impositions.

Each of these examples from the lower echelons of drug selling demonstrate how different a sellers experience of violence can be and that the these experiences can be affected by class, gender, culture and individual predisposition. Although it is far from highlighted or accepted as the norm some drug market research however provides further evidence of differentiation of personnel and of consequent activity within drug markets. Adler (1985:119) in her ethnography of an upper-level drug dealing and smuggling community for example only rarely observed (or became aware of) violence and cites the various alternative forms of action that some prefer to take:

Violent behaviour was least prevalent in the upper echelons of the prestige hierarchy. Individuals at these levels generally excluded others from their business dealings if they committed offensive acts.

Ostracism was considered sufficient retaliation for burns, rip-offs, security violations, and other disreputable behaviour. At the lower end of the prestige hierarchy, where rip-offs and burns were more common, drug traffickers chased, threatened, and occasionally hit each other. In the end, though, the guilty parties usually either capitulated to the threats or fled the area and hid. *Ultimately, little violence occurred even among this group* (my emphasis).

In reference to a sample of 80 cocaine dealers heavily loaded with individuals from middle-class backgrounds Murphy et al. (1990: 330) reported them to be mostly 'quite law abiding, with the obvious exception of their use and sales of an illicit substance...[and] When they were not dealing, our respondents engaged in activities that can only be described as mainstream American'. Denton and O'Malley (1999: 513) stress that for their sample of successful women drug dealers 'ruthlessness and violence are comparatively peripheral [in their dealing activities], even though the women demonstrated that these were well within their repertories of action'. Moreover, this was in a general dealing context (previously unnoticed by research) where 'it did not appear that the model of the ruthless, manipulative and threatening dealer had a central place, and the women's 'weakness' on this front did not thus appear as a significant problem (Denton and O'Malley, 1999: 528). Even traditional open street markets in areas considered a locus of drug market violence may in fact present less by the way of violence than might be assumed. In a study of street sellers (heroin and cocaine) at two of Sydney, Australia's more notorious open drug markets it was found that drug related violence was not something that impacted on them to any great extent with many reporting the areas to have an undeserved and exaggerated reputation for violence (Coomber & Maher, 1996). The dealers involved in the Australian study were predominately 'independents', nearly half were women and although the dealing scene they populated was 'competitive' the observed and reported relationships with the other dealers was largely supportive and tolerant. Hagedorn's (1988) study of drug dealing in Milwaukee similarly found that the experience of violence among drug dealers was of a lesser degree than that anticipated by the researchers and that suggested by the local media and observed that in the two locations under study that 'methods of business have been perfected that avoid violence' (p12). The closer one looks at different dealing populations in different contexts the easier it is to see how and why such populations that do not seem to simply conform to the assumed systemic norms do not.

Visible and non-visible market activity – the lesson from theories of addiction

Although Goldstein's model has its usefulness it should always be remembered that its focus has been on homicide and that homicide is some distance removed from most drug market violence. In this sense although the notion of systemic violence appears to have explanatory power to explain the most extreme forms of violence it may have much smaller explanatory power for other less extreme forms. This is important because those unlikely to be involved in less violent activities are also less likely to show up in homicide cases. The problem therefore is that by focussing on a particular set of behaviours and outcomes it tends to promote a picture of the drug market that may well be out of kilter with the drug market as a whole. Yes, homicides may be largely explicable in terms of systemic issues but not everyone is equally susceptible to those pressures. This picture is not an inevitable outcome of the method involved – much drug market violence may well be mostly explicable in systemic terms – but to overstate the *potential* of those systemic pressures is problematic. By focussing on seriously violent criminal justice populations as a means of understanding drug market violence does not help to understand the prevalence or essence of violence in drug markets beyond this population. A similar situation previously emerged in relation to how addiction to drugs such as heroin was understood. Earlier conceptions of addiction were strongly influenced by views of, and experience of, treatment populations. In the 1960s it was the case that most clinical experience and thus knowledge of those dependent on opiates came from observation of those in treatment. What was unknown at the time was the extent to which treatment populations could differ from non-treatment populations and so a fairly homogenous understanding of (mainly) opiate addiction emerged and was used as a basis of understanding the nature of the addictive state. Treatment populations, on the whole, tend to be more chronic than non-treatment populations and present a picture of the character of addiction as far more helpless (and hopeless) than many that never enter into treatment. Many heroin and cocaine addicts are in fact in fulfilling relationships (some few where their partners and family are unaware of their dependence), others hold down jobs and sit next to us on the bus or train raising nothing in the way of suspicion, and many leave their addiction behind without recourse to treatment. Visible drug addicts – as with visible alcoholics – may sit in street doorways, inebriated and apparently senseless. More purposive addicts have lifestyles that do not conform to this junkie stereotype (see: Preble and Casey, 1969; Waldorf, 1973). In the 1970s and 1980s theories of addiction had to adapt to also include those individuals whose behaviour was less chronic, less prone to relapse and those that managed to leave their addiction behind.

It is the contention of this chapter that most drug market activity is in fact of the invisible kind and that much of this is different in character to the kind of model pre-supposed by Goldstein and others. If this is the case then the general character of how we perceive the drug market may well also be different.

Markets differ and thus so does the level and form/s of violence therein

An obvious truism is that whilst drug markets will have their similarities they will of course all differ to a greater of lesser extent. This will be true of markets of essentially the same make-up but is even more so where the essential characteristics of the market are not so similar. The generalised view – as we have seen – tends to suggest something much more homogenous, ignoring broad but especially specific difference. The differences however are often not trivial and when considering the general nature of drug markets and the ways that violence is played out within them it is only by acknowledging and incorporating the differences into our perspective that a more meaningful understanding is achieved.

Drug markets differ in many significant ways: some are highly organised and as such will often have more routine forms of punishment/violence permeating them (Reuter, 1983). As we have seen many others are highly fragmented and fluid and in these markets – depending on the context, the permeation of violence may vary significantly both within and between the levels of distribution. In terms of the 'market' itself as opposed to the individuals that make it up four significant issues need to be taken into account: the 'maturity' of the market (e. g. whether it is burgeoning, established, declining); the culture of the market (e.g. whether it is dominated by a particular male inner-city machismo or other forms); the preponderate transactional form (e.g. predominately of the open or closed form) and lastly, the historical context in which it is located (e.g. traditions of selling, location – rural/urban etc.) Let us take each in turn.

Market maturity: levels of stability/instability

The disorganised and relatively violent crack cocaine market/s of New York ghettos in the 1980s were distinct from the heroin market that predominated and preceded them in the 1970s which was more ordered and comparatively less violent (Sommers et al. 1996; Johnson et al. 2000b). This market changed again in the late 1990s as heroin once again became resurgent along with cannabis, and crack lost its marketability (Jacobs, 1999; Andrade, 1999; Johnson et al. 2000b). Thus, depending on the what we might call the 'natural history' of any drug market and the particular phase that it is in, for example, 'incubation, expansion, plateau or decline' (Golub et al. 1994; 1997) and the particularities that pertain to it in terms of immediate environment (Curtis and Wendel, 2000) the level of violence likely to be present will vary. The particular context (see below) of the burgeoning New York crack market in its expansion phase produced a highly volatile and violent situation. Once the same market had plateaued however and then began to decline there was a decrease in violence and a shift of selling from aggressively competitive approaches to a more 'socially bonded' mode of organisation where co-operation and inter-reliance came to predominate (Curtis and Wendel, 1999). We should acknowledge however that not all drug markets reach such levels of violence when incubating/expanding and many remain relatively stable for many years. Indeed, once taken outside of its North American context and moment in time even burgeoning crack cocaine markets in other countries have tended not to be any where as near disorganised or violent in character. In this sense we need to acknowledge that whilst we might observe differences in market activity *between* drugs we need to be careful not to simply attribute those differences to pharmacology (i.e. crack user/sellers as more violent). Also, as was pointed out above New York's drug market has shown signs of relative stability for a number of years compared to those early days of the crack market which was more chaotic than that which had preceded it. In fact, and importantly, New York in the early 1980s was also experiencing a range of other problems that impacted disproportionately on the poorer communities, such as increased unemployment among African Americans and Hispanics (through manufacturing relocation) and the resultant 'distressed inner-city households' (Johnson et al. 2000b). These problems were then combined with the relative vacuum left by the diminution of organized crime in the distribution of heroin and the rapid emergence of crack through new groups not versed in the protocols of the extant market (Andrade et al. 1999). These factors led to a level of market destabilization that Jacobs (1999) is doubtful will ever be matched again. Although Fagan and Chin (1990) earlier characterised violence in crack-cocaine markets as typical and as the means through which regulation and control of the drug market is maintained, Brownstein et al. (2000b) similarly to Johnson et al. (1999) with the benefit of a retrospective view locate the level of violence in any one drug market at any one moment in time as indicative of how unstable the particular market is. In simple terms, the more stable a market is seen to be the less violence is thought likely to emerge – although measuring stability is in real terms a difficult thing to do (Brownstein et al. 2000b,c). Relative stability however, as we shall see, is itself an outcome effected by other facets of the market context.

Dominant cultures: traditional machismo and cultures of violence

Once again referring to New York, Johnson et al. (2000) have argued that the downward shift in drug market violence and the petering out of the crack cocaine market since the mid-1990s is as much to do with shifts in (sub) culture/s as it is in the structural decline of the market alone. Referring to a raft of research they argue that the observed mainstream culture and 'conduct norms' for many of those that took up crack selling in New York during the mid to late 1980s was imbued with parental domestic violence, parental alcoholism/intoxication, and that 'yelling, cursing and aggressive language were commonplace' in the family home. This 'transmitted violent conduct norms...which effectively prescribed use of loud aggressive and threatening language and physical assault of loved ones to dominate them' (Johnson et al. 2000: 170). This was combined with inner-city deprivation, lack of opportunities and a culture of 'hanging out on the street' where they learned other subcultural norms permeated with facets of hustling and 'getting by'. For many there was also an expectation – even from their parents – for them to be consuming cigarettes and alcohol at a young age. It was this generation and the formative conditions within which many of them grew up that for Johnson et al. helped to produce the particularly violent and chaotic crack markets of the 1980s. By way of consequent market decline and diminishment of violence they cite a shift in many of these subcultural norms for the generation that came up behind them – a generation that (at least in sufficient numbers to have an impact) rejected many of the negative social norms which promoted violent outcomes. A rejection of crack as drug of choice and a broad move to (less compulsive) cannabis use is now more characteristic of New York inner-city drug use. A diminution in positive views of drug selling but also of violence as a social norm to resolve conflict along with other measures such as policing have changed the nature of the New York drug market. It still exists, it is still vibrant but it is now different – and it is less violent than before. Not too dissimilarly and consistent with a wider literature on drug effects Sommers & Baskin (1997) found that violence among drug sellers (men and women both) tends to reflect 'the self selection of people who routinely use violence in their broader social and economic interactions' and the immediate environment where for some, 'violence is taught, practiced and maintained as a way of negotiating the social realities of street and domestic life'. Similarly Pearson and Hobbs (2001), whilst at times stressing the potential for violence at the middle-market level, are also at pains to disaggregate drug market violence from violence that is part and parcel of the macho cultural values that may be present within some of the groups involved. Thus, depending on the dominant cultural and subcultural values that permeate drug markets in different settings, particularly the way that violence is used and played out to resolve everyday life issues, we might expect there to be some significant impact in the way that violence is played out in those settings. Likewise, where violence is less culturally imbued (as in the case of Adler's upper-level dealers referred to earlier) other options come into play and dealers regardless of circumstance do not unerringly apply the same punishment/s as stated by Bean (2002) earlier.

Transactional forms: open and closed markets

Johnson et al. (2000b) whilst referring to the shift in subcultural attitudes towards both crack, crack market activity and towards the use of social violence that helped bring about a downward shift of violence also note the importance of policing activity at the time this took place. Drug dealing in New York in the 1980s was highly visible and very public with 'wide agreement... among public officials and community leaders that drug sellers effectively controlled many New York street and most parks' with Crack sellers active on virtually every block in inner-city New York City and at some locations in many middle-class and suburban neighbourhoods as well (Johnson et al. 2000b). Slowly over the 1980s the policing of drugs in New York was galvanised and campaigns that aimed to 'take back the streets' were implemented along with increased penalties for dealing in crack. One consequence of the increased pressure by policing was to displace the preponderance of open street markets with something closer to the closed market that operated for heroin in the 1960s. This has meant that clients now increasingly need to be 'referred' by someone known to the dealer (as a means of protection) where deals are either made somewhere inside, away from direct observation or via an agreed meeting place arranged by non-traceable mobile phone technology (Hough and Natarajan, 2000). Closed markets by their very nature – where nothing so physical as a literal street corner have to be protected and where risk of arrest is high on the agenda and so therefore is heightened care of operation – means that there is reduced opportunity for violent activity to take place. The level of risks attendant to any one kind of 'risk environment' can be affected by the presence or absence of risk factors. An example of this would be the rise in the ownership and use of guns among drug dealers in New York. When there were less guns being used (1960s) the risk of being killed in an altercation (where knives were the likely weapon of choice) was less than when guns became part of the general arsenal in the drug market place. Likewise when more selling takes place by arrangement with people 'known' to the seller there is less risk of unforeseen and opportunist violence from other dealers and those unknown to the dealer. The level of open street selling seen in New York in the 1970s and 1980s was comparatively unusual and not representative of markets in most other countries and cities in the West. Policing pressures and the protection offered by new communications technology (such as pagers and mobile phones) appear to be ensuring that closed markets are, for the most part, the primary way to deal drugs in the new millennium.

Historical and other contexts

This last 'structural' or risk environment condition overlaps to some degree with those already dealt with but sits slightly outside of them at the same time. Markets will often have their own traditions as regards drugs sold and used and the proportions therein. This will also be true of policing activity which is commonly highly varied between regions. The demographic make-up (ethnic or otherwise) of those involved in drug selling may also bring its own culture/s of trading which is/are more or less 'closed' to some groups and not others and where trust is cultivated more than in markets where all comers are welcome (cf. Lupton et al. 2002). Inner-cities appear to have greater levels of drug market related violence than rural areas where the 'town' or village dealer may have known all of his or her clients all their life (Few et al. 2004). The cultural milieu in which drugs are being sold (e.g. middle-class dealers dealing to privileged acquaintances) will affect decisions on how to manage conflict and 'drug markets' are an amalgam of many little markets within a bigger one in any one region, city or even country. This is important to remember when assessing 'the drug market'. Cannabis remains, easily, the most used and thus the most traded illicit drug and yet cannabis selling is not – as a rule – associated with anything like the same levels of violence as other sections of the drug market. In this spirit Curtis and Wendel (2000: 137) summarise that difference of structure is important in understanding typologies of drug markets as well as locating when, why and where violent episodes are most likely to occur:

> 'Street level corporations also may deal with the issue of trust and loyalty by instilling terror through the routine use of public "beat-downs," humiliations and killings, and many "enforcers" are hired expressly for this purpose. By contrast, indoor corporate distributors, such as the marijuana-selling "doors" (Lower East Side) and "herb-gates" (Brooklyn) relied more on a high degree of social cohesion based on long-standing neighborhoods friendships and ethnicity (Puerto Rican on the Lower East Side and West Indian in Brooklyn). Corporate delivery services are characterised by the highest degree of trust of employees, since they are routinely "fronted" (advanced on credit) drug supplies of a thousand dollars retail value. They tend to employ only close friends of existing employees and attempt to generate camaraderie and esprit de corps among members of the

organization through paying employees well, providing perks (e.g. free or discounted drug supplies for personal use), and sponsoring social functions such as Christmas parties.

Users that are dealers

In numerical terms perhaps the largest group of sellers is the user/dealer. That is individuals that we might understand as users first and dealers second who primarily supply to support their own drug use. Although there is inevitably a fair amount of overlap here and some users clearly progress to significant levels of dealing and/or do so for short periods of time there is none-the-less a large group of user/dealers that many have argued are not the same as the dealers that the numerous criminal justice systems purport to be pursuing – depending of course on the criminal justice system[3]. Even within this group there is a fair amount of differentiation depending on the drugs that they use and sell and thus (usually) the extent to which they are using. Heroin and cocaine user/dealers for example are often going to be dependent users that started selling drugs to enable themselves to provide for their own habitual use. Sellers of cannabis, ecstasy and other substances less addictive than heroin and cocaine may well be profit dealers but many of them will be friend dealers and many of them will not even see themselves as dealers nor be perceived that way by the friends they help to 'sort out' (Moore and Miles, 2004; Parker et al. 1998). The degree to which certain types of drug selling has, like some forms of drug use, become 'normalised' is unknown but if such activity is increasingly drawing in otherwise non-deviant individuals we might reasonably speculate that the drug market as a whole is populated increasingly with less violent personnel and as such needs to be viewed differently.

The prosaic and mundane, the hidden and the ignored

Drugs, drug use and drug users are alternatively represented by images of the exotic, of excitement, hedonism, experimentation – even enlightenment as well as danger and risk. Drug markets likewise are subject to represen-tations of intrigue, double-dealing, high-risk but high reward and of high-rollers, gangsters and organised crime. All of these representations have been found in research and as we have seen are commonly referred to in reports from the media, criminal justice authorities and politicians. Much drug use however, particularly dependent drug use is neither exciting nor exotic. Drug use (particularly dependent drug use) is often mundane and so is much that takes place in the drug market. This chapter has attempted to show that whilst drug markets often are violent places they may also be only notionally, if at all, more violent than 'normal' life for many of those involved and that market extremes – both violent extremes but also e.g. the crack markets of New York in the mid to late 1980s – are just that the extremes. For many sellers however the violence of the drug market will not impinge on their lives and for others it may only do so rarely and/or sporadically. The problem with drug market violence is that it is highly visible and of course frightening but this doesn't mean that it is what characterises drug markets – at least not to the degree commonly suggested. An analogy might be of traffic lights – we are continuously reminded of people's failure to stop at them on time or at all and how the consequences can be tragic. Other kinds of driving transgression are also commonplace but what really characterises the 'culture of the road' is that of conformity – the overwhelming conformity – even at night on a country road with no-one else around of those that do what they are supposed to. By and large this conformity is not noticed or acknowledged. It is an absence of something happening and as such it is the transgressions that gain attention. From an outsiders perspective, or a sociologist's (who job is – partly – to say how the world, and bits of it 'look' and are ordered) I would suggest that we would gain more from starting to understand road culture from the high levels of conformity. If we then want to look at how transgression is played out in different contexts with different populations with different cultures we should then do that. Drug markets are arguably non-too dissimilar in this respect.

Footnotes

[1] I make no apologies for calling alcohol a drug. Not only is it comfortably classifiable as a drug but it is also the drug most associated with all types of criminality including violence against others.

[2] Although Goldstein et al. do suggest a small minority of homicides were 'caused' by the psychopharmacological effects of crack as with his earlier (1985) paper the causal attributions are somewhat problematic conceptually and fit poorly with cross-cultural evidence vis-à-vis causality.

[3] At different points in time the 'addict/dealer' that sells to maintain their own use has been subject to greater or lesser persecution by criminal justice systems in the West. It is generally the case however that these individuals, whilst representing a useful symbolic arrest at times, are not the 'higher level' traffickers/dealers making money out of the suffering of others that Western criminal justice authorities purport to be pursuing.

Chapter 6:

Who and 'what' is the drug dealer?

> With the variation in persons and circumstances which affect who
> deals, how he deals, and what happens to him, one cannot conclude
> that the one label *dealer* embraces many persons, capabilities,
> commitments and outcomes (Blum et al. 1972: 350).

Who and what is the drug dealer? Drug dealers are often referred to in
common sense terms as something we all 'know' about as though we can
discern what kind of person a drug dealer is and what kind of things they
are likely to do. Likewise this knowledge tends, in a rather circular way, to
attest to how they should be known in essence – and thus how they should
be dealt with. As we have seen so far throughout the book there are a range
of common assumptions about the kind of person the drug dealer is and the
way they act within the drug market – many of which are reference points on
the defining characteristics of who/what drug dealers are. We have also seen
that many of these common assumptions are often unhelpful either because
they have little or no substance in reality (dangerous adulteration, seeking
to hook non-users, Blue Star legend) or at the very least are unreasonably
exaggerated, overstated or applied too broadly (pathological behaviour,
systemic violence). It is perhaps reasonably clear that if common assumption
about what drug dealers *do* needs to be substantially revised then the image
of who *the* drug dealer is also needs revision along with the characteristics of
their essential make-up. Thus, if drug dealers are not cutting the drugs they
sell hap-hazardly with any poisonous substance they can get their hands
on; if they are not an essentially predatory group looking to hook the drug
free and otherwise vulnerable on addictive drugs; if they are not standing at

the school gates dealing to school children; if they are not giving children LSD tattoos laced with strychnine; if they do not all succumb to systemic or other drug related violence, then – it follows – they must, as a group, be significantly different to how they are commonly understood.

In everyday reality, imagery of the 'evil drug dealer' is an amalgam of a number of types of popular representations of dealers and their place in the dealing hierarchy. Overall therefore we might suggest that it is the street or house dealer that comes immediately to mind when the term drug dealer is uttered and that this image is usually male, working class, of a criminal and relatively violent disposition, and largely amoral. Such an image makes common beliefs about dealers – such as those discussed in previous chapters – easy to believe, a situation that is circular and reinforcing. Beyond this, other stereotypes surrounding various ethnic groups, gangs, Mafioso and so on would blend with this basic mould to allow for the known differences in representation. In this sense *the* drug dealer has an essence and that essence is *bad*. Such a position however, just like that concerning violence in the previous chapter, is difficult to reconcile with a range of academic research. Some of that research suggests for example that there is sufficient individual variation in types of drug dealer and dealer activity that an overly homogenous depiction is unreasonably faulty. In turn research has shown that not only are there different types of people engaging in differing types of activity of differing levels of 'seriousness' but also that whole sections of the drug dealing community cannot be seen simply as problem (evil) individuals. An overly convenient focus on the drug dealer as a 'criminal individual', de facto ignores the ways that drug dealing, for some individuals and communities, may in fact be one outcome of a marginalised and relatively oppressed existence. It thus ignores the role of poverty and other structural influences that help *produce* involvement in crime, and by extension, in drug dealing. Lastly, for some, it is one of the least harmful (for others) choices of providing resources to support a drug habit.

Simple dealer demographics

This chapter is not overly concerned to outline 'who' is the dealer in simple demographic terms such as gender, ethnicity or age. It is more concerned to consider the 'who' and 'what' the drug dealer is in terms of a deeper essence, as to whether dealers fit the common demonised stereotypes which suggest an essence of being essentially evil/amoral and if not, why not. It is also concerned to outline how some drug field researchers have chosen to interpret the drug dealing role and locate it in relation to broader societal structures. There is however a range of dealer stereotypes that also relate to these simpler demographics. As such they do deserve some brief consideration as they do tend to contribute significantly, as reinforcers, of the essential behavioural stereotype itself. In the UK at least street drug dealers are often thought of as the tripartite of young black men[1] driving around in BMWs[2]. BMWs apart there is some evidence to suggest that the stereotype largely also holds for the US where some 80% of those convicted for drug offences are black or Latino (King and Mauer, 2002) and commonly believed to be males of this characteristic in inner-city areas (Hunt, 1990) if not more widely (Beckett, 2004). Our actual knowledge of dealer demographics is limited. As for many hidden or criminal groups, the shape, size and make-up of the population is largely unknown. In the case of drug dealers it is informed by adjunct research data on drug users, prison populations and on relatively small scale research on pockets of dealers or a focus on specific drug markets in particular locations at particular moments in time. Even here however, as for drug market violence, too much of a focus on any one kind of group or market can over homogenise the image presented. It may also be the case that, as with numerous crime statistics, the demographic evidence available may not be representative of the populations we want to know about. In the case of drug dealers this would largely mean the composition of arrestee statistics or drug dealers in prison populations. Along these lines, recently in the US, Beckett (2004 and Beckett et al. 2006) has argued that there is a disparity between both perceived racial involvement in the drug trade, the consequent police activity around it and the broader reality.

Ethnicity

Beckett et al. (2006) refer to a range of research that suggests that racial stereotypes impact meaningfully on how crime is perceived in any one geographical area and that an 'implicit racial bias' (unconscious perceptions) as opposed to overt racism can lead to an exaggerated assumption of the involvement of young black men to various types of criminality and of the amount of perceived criminality actually occurring. Beckett's own research

(2004) carried out in Seattle in the US goes some way to confirming such a position as just such a disparity emerged from observations of the drug market in that city:

> ...the majority of those who deliver serious drugs in Seattle are white, and that a smaller percentage of those who do so are black. And yet, according to Seattle Police Department arrest records, 64.2% of those purposefully arrested for this crime from January 1999-April 2001 were black; 14.1% were Latino, and 17.6% were white...This disparity assumes even greater significance in light of evidence that the Seattle Police Department conducts significantly more drug delivery arrests than comparably sized cities around the United States (Beckett, 2004: 7).

Reviewing the possible causes for this disparity Beckett et al. (2006) concluded that 'the organizational practices that produce this outcome are difficult to explain in race neutral terms' and that implicit bias in Seattle's police officers and officials had impacted on what (and who) constituted Seattle's drug problem. As such they argue, Seattle's police officers and officials were 'less likely to perceive whites who are involved in illicit drug activity as drug offenders'. The outcome of this was an unconscious focus on black men and more black men were then arrested and prosecuted. The perception, in turn, was thus reinforced and the enforcement policy justified. The image of the black drug dealer, even in a city where white dealers predominate, reigned supreme.

In the UK drug dealing had been a predominately white enterprise until the mid-1980s (Dorn et al. 1992) but at that point in the new wave of heroin use there was a shift towards a greater level of non-white selling. Although approximating the relative proportions of non-white dealers in the UK is difficult to do Dorn et al. usefully pointed to a different aspect of non-white dealing activity that is arguably as important – that of relative visibility. As with the Seattle findings above we might surmise it likely that increased visibility of one population over another will impact both on public perceptions about who drug dealers are as well as media and law enforcement responses to it.

The way in which they [black dealers] made heroin available to the point where they were very openly selling heroin in the shopping centre, on the streets, whereas...white dealers would probably do it from a house or a pub or have what they call runners, running around the district doing bits and pieces for them...[Whereas] if you walk into Moss Side centre and drug dealers are queuing up to sell you drugs. Well, there's one of the attractions. It's there all the time (White female 'informed observer of the Manchester scene' quoted in Dorn et al. 1992: 45).

In addition to this new visibility the late 1980s and early 1990s saw the UK drug scene increasingly associated with (scares around) crack cocaine and Jamaican 'Yardies' who were thought to be taking especially violent control of the cocaine trade (Green, 1998). Specifically in relation to the policing of crack in the London Borough of Lewisham – and with echoes of Beckett's research above – Pearson et al. (1991) noted that, whilst the evidence suggested that most crack users were white nearly all those arrested (around 95%) were black. On this issue Green (1998: 147) was prompted to declare:

The Lewisham research provides yet more evidence of a policing strategy based on racially informed stereotypes of drug use and criminality. Racism, of course, is not simply a feature of domestic drug enforcement. At the level of border controls the issue of targeting couriers is intimately bound up in racial and cultural stereotypes. The predominance of black foreign national drug couriers incarcerated in British jails...is testimony to an enforcement policy underpinned by an ethnically structured targeting strategy

Whatever the actual demographics as regards ethnicity in any one market – and these will vary in different locations depending on a range of historical and cultural factors – it seems clear that *perceptions* of 'who' the drug dealer is in ethnic terms is often not clear cut and may be subject to misrepresentation and serious misunderstanding.

As men

As for drug dealers being men it would seem once again that this may reflect issues of visibility and what people actually choose to *see*. My students, when asked to provide their idea of 'who' drug dealers are tend to be even more deterministic in their thinking around gender than they are even around race. In this sense it is also likely that one or two young women hanging furtively around a public telephone, or on a street corner, will not automatically suggest to the casual observer that they are waiting to make a 'connection' whereas this may often be the fate of young men. Further I would suggest that even drug field researchers will conjure an image of a man before they do a woman at the mention of a drug dealer – apart perhaps from those whose research has focussed on women dealers for most academic research has focused on male sellers (Denton and O'Malley, 1999). There is also very little mention in the media (drug mules apart) of women 'pushers' or dealers. In terms of reinforcement many of the ideas already put forward as preconceived behavioural stereotypes attaching to the dealer – aggressiveness, violence, pushing and dangerous adulteration – for most people signify a male presence, just as sexually violent crimes against children do likewise. Women however *are* drug dealers (Denton, 2001; Denton and O'Malley, 1999; Maher, 1997; Sommers et al. 1996; Dunlap et al. 1994). It is likely that women are dealers in fewer numbers than men, as they are in most drug *use* statistics, but whether they are proportionately fewer is unknown and contested (Jacobs and Miller, 1998). Moreover, as with ethnicity, the degree to which implicit bias points enforcement activity towards men is also an unknown. It may also be the case that an increased normalisation (Parker, 2000) of drug use and with it (to some extent) the relative normalisation of some parts of the drug market will bring about with it an increase in both the number and proportion of women drug sellers.

Dealer typologies

Descriptions by researchers of drug markets in different places and in different periods of time have led to the production of a range of dealer typologies. Many of these usefully depict dealers at different points in the chain of distribution with varying relationships to it. Often, meaningful descriptors of dealers are seen to be inextricably linked to the kind of market structure that they inhabit – for example whether they are freelance or part of some form of more organised distributional structure. Indeed, for the most part, what has been produced is more akin to typologies of distribution styles than that of dealers (Curtis and Wendel, 2000). Styles of distribution, as well as 'location' in the chain of distribution, are no doubt important typological considerations but they are, as we shall see, insufficient on their own. It isn't an aim of this chapter to provide an overview of typologies and market structures as such. More, it is an aim to show how the varieties reported provide evidence of difference – difference of form and *nature*.

Typologies such as those provided by Caulkins et al. (1999) of 'lower-level' crack sellers in New York City in the late 1990s provide some insight into one aspect of that city's drug market. Other typologies however have attempted to be broader and more encompassing. In this spirit Dorn et al.(1992) not only provided an overview of how drug dealing in England had evolved from the 1960s but more usefully they also provided an interpretation of types of dealer and forms of distribution practice and structure that can be used to analyse drug dealer typologies. Dorn et al.'s seven primary types included:

1. *Trading Charities* – enterprises involved in the drug business because of ideological commitments to drugs (e.g. cannabis, Ecstasy), with profit a secondary motive;
2. *Mutual Societies* – friendship networks of user-dealers who support each other and sell or exchange drugs amongst themselves in a reciprocal fashion;
3. *Sideliners* – the licit business enterprise that begins to trade in drugs as a 'sideline';
4. *Criminal Diversifiers* – the existing criminal enterprise that 'diversifies' its operations to include drugs
5. *Opportunist Irregulars* – individuals or small groups who get involved in a variety of activities in the 'irregular economy', including drugs;
6. *Retail Specialists* – enterprises with a manager employing people in a variety of specialist roles to distribute drugs to users;
7. *State-sponsored Traders* – enterprises that result from collaboration between control agents and their informants who may be allowed to trade; or 'buy bust' covert operations
   (Dorn et al. 1992: xiii)

In practice, they argued, these typologies are too rigid. The market is fluid. Individuals move from one to the other and/or are sometimes a complex mix of one or more of the given typologies. Some may not fit neatly into any of the descriptors at all. What Dorn et al. provided however was some rich detail of each of these broad types of dealer/trafficker. Two or three of Dorn et al's typology do not fit with dealer stereotypes at all. If we take those involved in what they described as *Trading Charities* for example, they are described as 'traffickers who initially at least, are not primarily (and definitely not solely) financially motivated' (Dorn et al. 1992: 3). Indeed some of these individuals had a broader life philosophy of which drug use; particularly psychedelic drug use was part and parcel. Being a conduit for drugs such as cannabis and other psychedelic drugs was for some of these individuals a way of practising commitment to these broader ideals or as Dorn et al. put it a 'hippy ethic'. Blum et al.(1972) writing about a wide variety of drug dealers in the US in the late 1960s and early 1970s also came across dealers who felt it to be almost an obligation to spread the freedom and enlightenment they perceived to come with psychedelic drug use. A similar advocate, Timothy Leary, with this mind and with great enthusiasm quotes the thinking of one such dealer;

> We believe that dope is the hope of the human race, it is the way to make people free and happy....We wouldn't feel good just sitting here smoking the dope we have...knowing that there are thirty million kids that need dope (Leary 1969, quoted in Blum et al. 1972: 5).

The almost proselytising hippy ethic of the 1960s and 1970s would have been writ larger in some individuals than in others but seeing recreational drug use as a broadly good thing and thus happily facilitating access to drugs such as cannabis in this vein would arguably characterise such individuals more meaningfully than that of the pusher.

Dorn et al.'s (1992) characterisation of *Mutual Societies* would have also had much credence (and often overlapped) with those connected to trading charities in the 1960s and 1970s. Arguably, from the mid-1980s up to the current day an analogous role has come to be played out by those we might simply define as 'friend dealers' and, in regard to dance drugs such as ecstasy, friends that 'sort' out people they know. Some such individuals (that in legal terms would be characterised and even prosecuted as dealers) do little more than pass a drug from one person to another taking no cut or benefit from the transaction. Individuals such as this may not either see themselves as dealers nor be perceived as such by their friends to whom they supply. In this sense drug dealing for some populations has been normalised in a way that has parallels with the normalisation of drug use (Parker et al. 1998).

> [Asked where he got his drugs cannabis and amphetamines] Depends, friends normally if I can, if not I'll send a friend to a dealer. [Asked if he ever goes to dealers himself] 'No I've *never* been to dealer (18 year old male recreational user quoted in Parker, 2000: 65).

Even at the 'mid' market level there can be ambiguity in this respect:

> I don't know, it's just friends that know friends isn't it? You know, I could say that I've sold to over like three hundred people, but they may go and sell it over to somebody else...I didn't run it like a business, not really, it's just a friend of mine knows a friend of mine knows someone, he says, "He can sort you out", and it goes from there (21 year old mid-market male ecstasy dealer quoted in Pearson and Hobbs, 2001: 32).

It is far from the case that all cannabis or ecstasy 'dealers' conform to these types but at the same time it is certain that many do (Murphy et al. 2005; Parker, 2000; Moore and Miles, 2004). Moreover, cannabis remains easily the most used drug in countries such as the UK, the US and most other western nations and as such a significant proportion of those understood as drug dealers in the West do not conform to traditional ideas of who or what the drug dealer is. Many of these individuals will be no more 'deviant' beyond their drug use and 'dealing' than other 'normal' law abiding citizens. We might speculate (as little work has been done on this) that it is the very recreational-ity of the use surrounding such 'dealing' that makes this more likely. Murphy et al. (1990) for example found that many of the individuals that drifted into dealing (see below) in their sample of cocaine dealers very much played the go-between role at first and that these 'middle-class' individuals were also – dealing/using apart – no different to other middle-class Americans. Cocaine, unlike heroin[3] has a large, middle-class recreational market and we might reasonably speculate that as with cannabis and ecstasy many of those involved with its supply could reasonably be characterised as an amalgam of trading charities, mutual societies or simply friend dealers. Rarely is the drug market considered in these terms but that is precisely the aim of this chapter – to suggest that *the* drug market and *the* drug dealer is something more than that normally suggested. We need to further acknowledge that many people that supply drugs at some point or another often do it for very short periods or do so only opportunistically – this will also be true of many members of a mutual society. Such individuals, once again will often not be as integrated into the 'system' sufficiently to be affected by it nor to have learned its rules and thus 'play' the role of drug dealer stereotypes.

The typology of *Criminal Diversifier* – the criminal that moves into drug selling or trafficking as one of a mix of other illicit activities probably conforms to some extent to the conventional mid and upper level 'player' in the dealing/trafficking scheme. The typology of *Retail Specialists* however whilst providing confirmation of the role to be played for moderate sized organisations dealing in drugs it also provides evidence of the division of labour within the drug scene. The various firms that employ people to be 'runners', look-outs, sellers or just transporters may well be construed to be full of 'dealers' and be liable of conviction under 'conspiracy to supply' but some will have significant roles to play in the dealing of drugs others will be marginal at best. Some individuals – such as the many female drug mules from overseas who make up nearly 16% of the UK's female prison population (Joseph, 2006; HM Prison Service, 2006) – may in fact have been forced to smuggle drugs or be ignorant of the extent of their wrongdoing (Green, 1998). This is not to say that many of those that attempt to smuggle drugs are not wilfully guilty but to acknowledge that many, quite simply, are not. In its deepest sense, to understand many of these women as 'traffickers' is to understand the runner as being akin to Mr Big.

The mix of individuals that inhabit the drugs market is thus heterogeneous. It is heterogeneous both in terms of the levels of dealing involvement and in terms of how far they are integrated into stereotypical dealing systems of the type outlined by Goldstein (1985) in chapter five. There is of course, a continuum. One 'friend' dealer will deal cannabis to three or four other people, perhaps with a supply grown at home. Another friend dealer may well have wider contacts, make small profits and source from a mid-level supply but still retain only a marginal connection to the system. Such heterogeneity also exists within the heroin and cocaine markets although it is likely that proportionally more individuals that conform to some of the dealing stereotypes inhabit this market than that of more recreational drugs[4]. Many user dealers, more reasonably defined as users than dealers, dip in and out of selling when they need to, barely integrating themselves into the dealing system whilst others sell to a select few and are happy to do so.

Whilst these typologies are helpful in showing that individual drug dealers conform to a greater or lesser degree to the archetypal imagery they none-the-less tend (by default) to understand drug dealers in individual terms relating to the broader drug market. Others have argued that rather than seeing drug dealers simply as individuals located within a system (market) that sits outside normal society that we need to understand (many of) them, and their dealing, as having a relationship to society that is meaningfully interconnected. From some of these perspectives drug dealing is not seen as inherently negative, either for the individuals involved in it or necessarily for the communities which they inhabit.

Alternative views of drug dealing and of the drug dealer

As victims of marginalisation

Rather than simply understanding drug dealers as 'bad' individuals, some research has chosen to instead place (some of) them and their activities within broader societal cultural and economic explanatory contexts. Ethnographic immersion into the lives of Puerto Rican crack sellers of El Barrio in New York's East Harlem led Bourgois (1995), for example, to witness (and become privy to) aspects of 'inner-city street culture' that in terms of violence and chaotic lifestyle conform to much of the dealer stereotype outlined previously. Bourgois (1995: 10) relates story after story of conflict, apparent lack of care for others and violence in a neighbourhood where 'Most of them live in fear, or even in contempt, of their neighborhood'. Explanation for Bourgois however lies not in analysis of the evil individual(s) but in the complex mix of macho street culture that was spawned in a context of economic and social marginalisation. According to Bourgois this particular type of street culture encapsulated:

> a complex and conflictual web of beliefs, symbols, modes of interaction, values and ideologies...have emerged in opposition to exclusion from

mainstream society. Street culture offers an alternative forum for autonomous personal dignity...This "street culture of resistance" is not a coherent, conscious universe of political opposition but, rather, a spontaneous set of rebellious practices that in the long term have emerged as an oppositional style (Bourgois, 1995: 8).

The selling of drugs and their use is thus seen as a means for such resistance to be played out – drug use is, in part at least, resistance and drug sales provide the material means to obtain aspects of lifestyle otherwise out of reach. In this sense it is about understanding the emergent street culture as both resistance to mainstream values through the building up of a street culture through which to nurture self defined dignity (that is otherwise denied), whilst at the same time embracing aspects of that mainstream materialist culture which determines how success and dignity are to be defined. Crack dealers in El Barrio are thus redefined by Bourgois as victims of a racialised system that has left them marginalised and subjugated to such an extent that one of the ways that they have chosen to (unconsciously for the most part) resist its burden and denigration is to 'contradictorily' engage in a 'street culture...predicated on the destruction of its participants and the community harbouring them' (Bourgois, 1995: 9). Yes the drug dealers do bad things but the explanation for these behaviours is to be found in the broader social milieu in which they have grown up.

The ethnographic work of Bourgois really applies to poor working class members of New York's inner city – although, as stated before we should not underestimate the power of such narratives to appear to be representative of dealing populations in general – and as such is really a narrative about how *some* members of populations living in such conditions *might* respond to their circumstances. In this sense it is a social-structural[5] understanding of why certain behavioural patterns exist and are perpetuated (in this case drug dealing) as opposed to one solely located in the individual. Moreover, it sees those affected (at least in part) as victim as opposed to simple perpetrator.

The analysis of drug user/seller as victim has also been applied to women involved in the illicit drug trade. Women have commonly been portrayed as weaker variants than their male counterparts: as largely subjugated by men and/or the female role and as a consequence being overly dependent on them. This, it is argued, is in part reflected in their drug use, much of which has been portrayed as self-medication to manage these frustrations (see Denton, 2001 for overview). Other literature, again essentially suggesting self-medication, focuses on women's drug use and involvement as having its routes in being victims of sexual and other physical violence. All in all women have been portrayed as 'lesser' users and 'lesser' dealers. In terms of dealing they are portrayed as weaker and less able to function in a male domain. Their drug use is of a lesser status as well, often portrayed as having been led to it by boyfriends or the need for self-medication. As if this overly masculine reading isn't enough, women drug users also suffer the 'double-whammy' of being viewed as 'less' than even male drug users in terms of their character. This is because, as women, they had further to 'fall' (Boyd, 2004) than the men, and stereotypes of women drug users ending up as prostitutes – a view that is overstated[6] (Denton, 2001; Goldstein, 1979; Maxwell and Maxwell, 2000; Sommers et al. 1996; Fagan, 1994; Dunlap, Johnson and Maher, 1997) – only reinforces such views. Positions such as this however have often been as much the stuff of assumption as they have fact. As Denton (2001: 163-4) states:

> Whatever the possible accuracy of their claims, these are based more on commonsense or political principles than observation or evidence, for there has been little or no research on which such assumptions could have been based' [and further specific to sexual and other abuse] '...Margaret Hamilton argues that clinicians, without research to back them up, readily accept the causal link between sexual abuse and drug use

Thus women are often portrayed as becoming drug users to 'dull the pain' brought on by 'outside forces' such as subjugation in a patriarchal system or the more specific consequences of such a culture such as sexual violence. Women drug sellers are more often than men linked to having become so through their drug use and having learned through men. Women drug sellers are not generally portrayed as entrepreneurs as male sellers sometimes are but as women that have entered the drug market on the 'shirt-tails' of their boyfriends or male partners and as once again performing a generally subjugated and lesser role. Of course it follows that working class women in inner-city areas like those described by Bourgois are subject to marginalisation both by class as well as gender and this is further enhanced when a member of an under-privileged ethnic minority. In such contexts, as Maher (1997) has shown, women dealers can also suffer further marginalisation within the local dealing scene which is dominated by male dealers and macho male culture. Although research *on* women drug dealers (or that which includes them) betrays the simple stereotype of the *male* drug dealer it has tended to only 'see' those women that reinforce other common gender stereotypes (e.g. those that portray women as weak and inferior). Some research however has shown that many women drug dealers do not conform to these perhaps overly simple stereotypes (Dunlap, Johnson and Maher, 1997; Denton and O'Malley, 1999; Mieczkowski, 1994).

In addition to acknowledging that women sellers of heroin and cocaine can be successful, in control, capable, entrepreneurial and even capable of managing their business with violence if necessary we need to remind ourselves again that not all drug markets function in the manner of the stereotype heroin/cocaine market – the market that most research pertaining to women has focussed on. Many markets (of e.g. different drugs) and positions in the market, as we saw in chapter five, require little by way of violent activity. Just as men that do not resort to violence inhabit these markets then women can also do the same without too much need to worry about 'doing business like a man'.

Drug dealers...earning big or small?

One common dealer stereotype depicts them as earning huge sums of money on the back of the misery of those they supply, a view that often justifies harsh penalties.

> Drug traffickers and drug dealers earn immense profits from the destruction of other people's lives. The Government have increased the penalties for drug peddlers. The maximum sentence for trafficking in class A drugs, such as heroin, cocaine and Ecstasy, has been raised from 14 years to life. The Criminal Justice Act 1993 strengthened the powers of the courts to confiscate the profits of drug trafficking and laundering drugs money. The Crime (Sentences) Bill will introduce a stiff minimum mandatory sentence of seven years for those who are

convicted on three separate occasions for trafficking in hard drugs. The Security Service Act 1996 has enabled the Security Service to support the efforts of law enforcers to fight drug trafficking (David Evans, MP. Hansard, 17 Jan 1997: Column 546).

A range of research however has shown that this image of dealers making vast profits is far from the case for many if not most drug dealers. Once again we are dealing with the issue of the visible and the invisible. There are always those that will make good money from the drug market and there will likewise be those that make good money and want to show that this is the case with an ostentatious lifestyle that suggests a high disposable income. There are also those high profile 'king-pin' prosecutions that the media in particular is keen to focus on: 'Drug baron who 'earned £640m' gets 20 years' (*The Guardian*, September, 19, 2000) as well as the ordinary dealer: 'It varies drastically, some weekend nights I could make up to $2,000 alone in-pocket from a club' (Webster, 2002). That such individuals exist does not mean that we should either characterise or understand the drug market as likely to produce such outcomes for those that work in it. Many of those 'employed' in the drugs market as lower level employees such as runners, look-outs or even sellers may be paid in drugs rather than cash. Hagedorn (1988) for example found that up to two-thirds of the drug market employees in the two areas of Milwaukee that he studied were paid in this way. Moreover it was the case that most of the small outfits doing the employing were themselves only grossing between $6,000 and $12,000 a year with about 1 in 6 grossing around $60,000 a year. In real terms these were akin to small businesses earning only moderate, often small sums of money whilst many of the 'dealers' were paid in drugs alone. Reuter et al.(1990) in their study of dealing in Washington D.C. found that two thirds of the 186 men they sampled also held down regular paid jobs; that only three in eight sold daily with a quarter selling only once a week or less frequently. On average all of those selling reported incomes from selling that were better than those likely through legitimate means but 'few of the street dealers who made up most of this sample reported the kinds of incomes from which Mercedes and great fortunes spring' (viii) whilst infrequent sellers made little money at all. In addition, an average of around 25% of earnings was spent/consumed on drugs for personal use. Caulkins et al. (1999) found that in late 1990s New York City the rewards accrued related to proximity to ownership of the drugs being sold. 'Entrepreneurs', those that owned the drugs they sold retained an average of 53% of the sale price. 'Independent consignment sellers' who obtained the drugs they sold from a supplier and then paid for the drugs once sold, retained on average 25% of the sale revenue. The last two categories listed 'spot consignment sellers' – paid a proportion of what they sell – and 'spot wage sellers' who were paid hourly to sell at particular locations received 11% and 3% respectively. Levitt and Venkatesh (2000) reported that the 'earn more at the top earn little at the bottom' picture was also true of gang based drug dealers in Chicago during the 1990s but that those earning little were often vying for opportunities to rise higher in the organisation and thus earn more money. More recently in a study of drug markets in four English communities, May et al. (2005) found that whilst the full-time 'for profit' dealers made very good money (approx £7,500 weekly) the user-dealers and runners made something closer to £450 per week. Again, we find that over half the sample reported spending the majority of their earnings on drugs for personal consumption although many made enough for luxury consumption and enhanced lifestyles those at the lower end of the earnings scale were clearly barley surviving. Stewart (1987:116-7), for example provides a graphic example of the way personal consumption can impact on earnings and disposable income for even those turning over large amounts of drugs and large sums of money:

> Money ceases to have any meaning for a dealer who regularly moves ounces of smack. He may be using hundreds of pounds' worth of heroin everyday. He can find himself sitting counting out dozens of £10 notes and asking someone to lend him a fiver to make up the money to score. Roger laughed as he reported one such occasion. 'I was down at Macker's and he said to me, "Lend us two quid for petrol. I've only got three grand and I need that to score"

What the various research on income from drug dealing suggests is that a number of variables will determine how much any one individual profits from their involvement in selling drugs. Again, differing contexts will produce different scenarios and depending on where an individual is 'located' (e.g. as a 'runner', someone who stores drugs, a low-level dealer as compared to a freelancer with a small stable of constant reliable customers) will affect incomes dramatically. The state of the market will also affect price, competition and the selling context. The early, highly profitable crack market in New York for example later became one with much lower earning potential. Overall, research does suggest that on average, full-time dealing in drugs – particularly if a dealer owns the drugs they sell, or sells on consignment – will provide a better income for many of those involved in it than they can get from legitimate employment (Fairlie, 1999; Caulkins et al. 1999; MacCoun and Reuter, 1992). It also suggests that many drug dealers earn very little money – that sometimes payment is in kind as opposed to cash – and that much of what is earned is spent on drugs for personal consumption. Interestingly, many drug sellers (probably most) also appear to be supplementing legitimate incomes with money from drug sales and are thus effectively part-time dealers – probably reflecting the fact that as a whole it is a less profitable activity than the media suggests (MacCoun and Reuter, 1992). In addition to this, risk of arrest and attendant high penalties for drug supply make being involved in the drugs trade (at any level) a hazardous business and in some dealing contexts the risk of violence is also extremely high (cf. Levitt and Venkatesh, 2000; Jacobs, 2000; Brownstein et al. 2000; Goldstein et al. 1992). As such, a cost benefit analysis of the worth of drug dealing overall has to be married up with a number of aspects of dealing that lessen the worth of any profits made, particularly for those making relatively small profits.

Becoming a drug dealer – pathology or circumstance?

Even if we accept that there is a great deal of exaggeration regarding the attendant riskiness of illicit drugs it none-the-less remains the case that drug use, particularly the use of drugs such as heroin and crack cocaine, but also numerous others, *is* a comparatively risky activity. Given that this is the case, what would possess any individual to sell addictive and/or potentially dangerous, mind-altering substances that have no quality control (in terms of consistent purity etc) to other people? It is perhaps this part of drug dealing that many people have the most difficulty understanding and arguably the aspect that condemns drug dealers most definitively in their eyes. Couched in its simplest terms, any individual that knowingly sells dangerous drugs on to others is committing a highly immoral act, tantamount to murder (if someone dies) or physical abuse. To many the act is simply an incredulous one. Add to this a general sense that such individuals 'push' these dangerous substances onto people, or even children, who otherwise would not have used them, then the indignation that they inspire is often without equal. Explanations of how and why an individual could stoop so low, as we have already seen, tend to be expressed in the essential 'badness' of the individuals involved or that they have been turned bad by the drugs the use and then sell. Some combination of both is also compatible. In a way it assumes a kind of pathological cause, you have to be (or become) a particularly bad person to do this kind of criminal act just for financial reward.

The evidence however is more prosaic. There are for example, what I will call surface level reasons for selling drugs that some researchers have pointed to. These are usually self-report reasons such as the pursuit of simple financial gain, drug selling as an alternative to poorly paid work, hedonism, the need to support a habit, the pursuit of culturally located status or power or perhaps as Van Nostrand and Tewksbury (1999: 59) have put it, the 'realizing of socially valued goals'. Such reasons however do not get to the essence of why some people involve themselves in a criminal activity that to much of society is an act of evil – unless those people are, simply bad. Although under-researched, some of the pathways into drug dealing literature goes beyond such surface level explanation to a deeper level, one that provides a basis for understanding how individuals come to try to realise those desires in ways that are, to others, unreasonably deviant.

A number of researchers, with regard to the dealers in their samples, have alluded to, or specifically theorised, how dealers become dealers by referring to the connected concepts of 'career', 'neutralisation' and 'drift' (Murphy et al. 1990; Tunnell, 1993; Curcione, 1997; Lieb and Olsen, 1976). The concepts, predominately developed from Becker (1963) and Matza (1969), are to some extent wedded to social theories that seek to explain how and why deviant careers develop, that are now out of vogue. As with many such theories however we can accept that there may well be much about what is described or theorised that is useful without needing to accept the theoretical model/s used in total. The idea of the criminal *career* is now well established (Blumstein et al. 1986). In the drugs field it is also well established that most drug users tend to have a drug using career – that is, it has a beginning, middle and an end (Hser, 2000). The process through which this takes place can be complex and individual biographies highly divergent (cf. Coomber and Sutton, 2006; Moore, 1993; Zinberg, 1985; Waldorf, 1973) but clear trends are discernable in the sense that becoming a drug user, maintaining levels of use and desisting from use involve decision making activities and that these are affected by circumstance and time. The concepts of 'natural history' and 'maturing out' (Winick, 1962; Waldorf and Biernacki, 1982) for example have been used as shorthand descriptors for the process where, after even a lengthy period of drug use many heroin dependent users take action, with or without treatment, to successfully stop using. The concepts of neutralisation and drift to some degree complement the notion of career. Neutralisation refers to the way that those involved in activities frowned upon by others seek to rationalise and justify their behaviour as being not particularly problematic whereas drift refers to the idea that individuals in reality tend to take small incremental steps towards disapproved behaviour such that by the time they are committing serious acts of crime they have barely noticed the progression. At each small stage (e.g. tobacco use, prior to cannabis use, cannabis use prior to other drug use, sharing drugs prior to selling them) the employment of neutralisation techniques (this is victimless crime, they came to me, the drugs I sell are good quality) will be used to make the behaviour acceptable. Taken together they provide part of a framework to start to understand some of the processes through which some people become drug dealers. Once again, some examples may once again help by way of illustration:

1. Steve grew up on a housing estate in an inner-city area where cannabis use among his peers was not uncommon from his early teens. He himself had been initiated into cannabis at the age of twelve by his older brother and each of his other three siblings all smoked cannabis and/or took amphetamines. Drug use was not considered anything particularly special and it was simply part and parcel of Steve's formative teenage years. Although there was a great deal of criminal activity, mostly vehicle related, committed by Steve's peers, Steve himself had never been arrested and apart from some very infrequent and minor shoplifting episodes he did not involved himself in crime. One of Steve's older siblings supplied Steve with his drugs and by the time Steve was seventeen he had shared his drugs with others on numerous occasions in social settings and others had shared theirs with him. Sometimes Steve was asked by his friends to get them drugs from his brother and

sometimes his brother would ask him to pass on an order to one of his friends. None of these activities were particularly meaningful to Steve – they were just part of his life and cannabis was consumed in a way not too dissimilar to the way others consume alcohol non-problematically. As it became known that Steve could be a conduit for drugs Steve was approached by others – nearly all of whom he knew – to procure drugs for them. Steve, reluctant to be 'used', began to receive minor payments (either money or part of the drugs supplied) from both his older sibling and the person he supplied to. When Steve's older sibling moved away from the area Steve took his place. This was a smooth transition because Steve knew his sibling's supplier and users quickly learned of the change in setup.

2. Gill was nineteen when she first used ecstasy. She was introduced to it by friends at university with whom she shared a house and she quickly became a regular (every weekend whilst clubbing) user. Her background was both loving and stable and she has a postgraduate degree in physics. She has no known criminality in her family, in her own past and none of her close peers had ever been in trouble with the police. After using ecstasy for six months the friend that she normally sourced her ecstasy from stopped going to clubs and stopped facilitating her and her others friends supply. Needing to find a new source Gill, by word of mouth in her clubbing network, found out about someone she could obtain ecstasy from. On informing her close friends of this Gill collected their orders and contacted her prospective supplier. Gill's first order was for forty tablets and she was given an extra five by the supplier for the 'bulk' order. Gill sold the extra five for profit and to pay for her own drugs – she had after all (she reasoned) sourced the new supplier and taken the risk. Gill quickly became the conduit for all of her friends and soon after that for others who, through friends, contacted her. After three years Gill also stopped going to clubs and slowly also stopped taking ecstasy and supplying it.

3. Boon became involved in drug use from an early age starting with cigarettes, alcohol and cannabis then, later, amphetamine and finally heroin. Petty criminality preceded all illicit drug use but

by the time he was 20 he was using amphetamine very regularly and his involvement in crime had progressed to burglary and numerous other forms of criminal activity. Boon mixed with a number of individuals who supplied illicit drugs, some were friend suppliers, some were part-time dealers and also those who would be classified as middle level or wholesale dealers. When Boon became dependent on heroin at 22, after using irregularly for one and a half years, he combined dealing heroin and cocaine within his repertoire of illicit activities.

These examples go some way towards providing an explanatory framework for how some drug dealers become drug dealers without recourse to notions of inherent badness or drug induced transition. In the first two cases the individuals were already drug users. The drugs involved (cannabis and ecstasy) were perceived in a positive light by both individuals, in Steve's case it was what people that were 'like him' just did. Selling cannabis for Steve then, in terms of either 'drift' towards criminality or in terms of neutralisation was almost non-existent the cultural milieu in which he grew up was as important. Yes, he was aware that the outside world would condemn his selling but the outside world was not (to some extent) his world and he saw little wrong with it. Gill on the other hand had 'drifted' much more significantly. For Gill, the initial drift was to do something illegal, to use an illicit drug. Her neutralisation rationale was that this was to be a one time event so that she could fit in with her new peer group who appeared to be regular and committed users. Having enjoyed the experience of ecstasy combined with clubbing she felt less anxious using a second time. Her new neutralisation rationale focussed around how scares around ecstasy were exaggerated and that this, like many other social controls, was unjust. Soon, now an enthusiastic user, Gill found the step up to facilitating supply a slight concern in the sense that she was aware that others outside the 'scene' might see her as a dealer but in her mind this was ludicrous. Her friend had not been a dealer and neither was getting drugs for others, who had asked her to do so, the same as being a dealer. She looked on the supply of ecstasy, a drug she considered relatively benign, as not very serious, only supplied to those that asked and made moderate amounts of money from selling. Regardless of whether Gill or Steve could be considered by some to be deluded in terms their perspective on the drugs they sold the point is that for them they were not doing too much wrong.

Boon is slightly different. He only drifted into drug dealing if we choose to see drug dealing as something 'more' than the other kinds of criminality he was already involved in. Drift still probably applies usefully to Boon's criminal career overall but prior to selling he was a drug user, had friends and acquaintances who were users/sellers and had long been so and such a way of life was neither alien, new or in any way anathema to him.

How people become drug dealers is of course a multi-layered and contingent process with varying contexts, influences and opportunities impacting on the career of any one individual. When we also consider that drug dealers do not in fact do most of the 'evil' things they are supposed to, it by default, also means that many drug dealers do not actually have as far to 'fall' as the is usually assumed. As such, it is far easier to understand how people like Gill, the middle-class cocaine dealers in Murphy et al. (1990) and even Steve become drug sellers. Once we have an understanding that drug selling is not too far removed from an individual's drug use and social sharing (i.e. their everyday life) and that initial drug sales will commonly be to friends that are already drug users, we can then transpose on top some of the surface level motivations mentioned earlier – desire for money, material goods and see, that as 'motivations', they are only ever part of the picture.

Other confounding aspects.

Johnny Swan the heroin dealer in Irvine Welsh's *Trainspotting* perhaps sums up many people's view of the archetypal drug dealer. Swan is rough, tough, not to be crossed and carries out his business without compassion. In short the drug dealer is generally relieved of having too much humanity – as has been common for representations of terrorists over the years (Schlesinger et al. 1983). Once their humanity is relieved from them they become capable of any kind of heinous crime, attributed with evilness and often subject to harsh penalties. Yet, this depiction runs counter to many actual and intuitive (at least now you have got this far in this book) accounts of drug dealer behaviour. Throughout my research on dangerous drug adulteration, nearly all of those interviewed had a strong desire to be known as someone from whom 'quality drugs' could be bought. The meaning attached to this was usually depicted as somewhere between needing such a 'rep' (reputation) to maintain a client base and/or to attract a new one by word of mouth but also the desire for respect – both from others (buyers, other sellers) but also for themselves. As relayed in chapter three, it was also the case that many of the dealers expressed a concern that the 'comeback' for dealing 'dodgy deals' was not worth the risk. The inference being that in many cases that some of the people they sold to were more dangerous than they were. Indeed many of the men I have spoken to over the last ten years or so have not cut a figure of fear or intimidation however you might depict it. They were ordinary men and as such could (if they chose) elicit fear in some and fail to do so in others; they were working in an area of criminality where those they sold to would often be no less criminal – just differently so. Anyway, this image tends to reflect the image of the heroin, crack or powder cocaine dealer, but as we have seen it doesn't even conform to that market never mind other segments of the market such as that where cannabis predominates. Even in this (powder) market however I had people tell me about cutting the cocaine they sold with a homeopathic remedy that helps rhinitis to allay the side-effects of cocaine[7]. Now that's a level of customer care that goes beyond most licit retailers. I am not suggesting that such as case is 'typical' but Stewart (1987: 119) relates a similar tale:

> One big dealer could never bear to see anyone sick. Customers who turned up on his doorstep without money would be sure of a free turn-on however much they owed him. On one occasion he heard of someone mugging other users for their gear. Angrily, he sent the man a message, telling him that instead of attacking users he should come down and see him for a free hit when he was sick

The point Stewart is trying to make here is that the dealing fraternity is a complex mix of individuals and although such examples may not be typical they 'must come as a shock to anyone who has read the papers and been convinced that dealers are all monsters whose closest relatives probably hailed from Transylvania' (p119).

We can see then that a simple demonisation of the dealer whereby 'he' is stripped of most of his humanity simply ignores that many dealers are relatively ordinary individuals, with ordinary thoughts, feelings and even morals. When we consider, as this book has shown, that most of the activities that commonly underpin why the dealer is thought to be evil, or particularly 'bad', are either largely mythical or a gross exaggeration the idea that the drug dealer is not so special or unusual is not so difficult re-imagine.

Footnotes

[1] In the absence of research that has purposively sought to obtain lay views on what kind of person drug dealers are I refer here to the consistent annual finding in one of my classes (a class on this very topic) that the students hold the stereotyped view that drug dealers are mostly 'black'. It also concurs with a range of media reporting (cf. Murji, 1998).

[2] Reference to the BMW is significant for BMWs are, as the stereotype goes – melding with other stereotypes about black men being poor – likely to be too expensive for most young black men and as such, in circular fashion, a black man driving a BMW is a dealer, how else would he get such a car.

[3] Heroin too has its share of recreational and occasional users (cf. Zinberg, 1985; Warburton et al. 2005)

[4] Obviously 'hard' drug and recreational drug markets often overlap but it is also the case that they often do not. Many recreational drug users perceive drugs such as heroin as significantly different (worse) than the drugs they use and sell and avoid that market. Some cocaine dealers even feel that way about heroin (cf. Coomber, 1997a)

[5] Or indeed one of political economy depending on your preferred emphasis

[6] It has been shown however (e.g. Maher, 1997; May et al. 1999), that there are some contexts within which women are more likely to become involved in sex work. To suggest that this is applicable to nearly all drug addicted women however ignores the alternative choices many women make which enables them to avoid it and pays lip-service once again to that which is visible and the ways that the visible (especially those that have fallen further) are magnified in accounts of drug use. It also pays conventional lip-service to banal accounts of the way that drugs such as heroin and cocaine strip the user of morality and makes the user 'do' things they otherwise would not.

[7] The point here isn't that this would prevent nasal problems but that the intent was to do so.

Chapter 7:

Complexity not simplicity – re-situating the drug dealer and the drug market

Why, then, have claims makers in the United States in the later years
of the twentieth century vilified drug dealers as violent, evil people?
(Brownstein, 2000: 54).

To what extent might the topics covered in this book be reasonable ones?
Might it be the case that the depictions of drug dealers and drug markets
focussed upon have been overstated, or perhaps more importantly, is it the
really the case that 'people' commonly believe the things about dealers that
I have suggested? These are important questions to ask for there is no point
in fashioning an amalgamation of 'straw-man' depictions and beliefs whose
importance in understanding drug dealers and drug markets is in reality
overstated.

When I first started researching the issue of dangerous drug adulteration
the answer to such questions appeared to be unambiguous. Regular reports
by the media were clear: dealers used rat poison and other dangerous
products to cut the drugs that they sold, and people, it was being claimed,
died because of this. The police and other authorities – as we have seen
in chapter three – either provided the statements or supported them. A
minor piece of research on a student population seemed to confirm that the
belief was (apart from that those that had not heard of such things at all)
widespread and almost totally uncontested. In addition to all of the media

reporting and political statements that have sustained such images, over the last ten years, numerous stories, such as the 'van in the playground' account from chapter two, have been relayed to me. In presenting my research findings at conferences, police training days, and on my own undergraduate courses, they are consistently met with surprise and to some degree a level of bewilderment simply because they have often contradicted aspects of the drug problem that people took for granted and felt that they could reasonably do so. I have seen little over the last ten years to suggest that very much is changing or that the growing body of research into drug markets is having much impact in changing perceptions at either the more 'informed' of levels or for 'ordinary' people.

Three very recent incidents both reinforce this notion and, within reason, illustrate the point. The first (May 2006) involved a high ranking UK police officer with some national responsibility for drug issues. The context was a meeting of drug field 'experts' regarding drug market activity around cannabis. The conversation had been focussing on the likelihood that most cannabis supply to young people was 'social supply' by other young people when the officer interjected. We had to be wary of making such assumptions he argued because, he had in fact heard only that morning, that drug dealers in a particular London Borough were putting crack cocaine into cannabis cigarettes. The inference was twofold: that cannabis dealers are not in some way lower-level dealers, and that this practice was particularly sneaky as those buying cannabis wouldn't know there was crack in it. A later prompting of his source revealed a perspective that suggested that, on top of trying to avoid prosecution for selling crack cocaine[1], this was another way of trying to hook those that thought they were just buying cannabis. Initially the tenor was of an announcement of fact but a gentle prompting for sources and the suggestion that such stories, despite being common fare, were often unsubstantiated, a little backtracking took place and it was revealed that this was in fact hearsay, that no cannabis cigarettes with crack had been seized and that the source was 'a source of the source'. Rather than such activities being 'taken with a pinch of salt' the police, and no doubt many others continue to accept them as proof of particular activities that are simply taken for granted as what is 'going on'. New practices (if they exist) are rationalised into existing assumptions about what dealers do. So in this instance the story appeared to confirm, once again without 'proof' because no proof is needed (we know it happens) how dealers cut their drugs with more dangerous drugs/substances – in this case crack cocaine.

The second event (June 2006) involved a criminal justice/health information email 'cascade'. This is where some important information is 'cascaded' out to a wide variety of relevant organisations for them to act on or note. In this instance the cascade was initiated by a Detective Inspector local to the region where I work. The information bluntly stated that in relation to a 'recent spate of drugs deaths relating to intravenous heroin users... Intelligence suggests that the Heroin may be cut with cement and this is causing fatalities. We will do a press release...' The message was headed as of 'high importance' and as 'Informed by intelligence'. As it turned out however the 'intelligence' consisted of some comments by local informants, and outreach workers passing comment on the likely causes of the five deaths. The 'intelligence' upon which it was based was not accompanied by any forensic evidence and the postmortems were inconclusive. This cascade, backed up by 'intelligence', just like Blue Star LSD tattoo hoaxes, is working its way around the region and country as I write.

The third 'event' (April 2006) involved a conversation with a PhD student who wanted to compare the risks related to drug trafficking with those of the trade in international fuel. In practice the conversation revolved around 'how drug dealers' operate and this was prefaced by the student (and reinforced at other times) with comments alluding to how the area he came from was full of drugs and drug dealers and as such that he knew how 'it all worked'. During the conversation he referred to 'pusher' (his words) stereotype after pusher stereotype and as the conversation developed and we discussed his conceptual framework it became clear – to us both – that his 'knowledge' was based not on experience but on assumption and 'commonsense knowledge'. It provides a reminder once again that the most simple of stereotypes continue to hold power even for those supposedly immersed in an environment where dealing is common.

Although these three events do not prove my case there are other examples that I can reasonably refer to that go some way to supporting it. The continued success of the Blue Star Tattoo speaks volumes for what people in authority and the lay public believe about what dealers do to drugs and that what they do is predatory and highly dangerous. Belief in dangerous adulteration continues and drug markets, when mentioned in the media, are never considered benign in character – where is the story after all in that[2]. As was shown in chapter three, even drug dealers believe and invest in many of these images – even though they may not in fact correspond to what they themselves do or what other dealers that they know do. Moreover, I would ask the reader to reflect on their own views and perspectives. How did you see the drug dealer? Which beliefs covered in this book are/were part and parcel of your own world view? The extent to which all or parts of these images are embedded within popular culture, as well as the Western sense of what drug dealers are, or what the drug market is, is also important – and I hope – demonstrated in the chapters in this book.

What is the drug problem?

This book has suggested that there are a number of common beliefs about drugs, about addiction, about the effect of these on communities and society, and about drug dealers and drug markets. It has further suggested that many of these beliefs are highly problematic in the sense that there appears to be little evidence of the existence of the effects or behaviours (as they are commonly conceptualised) or that they are unreasonably exaggerated or overly homogenised.

In chapter one we saw that drugs such as opium, cocaine, heroin, but even cannabis, were long ago blamed for creating the 'unmoral savage' (Hubbard, quoted in Trebach, 1982: 50). Little by way of credence is today given to these early depictions – although much uninformed, similar scaremongering continues, around crack for instance (Reinarman and Levine, 1997). The Chinese experience 'taught' the West what could happen to a society that allowed the horrors of opium to catch hold and yet today we are starting to see that this proof is highly suspect. It appears that reporting on the devastation was largely anecdotal and politically infused from the earliest of days. Official accounts were uncritically accepted and the extent of ravaged addiction certainly appears to have been overstated whilst the widespread social and cultural use of opium, was either ignored (usually) or greatly understated. Opium it seems did not simply have the power to transform and addict, but the fear that it did was strong. This indignant fear was writ large in the temperance, and other puritan movements that abhorred excess and preached moderation as a principle. The immoderate claims they made however, about the 'evil' of alcohol and other drugs such as opium, were and remain, unproven and testament to overstatement. As Morone showed with regard to the 'white slave' scare, evidence was not a pre-requisite. Reasoned, often evangelical argumentation that preyed on fears (we would never want this to happen, it seems it is happening, it could be your child/sister/daughter next) and took advantage of contemporary prejudices was sufficient. By the 1930s dealers were portrayed as preying on those they could, particularly the young and innocent, giving away free drugs to get them addicted – a view that remains common even today. Yet, as related in chapter two, research shows that addiction is neither instant nor even particularly rapid and that most new experimenters are exposed to, and given a drug by those close to them, such as other family members, friends or acquaintances (McIntosh et al. 2003). On top of this, dangerous adulteration is largely mythical, free drugs are not provided in the ways assumed, the Blue Star Tattoo is a hoax, and although drug markets certainly can be violent and brutal places they often are no more so than the culture within which they operate. For many that work in the drug market, violence is not an oppressive or prominent part of their experience, and many do not conform to the dealer stereotype in the slightest.

What are we to make of all this? Is *the* drug problem as it is conventionally presented still the same if drugs such as heroin and crack cocaine do not possess the transformative powers suggested, if they are not instantly addictive, if it were known that most drug users 'mature' out of use – even many (perhaps most) dependent on heroin and cocaine? Would the problem still be the same if it were known that the primary dangers of street drugs like heroin do not lay in poisonous cutting agents or even in the heroin itself but, most commonly in using heroin excessively with other drugs, particularly alcohol (Darke and Zador, 1996)? Would the problem still be the same if it were known that drug markets did not all present the kind of risk associated with 1980s New York and that many are positively demure in comparison? Surely a drug problem, even partly constructed on beliefs such as these, is itself transformed if many of the demons it was thought to possess can be shown to be false? If so, then the problem is perhaps lessened. If it is not lessened then it is changed, and activity and ire against the problem can be redirected to where issues of greater substance rest?

In criminal justice terms a re-orientation or repositioning of perspective on the drug dealer could lead to new criminal justice responses in relation to policing approaches and to punishment. Awareness for example, as we saw in chapter six, that the police may 'police' black drug dealers differently based on their presuppositions about *who* the drug dealer is, could lead to revised procedures and training programmes around this issue. Likewise, greater acknowledgement of the role played by different individuals convicted of drug dealing could lead to more informed and more appropriate punishment. On the one hand, many so-called 'drug mules' might receive less overtly punitive treatment, reflective of their often nominal role, whilst on the other hand, the increasingly problematic (in criminal justice terms) 'social supplier' who is far removed from the archetypal dealer, could also be dealt with appropriately, that is – differently. That this latter issue is a real one is reflected in a fairly recent case where a Scottish teenager died after taking ecstasy but the Sherriff (judge) ruled the friend who had supplied the tablet not prosecutable as a dealer:

> You are not a drugs dealer. You passed it on at the request of someone else. That makes this a much less serious charge … Had you been a dealer I would have been thinking in terms of imprisonment, but you are not (Sheriff John McInness, quoted in BBC News, 2000).

A shift in perspective has clearly taken place here but this is inevitably piecemeal. That there is continuing tension on such issues is evidenced by the introduction, even more recently, of tougher new measures in the recent 2005 Drugs Act (UK):

> The new measures will make sure courts are taking into account the vulnerability of young people when punishing those who target our schools to sell drugs to children (Paul Goggins, Home Office minister with responsibility for drugs policy, quoted in *The Guardian*, January 3, 2006).

This news article, reflective of my entire experience with 'drug dealer at the school gates' type stories, does not refer to any specific evidence of dealers targeting schools or school children. The Home Office minister's statement however justifies the new tougher measures explicitly in these terms. Drug dealer's are again 'one group' and they are again preying on children but once again no evidence is presented because there is no need for it.

The normalisation of drug use and thus of drug dealing however is an issue that will not go away. The criminal justice system has an uncomfortable decision to make. It can, as it has in the past, punish such individuals with the full severity of the law or it can come to terms with changed times and adopt a more complex and sensitive understanding of the personnel they are dealing with, as did the Scottish Sherriff in 2000.

Scapegoating, myth, rumour, ideology and explanation

In chapter one I attempted to outline some of the processes through which we might understand how the drug dealer and the drug market came to be understood in the ways that they did. It tries to show the complex overlapping of discourses on excess, on appropriate (often class based) behaviour, on why certain groups were thought to be worthy of denigration, prejudice and fear. It also shows how other movements such as the professionalisation of medicine and pharmacy impacted on issues of drug control but also how there had long been a struggle to wrestle control of potions away from quacks, itinerants and wanderers. It is a history about how certain discourses became dominant and it, to some extent, also tries to explain why. This explanation however, dependent on empirical and historical detail only tells us so much. Interpretation plays some role in this. Interpretation leads sometimes to theoretical explanation and/or to the privileging of emphasis of one part, or some parts of the process over others. To some degree this is inevitable in social scientific research. All history is an interpretation and we read interpretations of those that have gone before. The Chinese experience for example is being redefined as I write, whereas for many years this history was little more than a reproduction of the official Chinese standpoint and those of evangelists. Over time however we hope that some interpretations, subject to critical scrutiny, will be shown to be weaker and less credible than others. This is, after all, how we move forward. As far as the issues encapsulated in this book go I am aware that I could have delved so much further than I have for the historical processes that impact upon them.

There are histories of scapegoating for example that show how the ritual persecution of certain persons or groups has been used to 'cleanse' society for thousands of years. Sins of the wider group have to be removed – or God will punish – and by locating or transferring those sins *in* something 'other' (often a goat was sent (cast) out – hence scape-goat) the group doing the casting out cleanses itself not just symbolically but literally (Douglas, 1995). Such histories are numerous and even if they do not relate to universal human behaviour they certainly allude to common concerns within human society about the existence of purity and danger, of good and bad and of how to protect from that which is impure. Such interpretations of course suggest that human societies seek to protect themselves not only from the sins of their own but also that they are on the look out for the sins of others. For if the sins of these others are greater, and they are purged, it will by default cleanse those doing the purging. Other histories, particularly those of 'myth' have suggested that these ancient oral histories are stories that seek to embed, within their respective culture, that which is profane and that which is righteous, guiding it towards accepted norms and values and providing exemplas of how divergence leads to catastrophe (Cohen, 1969). Read in this way – and most myth is read as though it contains some kind of message regarding appropriate norms – we can see again how there is a human concern for counterbalancing the potential for chaos or societal collapse. If a threat to that societal fabric is perceived then it has to be countered (Douglas, 1995). More recently, Tudor (2003: 239) has suggested that fear is everywhere in modern society and that demons are all around us:

> Our children are no longer allowed to walk to school, and the landscapes of fear that we paint for them are populated not with trolls, wolves or wicked witches, but with paedophiles, satanic abusers, and generically untrustworthy adults. Of course, none of these fears may be merited. But they have become part of the common currency of late modern society, and we do not have an adequate understanding of their genesis, their character, or their consequences.

Tudor suggests that we need a new sociology of fear to better understand the ways through which many of us live our everyday lives. Such a sociology of fear:

> ...must examine the cultural matrix within which fear is realised and attend to the patterns of social activity routinely associated with it. Nor is it enough to develop a social psychology of fear of the kind that we typically find in the sociology of the emotions. Fear must also be examined at the societal level where it may even become the very foundation of forms of social organization. As many have known to their cost, whole regimes of domination can be founded on fear (Tudor, 2003: 244).

Drugs, drug users, and drug dealers have long been attributed by drug field researchers as 'victims' of unreasonable scapegoating and demonisation (e.g. Lindesmith, 1941; Szasz, 2003; Boyd, 2004; Green, 1998; Miller, 1991; Friedman, 2002). Moreover, it is relatively easy to show how such events are littered throughout the history of the development of drug control. Without needing to question conventional views of drug related danger we can point to examples where drugs, drug users and suppliers are literally considered evil and amoral. We can also readily point to examples where drug use only becomes a problem when associated with particular groups. However, although we can point to moments in history – as I have done throughout this book – where fear is galvanised around particular issues and peoples, we need something more than this narrow focus to fully situate our understanding (and fear of) drug dealers and drug users more meaningfully. A certain syncretism of these various, often overlapping but conceptually distinct, approaches (scapegoating, myth, fear) would I believe provide some valuable insight. That however, is a project for another time. For now I have sought merely to reposition the surface level (testable) understanding of the drug dealer to something more complex. To show that how the drug dealer is currently understood has a traceable basis that is located in the shifting sands of what was assumed rather than what was known and that there is much about those assumptions which was and remains highly questionable. When we looked closely at this thing called the drug dealer we found that most of what is commonly believed is either false, misconstrued or incorrectly applied to too broad a population. A deeper understanding of how and why fear is such a potent force in modern society might tell us why current perceptions of who the drug dealer is continue in the form/s that they do.

Footnotes

[1] If true it is almost certain that putting crack in cannabis would have had a rationale beyond trying to hook the unsuspecting. Most likely is that this was indeed an attempt to – if caught – either to convince that no prosecution be mounted because it was 'only cannabis' or to be charged only with supplying cannabis as opposed to crack for which the penalties are more severe. Alternatively, but less likely, this combination is a new variant available for those that wish for such a mix.

[2] Depending on your perspective of course that is the story.

References

Adler, P. and Adler, P. (1994) 'Networking practices among drug-dealers', in Mary Lorenz Dietz, Robert Prus and William Shaffi, *Doing Everyday Life: Ethnography as Human Lived Experience*, Ontario: Copp Clark Longman.

Adler, P. A. (1985) *Wheeling and Dealing: An Ethnography of an Upper-Level Drug Dealing and Smuggling Community*, New York: Columbia University Press.

Adler, P. and Adler, P. (1983) 'Relationships between dealers: The social organization of illicit drug transactions', *Sociology and Social Research*, 67: 260-278.

Advisory Committee on the Mis-Use of Drugs. (1984) *Prevention*, London, HMSO.

Agar, M. (1973) *Ripping and Running: A Formal Ethnography of Urban Heroin Addicts*, New York: Seminar Press.

Alexander, B. K. & Wong, L. S. (1990) 'Adverse Effects of Cocaine on the Heart: A critical Review', in Trebach, A. and Zeese, B. (eds.) *The Great Issues of Drug Policy*, Washington: The Drug Policy Foundation.

Anderson, A. (2000) *Snake Oil, Hustlers and Hambones: The American Medicine Show*, Jefferson, North Carolina: McFarland & Company.

Andrade, X., Sifaneck, S. and Neargus, A. (1999) 'Dope sniffers in New York City: An ethnography of heroin markets and patterns of use', *Journal of Drug Issues*, 29(2): 271-298.

Anita an the wolf (2002) [online]. [Accessed: December 21, 2002]. Originally available from World Wide Web: http://www.homestead.com/brendanbeales/anita.html

Anslinger, H. J. (1937) 'Marijuana: Assassin of Youth', *The American Magazine*, July.

Aurin, M. (2000) 'Chasing the Dragon: The Cultural Metamorphosis of Opium in the United States, 1825-1935', *Medical Anthropology Quarterly*, 14(3): 414-441.

Baumler, A. (ed.) (2001) *Modern China and Opium: A Reader*, Ann Arbor: University of Michigan Press.

BBC News (2002) 'UK Zero tolerance for school drug dealers', May 21 [online]. [Accessed: May 21, 2002]. Available from World Wide Web: http://news.bbc.co.uk/1/hi/education/2000225.stm

BBC News (2000) 'Ecstasy victim's friend fined', Monday, 14 February, 2000, 16:19 GMT [online]. [Accessed: June 8, 2006]. Available from World Wide Web: http://news.bbc.co.uk/1/hi/scotland/642710.stm

Bean, P. (2002) *Drugs and Crime*, Cullompton: Willan Publishing.

Bean, P. (1993) 'Cocaine and Crack: The Promotion of an Epidemic', in Bean, P. (ed.) *Cocaine and Crack: Supply and Use.*, London: Macmillan.

Bean, P. (1974) *The Social Control of Drugs*, London: Martin Robertson.

Becchi, A. (1996)'Italy: Mafia-dominated drug market?', in Dorn, N., Jepsen, J. and Savona, S. (eds.), *European Drug Policies and Enforcement.* Basingstoke: Macmillan Press, pp 119-130.

Becker, H. (1963) *Outsiders: Studies in the Sociology of Deviance,* New York: Free Press.

Beckett, K., Nyrop, K. and Pfingst, L. (2006) 'Race, Drugs, and Policing: Understanding Disparities in Drug Delivery Arrests', *Criminology,* 44(1): 105-138.

Beckett, K. (2004) *Race and Drug law Enforcement in Seattle*, Report for the Racial Disparity Project, Seattle, Washington.

Bello, D. (2003) The Venomous Course of Southwestern Opium: Qing Prohibition in Yunnan, Sichuan, and Guizhou in the Early Nineteenth Century. The Journal of Asian Studies, 62(4), 1109-1142.

Bello, D.A. (2005) *Opium and the Limits of Empire: Drug Prohibition in the Chinese Interior1729-1850*, Harvard East Asian monographs; 241 Harvard University Asia Center.

Bennett, T. (1986) A decision-making approach to opioid addiction. In: Cornish D.B, Clarke R. V., (ed.) *The Reasoning Criminal: Rational Choice Perspectives in Offending.* pp.83-98. New York: Springer-Verlag.

Ben-Yehuda, B. (1994) 'The Sociology of Moral Panics: Towards a New Synthesis', in Ross Coomber (ed.), *Drugs and Drug Use in Society: A Critical Reader*, Dartford: Greenwich University Press.

Berridge, V. and Edwards, G. (1987) *Opium and the People: Opiate Use in Nineteenth Century England*, London: Yale University Press.

Berridge, V. (1984) 'Drugs and Social Policy: The Establishment of Drug Control in Britain 1900–30', *Addiction*, 79(1): 17-29.

Bigus, O. E. (1972) 'The milkman and his customer: A cultivated relationship', *Urban Life and Culture*, 1: 131-165.

Blum, R. H. and Associates (1972) *The Dream Sellers*, London: Jossey-Bass Inc.

Blumstein, A., Cohen, J., Roth, J.A. and Visher, C.A. (eds.) (1986) *Criminal Careers and "Career Criminals,"* Volume I, Commission on Behavioral and Social Sciences and Education, Washington, D.C.:National Academies Press.

Bourgois, P. (1995) *In Search of Respect: Selling Crack in El Barrio*, New York: Cambridge.

Boyd, S. C. (2004) *From Witches to Crack Moms: Women, Drug Law, and Policy*, Durham N.C.: Carolina University Press.

Brecher, E. M., and the editors of Consumer Reports. (1972) *Licit and Illicit Drugs: The Consumers Union Report on Narcotics, Stimulants, Depressants, Inhalants, Hallucinogens, and Marijuana--including Caffeine, Nicotine, and Alcohol.* Boston: Little Brown.

Brownstein, H. H. (1999) *The Social Reality of Violence and Violent Crime*, Boston: Allyn and Bacon.

Brownstein, H. H. (1996) *The Rise and Fall of a Violent Crime Wave: Crack Cocaine and the Social Construction of a Crime Problem*, New York: Criminal Justice Press.

Brunvand, J.H. (1986) *The Choking Doberman – And Other 'New' Urban Legends*, New York: W. W. Norton & Company.

Bruun, K., Pan, L. & Rexed, I. (1975) *The Gentlemen's Club: International Control of Drugs and Alcohol*. London: University of Chicago Press.

Bullington, B. (1998) 'America's Drug War: Fact or Fiction?', in Ross Coomber (ed.) *The Control of Drugs and Drug Users: Reason or Reaction?*, Amsterdam: Harwood Academic Publishers.

Carstairs, C. (2005) 'The stages of the international drug control system', *Drug and Alcohol Review*, 24: 57 – 65.

Caulkins, J. P., Johnson, B., Taylor, A., Taylor, L. (1999) 'What drug dealers tell us about their costs of doing business', *Journal of Drug Issues,* 29 (2), 323-340.

Center for Substance Abuse Research (CESAR) (2001) *Ecstasy in Maryland: Ecstasy Facts.* November 7 [online]. [Accessed: January 7, 2002]. Available from World Wide Web: http://www. ecstasyfacts.org/xtc/pubs/xtcreport.asp

Chaiken, J. J. and Chaiken, M. R. (1994) 'Drugs and Predatory Crime', in Coomber, R. (ed.), Drugs and Drug Use in Society: A Critical Reader, Dartford: Greenwich University Press.

Chen, K. and Kandel, D. B. (1995) 'The natural history of drug use from adolescence to the mid-thirties in a general population sample', *American Journal of Public Health*, 85(1): 41-7.

Chitwood, D. D., Rivers, J. E. and Inciardi, J. A. (1996) *The American Pipe Dream: Crack Cocaine and the Inner City*, Fort Worth, TX: Harcourt Brace.

Chung, T. (1978*) China and the brave new world: A study of the origins of the Opium War (1840-42)*, Durham, NC: Carolina Academic Press.

CNN.Com (1999) Book Chat Interview with Jan Harold Brunvand. Online chat broadcast on Tuesday, September 21st, from Salt Lake City, Utah.[online]. [Accessed: November 11, 2001]. Available from World Wide Web: http://www.cnn.com/COMMUNITY/transcripts/jan.harold. brunvand.html

Coc, T. C. Jacobs, M. R. LeBlanc, A. E. and Marshman, J. A. (1987) 'Understanding Drug Use', in Tom Heller, Marjorie Gott, and Carole Jeffery (eds.) *Drug Use and Misuse: A Reader*, Cambridge: Open University Press.

Cohen, P. (1989) *Cocaine Use in Amsterdam – in Non-Deviant Sub-Cultures*, University of Amsterdam Press. Amsterdam.

Cohen, P.S. (1969) 'Theories of myth', *Man*, 4(3): 337-353.

Collins, J. (1994) 'Summary Thoughts About Drugs and Violence', in Coomber, R. (ed.), *Drugs and Drug Use in Society: A Critical Reader*, Dartford, Greenwich University Press.

Condon, J. and Smith, N. (2003) *Prevalence of drug use: key findings from the 2002/2003 British Crime Survey*. Findings 229. London: Home Office

Coomber, R. and Sutton, C. (2006) 'How quick to heroin dependence', *Drug and Alcohol Review*, 25(5)

Coomber, R. and Maher, L. (2006) 'Street-level drug market activity in Sydney's primary heroin markets: organisation, adulteration practices, pricing, marketing and violence', *Journal of Drug Issues*, 36(3)

Coomber, R. and South, N. (eds.) (2004) *Drug Use and Cultural Contexts 'Beyond the West': Tradition, Change and Post-Colonialism*, London: Free Association Books.

Coomber, R. (2004) 'Drug Use and Drug Market Intersections', Editorial in, *Addiction Research & Theory*, 12(6): 1-5.

Coomber, R. (2003) 'There's no such thing as a free lunch: how 'freebies' and 'credit' operate as part of rational drug market activity not as a device for 'pushing' drugs onto the innocent and uninitiated' *Journal of Drug Issues*, Vol. 33, No. 4: 939-962.

Coomber, R. Morris, C. and Dunn, L. (2000) 'How the Media do Drugs: Quality Control and the Reporting of Drug Issues in the UK Print Media', *International Journal of Drug Policy*, 11: 217-225.

Coomber, R. (1999a) 'The 'Cutting' of Street Drugs in the USA in the 1990s', *Journal of Drug Issues*, 29(1): 17-36.

Coomber , R. (1999b) 'Lay Perceptions and Beliefs about the Adulteration of Illicit Drugs in the 1990's – A Student Sample', *Addiction Research*, 7(4): 323-338.

Coomber, R. (ed.) (1998) *The Control of Drug and Drug Users: Reason or Reaction*, Amsterdam: Harwood Academic Publishers.

Coomber, R. (1997a) Vim in the Veins – Fantasy or Fact: The Adulteration of Illicit Drugs, *Addiction Research*, 5(3): 195-212.

Coomber, R. (1997b) 'The Adulteration of Drugs: What Dealers Do, What Dealers Think', *Addiction Research*, 5(4): 297-306.

Coomber, R. (1997c) 'Adulteration of Drugs: The Discovery of a 'Myth'', *Contemporary Drug Problems*, 24(2): 239-271.

Coomber, R. (1997d) 'Dangerous Drug Adulteration – An International Survey of Drug Dealers Using the Internet and the World Wide Web (WWW)', *International Journal of Drug Policy*, 8(2): 18-28.

Coomber, R. (1997e) 'How Often Does the Adulteration/Dilution of Heroin Actually Occur: An Analysis of 228 'Street' Samples Across the UK (1995-1996) and Discussion of Monitoring Policy', *International Journal of Drug Policy*, 8(4): 178-186.

Courtwright, D. T. (2002) 'The Roads to H: the Emergence of the American Heroin Complex, 1898-1956', in David F. Musto (ed.) *One Hundred Years of Heroin*, Westport, Connecticut: Auburn House.

Courtwright, D. T. (2001a) *Forces of Habit: Drugs and the Making of the Modern World*, London: Harvard University Press.

Courtwright, D. T. (2001b) *Dark Paradise: A History of Opiate Addiction in America*, London: Harvard University Press.

Courtwright, D. T. (1995) 'The Rise and Fall and rise of Cocaine in the United States', in Jordan Goodman, Paul E. Lovejoy and Andrew Sherratt (eds.) *Consuming Habits: Drugs in History and Anthropology*, Chatham: Routledge.

Cox, M. (2000) 'Just in time for the holidays: deadly rave drugs', Seaox Air-Medical [online]. [Accessed: December, 12, 2002]. Available from World Wide Web: http://www.seaox.com/lz/lz30-b.html

Curcione, N. (1997) 'Suburban snowmen: facilitating factors in the careers of middle-class coke dealers', *Deviant Behavior: An Interdisciplinary Journal*, 18: 233-253.

Curtis, R. and Wendel, T. (2000) 'Toward the development of a typology of illegal drug markets', in Natarajan, M. and Hough, M. Illegal Drug Markets: *From Research to Prevention Policy*, Crime Prevention Studies: Vol. 11. New York, Criminal Justice Press.

Curtis, R., and Wendel, J.T. (1999) 'The evolution of drug markets in New York City, New York: Lindesmith Center. May 10. ca. 2 hours. Audio file on Web. English [online]. [Accessed: December, 12, 2002]. Available from World Wide Web: http://www.soros.org:8080/ramgen/tlc/nydrugmarkets051099.rm

Curtis, R. and Sviridoff, M. (1994). 'The Social Organization of Street-Level Drug Markets and Its Impact on the Displacement Effect', In R. McNamara (ed.), *Crime Displacement: The Other Side of Prevention*, (New York: Cummings and Hathaway)

CyberiaPC.com (2006) Drug Dealers vs. Computers [online]. [Accessed: June 8, 2006]. Available from World Wide Web: http://www.cyberiapc.com/jokes_expand.php?id=9

Daily Trojan (2000) Health and Medicine: 'Ecstasy can be a long strange trip for some' by Francesca Camino, Vol. 139, No. 61 (Wednesday, April 19, 2000), pp3-13 [online]. [Accessed: December, 12, 2002]. Available from World Wide Web: http://www.dailytrojan.com/media/paper679/previousarchive/V139/N61/04-ecstasy.61c.shtml

Darke, S. and Zador, D. (1996) 'Fatal heroin 'overdose': a review', *Addiction*, 91(12): 1765-1772.

Davies, J. B. (1993) *The Myth of Addiction*. Amsterdam: Harwood Academic Publishers.

Davies, J. B. and Coggans, N. (1991) *The facts about adolescent drug abuse*, London: Cassell Education Ltd.

Davies, N. (2001) Special report: drugs in Britain: 'Make heroin legal', *The Guardian*, Thursday, June 14.

Decorte, T. (2001) 'Quality Control by Cocaine Users: Underdeveloped Harm Reduction Strategies', *European Addiction Research*, 7:161-175.

Denton, B. (2001) *Dealing: Women in the Drug Economy*, Sydney: University of New South Wales Press.

Denton, B. and O'Malley, P.(2001) 'Property Crime and Women Drug Dealers in Australia', *Journal of Drug Issues*, 31 (2): 465-486.

Denton, B. and O'Malley, P. (1999) 'Gender, Trust and Business: women drug dealers in the illicit economy', *British Journal of Criminology*, 39(4): 513-530.

Dikötter, F., Laamann, L. and Xun, Z. (2004) *Narcotic Culture: A History of Drugs in China*, London: Hurst & Company.

Dorn, N. Murji, K. and South, N. (1992) *Traffickers: Drug Markets and Law Enforcement*, London: Routledge.

Douglas, T. (1995) Scapegoats: Transferring Blame, Padstow: Routledge.

Drug Abuse Trends (1993) No. 102. October-December, Home Office.

Drug Abuse Trends (2004) Issue 27. April-June, The Forensic Science Service.

Dubey , A. (1996) Tainted Ecstasy surfaces at raves, *The Journal*, 25(2), March/April [online]. [Accessed: August 12, 2002]. Available from World Wide Web: http://www.arf.org/Ecstacsy.html

Dunlap, E., Johnson, B. D. and Maher, L. (1997) 'Female Crack Sellers in New York City: Who They Are and What They Do', Women & Criminal Justice, 8(4): 25-55.

Dunlap, E. and Johnson, B. (1996) 'Family and human resources in the development of a female crack-seller career: case study of a hidden population', *Journal of Drug Issues*, 26(1): 175-198.

Edmunds, M., Hough, M. and Urquia, N. (1997). *Tackling Drug Markets: an analysis of six London Sites*. Crime Prevention and Detection Paper 80. Home Office: Police Research Group.

Elliot, M. (2000) 'Listen Live' CFRB. A.M. 1010 [online]. [Accessed: October 6, 2001]. Available from World Wide Web: http://www.markelliot.com/july2000.html

Eskes, D. and Brown, J. K. (1975) 'Heroin-caffeine-strychnine mixtures – Where and why?', *United Nations Bulletin on Narcotics*, 27, (1): 67-69.

Executive Office of the President (1998) *Pulse Check: National Trends in Drug Abuse.*

Fagan, J. and K. Chin. (1990) Violence as regulation and social control in the distribution of crack. In Mario de la Rosa, Bernard Gropper, and Elizabeth Lambert (eds.) *Drugs and Violence*, NIDA Research Monograph, Rockville, MD: National Institute of Drug Abuse, pp. 8-43.

Falk, J. L. (1994) 'Drug Dependence: Myth or Motive', in Coomber, R. (ed.), Drugs and Drug Use in Society: A Critical Reader, Dartford: Greenwich University Press.

Fairlie, R. W. (1999) *Drug Dealing and Legitimate Self-Employment*, Report, Department of Economics, University of California, Santa Cruz, April.

Faupel, C. E., Horowitz, A. M. and Weaver, G. S. (2004) *The Sociology of American Drug Use*, London: McGraw Hill.

Fazey, C. (1991) 'The Consequences of Illegal Drug Use', in, Whynes, D. K. and Bean, P. (eds.) *Policing and Prescribing: The British System of Drug Control*, London: Macmillan.

Feldman, S. P. (1997) 'The Revolt Against Cultural Authority: Power/Knowledge as an Assumption in Organization Theory', *Human Relations*, 50(8), 937-955.

Few, B., Turnbull, P.J., Duffy, M. and Hough, M. (2004 unpublished) *Drug markets in rural areas*, London: Home Office

Flanagan, P. (1993) 'Bitter Pills', in *Time Out*, Oct 27 – Nov 3

Florida Department of Law Enforcement (2000) News Release: Deadly Variant of Popular Drug Identified in Florida. September, 29 [online]. [Accessed: June 7, 2006]. Available from World Wide Web: http://www.tgorski.com/drug_updates/PMA%20&%20PMMA%20Alert%2001081 5.htm

Forensic Intelligence Bureau (2005) *FIB Drugs Update*, Issue 32, July-September.

Forsyth, A. J. M. (1995) 'Ecstasy and illegal drug design: a new concept in drug use', in *International Journal of Drug Policy*, 6 (3): 193-209.

Freemantle, B. (1986) *The Fix: Inside the World Drug Trade*, New York: Tor.

Friedman S.R. (2002) 'Sociopharmacology of drug use: initial thoughts', The International Journal of Drug Policy, 13(5): 341-347.

Friedman, W.A. (2004) *Birth of a Salesman: The Transformation of Selling in America*, Cambridge, MA: Harvard University Press.

Furst R. T. (2000) 'The re-engineering of heroin: An emerging heroin "cutting" trend in New York City', *Addiction Research* 8(4): 357-379.

Ganguly, K. (2004) 'Opium Use in Rajasthan India: A Socio-Cultural Perspective, pp83-100, in Ross Coomber and Nigel South (eds.) Drug Use and Cultural Contexts 'Beyond the West': Tradition, Change and Post-Colonialism, London: Free Association Books.

Gelber, H. G. (2004) *Opium, soldiers and evangelicals. England's 1840–42 war with China, and its aftermath*, Basingstoke: Palgrave Macmillan.

Gibbins, T. (1991) *Regulating the Media*, London, Sweet and Maxwell.

Gieringer, D. H. (1999) 'The Forgotten Origins of Cannabis Prohibition in California', *Contemporary Drug Problems*, 26(2): 237-288.

Goldstein, P. Brownstein, P. Ryan, P. Bellucci, P. A. (1997) 'Crack and Homicide in New York City: A Case Study in the Epidemiology of Violence', in Reinarman, C. and Levine, H. (eds.) Crack in America: Demon Drugs and Social Justice, London, University of California Press.

Goldstein, P. J., Ouellet, L. J. and Fendrich, M. (1992) 'From bag brides to skeezers: An historical perspective on sex-for-drugs behaviour', *Journal of Psychoactive Drugs*, 24: 349-61.

Goldstein, P. J. (1985) 'The Drugs/Violence Nexus: A Tripartite Conceptual Framework', *Journal of Drug Issues*, 39:143-174.

Goldstein, P.J. (1979) *Prostitution and drugs*, Lexington: Lexington Books.

Golub, A. L. And Johnson, B. D. (1997) *Crack's Decline: Some Surprises across U.S. Cities*. National Institute of Justice Research in Brief. Washington, DC: U.S. Department of Justice. National Institute of Justice, July, NCJ 165707.

Golub, A. and Johnson, B. D. (1994) 'A Recent Decline in Cocaine Use Among Youthful Arrestees in Manhattan (1987-1993), *American Journal of Public Health* 84(8):1250-1254.

Goode, E. (1997) *Between Politics and Reason: The Drug Legalization Debate*, New York: St. Martin's Press.

Gossop, M. (1996) *Living with Drugs*, Aldershot, Arena.

Green, P. *Drugs, Trafficking and Criminal Policy: The Scapegoat Strategy.* Criminal Policy Series, Vol. III. Winchester, U.K.: Waterside Press.

Guardian, The (2000) 'Drug baron who 'earned £640m' gets 20 years', Tuesday September 19 [online]. [Accessed: January 17, 2006]. Available from World Wide Web: http://www.guardian.co.uk/drugs/Story/0,2763,370160,00.html

Gusfield, J.R. (1986) *Symbolic crusade: status politics and the American Temperance Movement* (2nd edn). Urbana: University of Illinois Press.

Hagedorn, J. M. (1994) 'Neighborhoods, markets, and Gang Organization', Journal of Research in Crime and Delinquency', 31(3): 264-294.

Hagedorn, J. M. (1988) *People and Folks: Gangs, Crime and the Underclass in a Rustbelt City*, Chicago: Lakeview Press.

Hamburger, M. (1959) 'Aristotle and Confucius: A Comparison', *Journal of the History of Ideas*, 20(2): 236-249.

Hamilton, R.J., Hamilton, R., Perrone, J., Hoffman, R., Henretig, F.M., Karkevandian, E.H., Marcus, S., Shih, R.D., Blok, B. and Nordenholz, K. (2000) 'A Descriptive Study of an Epidemic of Poisoning Caused by Heroin Adulterated with Scopolamine', *Journal of Toxicology*, 38(6): 597-608.

Harding, G. (1998) 'Pathologising the Soul: The Construction of a 19th Century Anlaysis of Opiate Addiction', pp. 1-12, in Ross Coomber (ed.) *The Control of Drugs and Drug Users: Reason or Reaction?*, Amsterdam: Harwood Academic Publishers.

Health Education Authority. (1993) HIV and AIDS: a guide for journalists, London, HEA.

Health Education Authority. (1994) HIV/AIDS: mass media activities, London, HEA.

Heath, D. B. (2004) 'Camba (Bolivia) Drinking Patterns: Changes in Alcohol Use, Anthropology and Research Perspectives', in Coomber, R. and South, N. (eds.) Drug Use and Cultural Contexts 'Beyond the West': Tradition, Change and Post-Colonialism, Free Association Books, London.

Henry, J. (1992) 'Ecstasy and the dance of death: severe reactions are unpredictable', in *British Medical Journal*, 4th July, Vol. 305, pp. 5-6.

HM Customs and Excise (1995) Personal communication relating information on purity of seizures since 1986..

Holland, J. (2000) TLC Drug Policy Series Seminar Transcript MDMA ('Ecstasy') Research: When Science and Politics Collide. *Presentation made by Julie Holland, M.D., at a seminar held at TLC New York City, Thursday, March 30th, 2000* [online]. [Accessed: June 9, 2006]. Available from World Wide Web: http://www.drugpolicy.org/library/JHolland_seminar2.cfm

Home Office Statistical Bulletin (1995) *Statistics of Drug Seizures and Offenders Dealt with, United Kingdom, 1994*, Issue 24/95, December 1.

Hough, M. and Natarajan, M (2000) 'Introduction: Illegal Drug Markets, Research and Policy', in Natarajan, M. and Hough, M. (eds.) *Illegal Drug Markets: From Research to Prevention Policy*, Monsey, NY: Criminal Justice Press.

House of Commons Journal (1802) Volume 9. British History Online [online]. [Accessed: June 6, 2006]. Available from World Wide Web: http://www.british-history.ac.uk/report.asp?compid=27450

Howell, J. C. and Decker, S. H. (1999) *The Youth Gangs, Drugs and Violence Connection*, Juvenile Justice Bulletin [online]. [Accessed: January 20, 2006]. Available from World Wide Web: http://www.ncjrs.gov/html/ojjdp/171152/contents.html

Hser, Y. (2000). Substance Abuse and Aging Project: Drug Use Careers: Recovery and Mortality [online]. [Accessed: June 5, 2006]. Available from World Wide Web: http://www.oas.samhsa.gov/aging/chap3.htm

Hunt, D. E. (1990) 'Drugs and consensual crimes: Drug dealing and prostitution', in Michael Tonry and James Q. Wilson (eds.), *Drugs and Crime*, Chicago: University of Chicago Press.

Hunt, E.S. and Murray, J. (ed.) (1999) *A History of Business in Medieval Europe, 1200-1550*, Cambridge: Cambridge University Press.

Huizer, H. (1987) 'Analytical Studies on Illicit Heroin: Efficacy of Volatilization During Heroin Smoking', in *Pharmaceutisch Weekblad Scientific Edition*, Vol. 9. pp 203-211.

Iddon, B. (2005) HC Deb 18 Jan: Column 742.

Inciardi, J. A. (1986) *The war on Drugs: Heroin, Cocaine, Crime and Public Policy*, Palo Alto, Mayfield Publishing Company.

ISDD (1994) 'What's in a Drug?', Druglink Factsheet 10, in *Druglink* Nov/Dec.

Jacobs, B. A. (2000) *Robbing Drug Dealers: Violence Beyond the Law*, New York: Walter de Gruyter, Inc.

Jacobs, B. (1999) *Dealing Crack*, Northeastern University Press, Michigan.

Jacobs, B. and Miller, (1998) 'Crack dealing, gender and arrest avoidance', *Social Problems*, Vol. 45, No. 4, 550-569.

Joint Committee on Health and Children, (1998) Parliament of Ireland. Presentation on Health Promotion and No Smoking Campaigns. Thursday July 9 [online]. [Accessed: May 21, 2002]. Available from World Wide Web: http://www.irlgov.ie/committees-99/c-health/Rep-Evidence/page4.htm

Johnson, B. D., Dunlap, E. and Tourigny, S. C. (2000a) 'Crack distribution and abuse in New York', in Natarajan, M. and Hough, M. (eds.) *Illegal Drug Markets: From Research to Prevention Policy*, Monsey, NY: Criminal Justice Press.

Johnson, B., Golub, A. and Dulap, E. (2000b) 'The rise and decline of hard drugs, drug markets, and violence in inner-city New York', in Blumstein, A. and Wallman, J. (eds.) *The Crime Drop in America*, New York: Cambridge University Press.

Johnson, B. D., Golub, A. and Fagan, J. (1995) 'Careers in Crack, Drug Use, Drug Distribution, and Nondrug Criminality', *Crime & Delinquency*, 41(3): 275-295.

Johnson, B. D. Hamid, A. and Sanabria, H. (1992) 'Emerging models of crack distribution' in Thomas Mieczkowski (ed.) *Drugs and Crime: A Reader*, Boston, Allyn and Bacon.

Johnson Q, Petru A (199 1) 'Foreign body pulmonary granulomas in an abuser of nasally inhaled drugs', *Pediatrics* 88(l): 159-161.

Joseph, J. (2006) 'Drug Offenses, Gender, Ethnicity, and Nationality: Women in Prison in England and Wales', *The Prison Journal*, 86(1): 140-157.

Kaa, E. (1994) 'Impurities, adulterants and diluents of illicit heroin: Changes during a 12 year period', *Forensic Science International*, 64: 171-179.

Kaplan, J. (1983) *The Hardest Drug: Heroin and Public Policy*, Chicago: University of Chicago Press.

King, L. A. (1995), Head of The Drugs Intelligence Laboratory, The Forensic Science Service, Aldermaston. Personal Communication.

King, R. S. and Mauer, M. (2002) *Distorted priorities: Drug offenders in state prisons*, Washington, DC: The Sentencing Project.

King County Bar Association (2005) *Effective Drug Control: Toward A New Legal Framework State-Level Regulation as a Workable Alternative to the "War on Drugs"*, KCBA [online]. [Accessed: May 21, 2006]. Available from World Wide Web: http://www.erowid.org/psychoactives/law/law_policy_proposal1.pdf

Kirk, R. (2003) *More Terrible than Death: Massacres, Drugs, and America's War in Colombia*, New York: Public Affairs.

Kitzinger, J. and Reilly, J. (1997) Media and expert constructions of risk, *Risk and Human Behaviour*, Issue 1, March:11-13.

Kleiman, M. (1998) 'Drug Policy for Crime Control', Policy Options, 19(8): 15-18.

Knowles, G. J., (1999), 'Deception, Detection, and Evaluation: A Trade Craft Analysis of Honolulu, Hawaii's Street Crack-Cocaine Traffickers', *Journal of Criminal Justice*, 27(5): 443-455.

Kohn, M. (1992) *Dope Girls: the birth of the British underground*, London: Lawrence & Wisehart.

Kosak, H. (2000) *Cultures of Opposition: Jewish Immigrant Workers, New York City, 1881-1905*, Albany: State University of New York Press.

Kritikos, P. G. and Papadaki, S. P. (1967) 'The history of the poppy and of opium and their expansion in antiquity in the eastern Mediterranean area', *Bulletin on Narcotics*, Issue 4, pp5-10.

Krivanek, J. (1988) Heroin: Myths and Reality. Australia: Allen & Unwin Pty., Limited.

Langer, J. (1977) 'Drug Entrepreneurs and Dealing Culture', *Social Problems*, 24: 377-385

Laub, J.H. and Sampson, R.J.(2003 'Desistance from Crime over the Life Course', in Jeylan T. Mortimer and Michael Shanahan (eds.) *Handbook of the Life Course*, New York: Kluwer Academic/Plenum. Pp. 295-310.

La Motte, E.N. (1920) The Opium Monopoly, Macmillan. [online]. [Accessed: May 21, 2006]. Available from World Wide Web: http://www.druglibrary.org/schaffer/History/om/ommenu.htm

Leary, T., Metzner, R., Alpart, R. and Glin-Pa, K. (1995) *The Psychedelic Experience: A Manual Based on the Tibetan Book of the Dead*, Citadel Press.

Lehrer, T. (1953) The Old Dope Peddler, Cambridge 38, Massachusetts: Lehrer Records.

Lenton S, Boys A, Norcross K (1997) Raves, drugs and experience: drug use by a sample of people who attend raves in Western Australia. *Addiction*, 92: 1327-1337.

Levine, H. G. Reinarman, C. (1991) From Prohibition to Regulation: Lessons from Alcohol Policy for Drug Policy.

Levitt, S. and Venkatesh, S. A. (2000). 'An Economic Analysis of a Drug-Selling Gang's Finances' Quarterly Journal of Economics 13(4): 755-789.

Lewis, R, (1994) Flexible hierarchies and dynamic disorder – the trading and distribution of illicit heroin in Britain and Europe, 1970-90', in John Strand and Michael Gossop (eds.) *Heroin Addiction and Drug Policy: the British System*, Oxford: Oxford University Press

Lewis, R., Hartnoll, R., Bryer, S., Daviaud, E. and Mitcheson, M. (1985) 'Scoring Smack: The Illicit Heroin Market in London,1980-83,' *British Journal of Addiction* 80(3):281-90.

Lieb, J. and Olsen, S. (1976) 'Prestige, Paranoia and Profit: On Becoming a Dealer of Illicit Drugs in a University Community', Journal of Drug Issues, 6: 356-367.

Lilly, J. C. (1987) *Programming and Metaprogramming in the Human Biocomputer*, Crown Publishers.

Lindesmith, A. R. (1941) '"Dope Fiend Mythology"', *Journal of Criminal Law and Criminology*, 32: 199-208.

Lo-shu Fu, (1966) *A Documentary Chronicle of Sino-Western relations 1644-1820*, Vol. 1. Tucson: University of Arizona Press.

Lupton, R., Wilson, A., May, T., Warburton, H., and Turnball, P. J., (2002), *A Rock and a Hard Place: Drug Markets in Deprived Neighbourhoods*. Home Office Research Study 240. London: Home Office.

MacCoun, R. and Reuter, P. (1992) 'Are then wages of sin $30 an hour? Economic aspects of street-level drug dealing', *Crime & Delinquency* 38 (4): 477-91.

Madancy, J. (2001) 'Unearthing Popular Attitudes toward the Opium Trade and Opium Suppression in Late Qing and Early Republican Fujian', *Modern China*, 27(4): 436-483.

Maher, L., Swift, W. and Dawson, M. (2001) 'Heroin purity and composition in Sydney, Australia', *Drug and Alcohol Review*, 20(4): 439-448.

Maher, L. (1997*) Sexed work: Gender, race and resistance in a Brooklyn drug market*, Oxford: Oxford University Press.

Maher, L. (1996) 'Hidden in the light: Discrimination and occupational norms among crack using street-level sexworkers', *Journal of Drug Issues* 26(1): 145-175.

Maher, L. and Daly, K. (1996) 'Women in the street-level drug economy: Continuity or Change?', *Criminology* 34(4): 465-491.

Mari, F, Bertol, E. and Tosti, M. (1982) 'Heroin in the Florence area, Italy, United Nations Office for Drug Control and Crime Prevention', *Bulletin on Narcotics*, Issue 1: 37-44.

Marschke G, Haber L, Feinberg M (1975) 'Pulmonary talc embolization', *Chest* 68:824-826.

Marumo, Y., Inoue, S. and Seta, S. (1994) 'Analysis of inorganic impurities in seized methamphetamine samples', in, *Forensic Science International*, 69, pp89-95.

Maryland Drug Early Warning System Report (2002) DEWS News. Vol. 3, No. 2. September [online]. [Accessed: June 8, 2006]. Available from World Wide Web: http://www.cesar.umd.edu/cesar/pubs/20020904.pdf

Matthee, R. (1995) 'Exotic substances: the introduction and global spread of tobacco, coffee, cocoa, tea, and distilled liquor, sixteenth to eighteenth centuries', pp.24-51, in Roy Porter and Mikuláš Teich (eds.) Drugs and Narcotics in History, Cambridge: Cambridge University Press.

Matza, D. (1969) *Becoming Deviant*, Englewood Cliffs, New Jersey, Prentice-Hall.

Matza, D. (1964) *Delinquency and Drift*, New York, Wiley.

Maxwell, S. R. and Maxwell, C. D. (2000) Examining the "Criminal Careers" of Prostitutes Within the Nexus of Drug Use, Drug Selling, and other Illicit Activities', Criminology, 38(3): 787-810.

May, T., Duffy, M., Few, B. and Hough, M. (2005) Understanding drug selling in communities: Insider or outsider trading? York: Joseph Rowntree Foundation.

May, T., Harocopos, A., Turnbull, P.J. and Hough, M. (2000) *Serving up: The impact of low-level police enforcement on drug markets*, Home Office Policing and Reducing Crime Unit, Paper 133.

May, T., Edmunds, M. and Hough, M. (1999) Police Street Business: The links between sex and drug markets, Research Series Paper 118. Home Office Policing and Reducing Crime Unit, Research, Development and Statistics Directorate [online]. [Accessed: June 9, 2006]. Available from World Wide Web: http://www.kcl.ac.uk/depsta/law/research/icpr/publications/fprs118.pdf

May, T., Edmunds, M. & Hough, M. (1999). *Street Business: The Links between Sex and Drug Markets*. Police Research Series Paper 118. Policing and Reducing Crime Unit. Home Office.

McAndrew, C. and Edgerton, R. B. (1969) *Drunken comportment*. Chicago, IL: Adline Publications.

MacCoun, R. and Reuter, P. (1992) 'Are the Wages of Sin $30 an Hour? Economic Aspects of Street-Level Drug Dealing', Crime & Delinquency, 38(4): 477-492.

McCoy, A. W. (1991) *The Politics of Heroin: CIA Complicity in the Global Drug Trade*, New York: Lawrence Hill.

McElrath, K. and McEvoy, K. (2001).' Heroin as evil: Ecstasy users' perceptions about heroin'. *Drugs: Education, Prevention and Policy*, 8:177-189.

McIntosh J., Gannon M., McKeganey N. and MacDonald F. (2003) 'Exposure to drugs among pre-teenage schoolchildren', *Addiction*, 98(11): 1615-1623.

McQuail, Denis (1987): *Mass Communication Theory: An Introduction* (2nd edn.). London: Sage.

Mieczkowski, T. (1994) 'The experiences of women who sell crack: some descriptive data from the Detroit crack ethnography project', *Journal of Drug Issues*, 24(2): 227-248.

Mieczkowski, T., (1990), 'Crack Distribution in Detroit', *Contemporary Drug Problems*, 17: 9-30.

Miller, R. M. (1991) *The Case for Legalising Drugs*, New York: Praeger.

Monmouth County Archives (1994) *Peddler Licenses* [online]. [Accessed: May 18, 2006]. Available from World Wide Web: http://www.visitmonmouth.com/archives/lgpedlr.asp#HISTORY

Moore, D. (1993) 'Beyond Zinberg's 'social setting': a processural view of illicit drug use', *Drug and Alcohol Review*, 12, 413-421.

Moore, D. (1992) 'Deconstructing 'dependence': an ethnographic critique of an influential concept, *Contemporary Drug Problems*, 19(3): 459-90.

Moore, K. and Miles, S. (2004) 'Young people, dance and the sub-cultural consumption of drugs', *Addiction Research and Theory*, 12(6): 507–23.

Morley, David (1992) *Television, Audiences and Cultural Studies*. London: Routledge
Morone, J. A. (2003) *Hellfire Nation: The politics of Sin in American History*, New Haven: Yale University Press.

Moynihan, D. P. (2002) 'One Hundred Years of Heroics', pp. 23-38, in David F. Musto (ed.) *One Hundred Years of Heroin*, Westport, Connecticut: Auburn House.

Murji, K. (1998) 'The Agony and the Ecstasy: Drugs, Media and Morality', in Coomber, R. (ed.) *The Control of Drug and Drug Users: Reason or Reaction*, Amsterdam: Harwood Academic Publishers.

Murphy, S., Sales, P., Duterte, M and Jacinto, C. (2005) A Qualitative Study of Ecstasy Sellers in the San Francisco Bay Area, Final Report to the National Institute of Justice Grant # 2002-IJ-CX-0018 [online]. [Accessed: May 18, 2006]. Available from World Wide Web: http://www.ncjrs.gov/pdffiles1/nij/grants/209267.pdf

Murphy, S., Waldorf, D. and Reinarman, C. (1990), 'Drifting into Dealing: Becoming a Cocaine Seller', *Qualitative Sociology*, 13 (4): 321-343.

Musto, D. F. (1987) *The American Disease: Origins of Narcotic Control*, Oxford: Oxford University Press.

Myles, J. (1995) 'Relative risks of amphetamine prescribing – the doctor's dilemma', Paper given to the Annual Symposium of the Society for the Study of addiction to Alcohol and Other Drugs, Thursday 19th October, Brighton.

Naggar, B. (1992) *Jewish Pedlars and Hawkers 1740-1940*, Camberley: Porphyrogenitus.

National Criminal Intelligence Service (1994) *Drug Valuation Guide*, Strategic Research Unit, June.

National Institute on Drug Abuse (1990) *Drugs* and Violence: Causes, Correlates, and Consequences, NIDA Research Monograph, Number 103.

Neumann, H. (1994) 'Comparison of heroin by capillary gas chromatography in Germany', in *Forensic Science International*, 69: 7-16.

Newman, R. K. (1995) 'Opium Smoking in Late Imperial China: A Reconsideration', Modern Asian Studies, 29: 765-794.

O'Callaghan, W.G., Joyce, N., Counihan, H.E., Ward, M., Lavelle, P., O'Brien, E. (1982) 'Unusual Strychnine Poisoning and its Treatment: Report of Eight Cases', in, *British Medical Journal*, Volume 285, 14 August, p478.

Observer, The (1999) 'Heroin users start at eight. It's £5 a bag. We'll need body bags, too', John Sweeney, Drugs in Britain: special report, September 26.

Office of National Drug Control Policy: National Drug Intelligence Centre (2000) *Heroin Distribution in Three Cities*, November, Washington, D.C.: Government Printing Office. Document ID: 2001-R0370-001.

Office of National Drug Control Policy 91989) *National Drug Control Strategy*, Wsahington D.C. Executive Office of the President.

Orcutt, J. D. and Turner, J. B. (1993) 'Shocking numbers and graphic accounts: quantified images of drug problems in the print media', *Social Problems*, 1993; 40 (2): 190-206.

Padilla, F. (1995) 'The working gang', in Malcom, W. Klein, Cheryl, L. Maxson, and Jody Miller (eds.) *The Modern Gang Reader*, Los Angeles, Roxbury Publishing Company.

Parker, H. (2000) How young Britons obtain their drugs: drugs transactions at the point of consumption. In Natarajan, M. and Hough, M. Editors. *Illegal Drug Markets: From Research to Prevention Policy*, New York: Criminal Justice Press.

Parker, H., Aldridge, J. and Measham, F. (1998) *Illegal Leisure: The normalisation of adolescent recreational drug use among English youth*, St Ives: Routledge.

Parker, R.N. (1993) 'The effects of context on alcohol and violence', *Alcohol Health and Research World*, 17, 117-122.

Parkin, S. and McKegany, N. P. (2000) 'The Rise and Rise of Peer Education Approaches', *Drugs: Education, Prevention and Policy*, 7, 3, 293-310.

Paoli, L. (2002) 'Flexible Hierarchies and Dynamic Disorder: The Drug Distribution System in Frankfurt and Milan', *Drugs: Education, Prevention and Policy*, 9 (2): 143-151.

Parssinen, T. M. (1983) *Secret Passions, Secret Remedies: Narcotic Drugs in British Society 1820-1930*, Manchester: Manchester University Press.

Pearson, G. and Hobbs, D. (2001) *Middle Market Drug Distribution*. Home Office Research Study 224. London: Home Office.

Pearson, G. (1987) *The New Heroin Users*, Oxford: Basil Blackwell.

Perrone, J., Shaw, L. and De Roos, F. (1999) 'Laboratory Confirmation of Scopolamine Co-Intoxication in Patients using Tainted Heroin', *Journal of Toxicology*, 37(4): 491-496.

Porter, R. (2003) *Quacks: Fakers and Charlatans in Medicine*, Wiltshire: Tempus

Postgate, J. (1990) 'Sticky Breeches and Poisoned Lozenges', in *New Scientist*, Vol 128, No. 1748, 22 December.

Prebel, E and Casey, J. (1969) 'Taking Care of Business: The Heroin User's Life on the Street.' *International Journal of Addictions* 23, 4 : 1-24.

Press Complaints Commission. (1996) Code of Practice and Report No. 35, London, PPC.

Prus, R. (1989a) *Pursuing Customers: An Ethnography of Marketing Activities,* California, Sage.

Prus, R. (1989b) *Making Sales: Influence as Interpersonal Accomplishment*, California, Sage.

Quigley, S. (2004) *Run for Home*, Century.

Reinarman, C. and Duskin, C. (1992) 'Dominant Ideology and Drugs in the Media', *International Journal on Drugs Policy*, 3 (1): 6-15.

Reinarman, C., and Levine, H. G. (eds.) (1997) *Crack in America: Demon Drugs and Social Justice*, London, University of California Press.

Rengert, G. F. (1996) *The Geography of Illegal Drugs*, Colorado, Westview Press.

Reuter, P., MacCoun, R., and Murphy, P. (1990) *Money from Crime: A Study of the Economics of Drug Dealing in Washington, D.C.* , R-3594-USDP, The RAND Corporation.

Reuter, P. (1983) Disorganized Crime. Cambridge, Mass: MIT Press.

Rhodes, T. (1990) 'The Politics of Anti-Drugs Campaigns', *Druglink*, May/June.

Robbins, L. (1995) Editorial: 'The Natural History of Substance Use as a Guide to Setting Drug Policy', *American Journal of Public Health*, 85(1): 12-13.

Roden, C. (1981*) Coffee*, London: Harmondsworth.

Rohmer, S. (1919) *Dope: A story of Chinatown and the drug traffic*, London: Cassell & Co.

Rohmer, S. (1922) *Tales of Chinatown*, London: Cassell & Co.

Rudgley, R. (1995) Essential Substances: A Cultural History of Intoxicants in Society, New York: Kodansha International.

Ruggiero, V. and South, N, (1995) *Eurodrugs: Drug Use, Markets and Trafficking in Europe*, Norwich: UCL Press

Saunders, J. (2000) 'The control of pain in palliative care', *Journal of the Royal College of Physicians*, 34:326-8.

Saunders, N. (1994) 'Ecstasy spiked with heroin and other rumours', *nicholas@neals.cityscape. co.uk*, at http://www/alt.drugs Newsgroup. 27 November [online]. [Accessed: April 19, 1996]. Available from World Wide Web: http://www.erowid.org/chemicals/mdma/mdma_info5.shtml

Schlesinger, P., Murdock, G. and Elliott, P.R. (1983) *Televising "terrorism": political violence in popular culture*, London: Comedia.

Schivelbusch, W. (1993) *Tastes of Paradise: A Social History of Spices, Stimulants, and Intoxicants*, New York: Vintage.

Seal, G. (2001) *Great Australian Urban Myths (Revised Edition): The Cane Toad High*, Sydney: Harper Collins.

Severns, J. R. (2004) 'A Sociohistorical View of Addiction and Alcoholism', *Janus Head, 7(1), 149-166.*

Shafer, R.P, et al, (1972) *Marihuana: A Signal of Misunderstanding*, Washington, DC: National Commissions on Marihuana and Drug Abuse.

Shotsmag (2005) Sheila Quigley – The new grandmother of crime?, by Ayo Onatade [online]. [Accessed: September 19, 2005]. Available from World Wide Web: http://www.shotsmag. co.uk/shots22/intvus_22/quigley.html

Shulgin, A. T. (1996) Personal Communication.

Shulgin, A. T. (1993) Post to newsgroup *alt.drugs* titled 'On the issue of strychnine in LSD', April 8 [online]. [Accessed: August 21, 1996]. Available from World Wide Web: http://www.lycaeum. org/drugs.old/synthetics/lsd/strychnine.html

Skolnick, J., Correl, T., Navarro, E., Rabb, R. (1997) The Social Structure of Street Dealing. In Larry K. Gaines and Peter B. Kraska, eds., *Drugs Crime and Justice*. (159-91) Prospect Heights, Illinois. Waveland Press.

Sommers, I., Baskin, D. and Fagan, J. (1996) 'The structural relationship between drug use, drug dealing, and other income support activities among women drug sellers', *Journal of Drug Issues*, 26(4): 975-1006.

Sommers, I. and Baskin, D. R. (1997) 'Situational or Generalized Violence in Drug Dealing Networks', *Journal of Drug Issues*, 27(4): 833-849

Speaker, S (2002) 'Creating a Monster: Newspapers, Magazines, and America's Drug Problem', *Molecular Interventions* 2:201-204.

Speaker, Susan L. (2001) 'The Struggle of Mankind Against its Deadliest Foe: Themes of Counter-subversion in Anti-Narcotic Campaigns, 1920-1940', *Journal of Social History*, 34(3): 591-610.

Spear, B. (1994) 'The early years of the 'British System' in practice', in John Strang and Michael Gossop (eds.) *Heroin Addiction and Drug Policy*, Oxford: Oxford University Press. pp. 3-27.

Spillane, J. (1998) 'The making of an underground market: drug selling in Chicago, 1900-1940', *Journal of Social History*, Fall.

Stafford, P. (1992) (3rd Edition) *Psychedelics Encyclopedia*, Ronin Publishing.

Strang, J. (1990) 'Heroin and Cocaine: New Technologies, New Problems', in, Warburton, D. *Addiction Controversies*, Harwood Academic Press, London. pp. 201-211

Stewart, T. (1987) *The Heroin Users*, Glasgow: Pandora.

Szasz, T. (1998) ' The Perils of Prohibition', in Coomber, R. (ed.), *The Control of Drugs and Drug Users: Reason or Reaction*, Amsterdam: Harwood Academic Publishers, 155-159

Taylor, A. (1993) *Women Drug Users. An Ethnography of a Female Injecting Community*, Oxford: Clarendon Press.

Terry, C. E. and Pellens, M. (1928) The Opium Problem, New York: Committee on Drug Addictions, Bureau of Social Hygiene, Inc.

Third Age (2006) 'Ask the Brodys – Your Midlife Relationship Advisers' [online]. [Accessed: June 8, 2006]. Available from World Wide Web: http://www.thirdage.com/romance/marriage/brodys/marriage/992367320.html

Time (2005) 'Fighting the Freebies: Citing Conflict of Interest, Acticvists are Targeting Doctors who Accept Big Pharma's Gifts', by G. Jeffrey Macdonald.
November 6, 2005 January 19 Foundation [online]. [Accessed: June 9, 2006]. Available from World Wide Web: http://www.time.com/time/insidebiz/article/0,9171,1126716,00.html

Topalli, V., Wright, R. and Fornango, R. (2002) Drug Dealers, Robbery and Retaliation. Vulnerability, Deterrence and the Contagion of Violence, *The British Journal of Criminology*, 42:337-351.

Trocki, C. (1999). Opium, Empire and the Global Political Economy: A Study of the *Asian Opium Trade 1750-1950*, London: Routledge.

Trocki, C. A. (2004) A Drug on the Market: Opium and the Chinese in Southeast Asia, 1750-1880. A paper presented to the International Society for the Study of the Chinese Overseas, Elsinore, Denmark, 5-10 May 2004 [online]. [Accessed: May 21, 2002]. Available from World Wide Web: http://eprints.qut.edu.au/archive/00000681/01/trocki_drug.PDF

Trebach, A. S. (1987) *The Great Drug War: And Radical Proposals Which Could Make America Safe Again*, New York: Macmillan.

Trebach, A. S. (1982) *The Heroin Solution,* New Haven: Yale University Press.

Tudor, A. (2003) 'A (macro) sociology of fear?' *The Sociological Review*, 51(2): 238-256.

Tunnell, K. D. (1993) 'Inside the Drug Trade: Tafficking from the Dealer's Perspective', Qualitative Sociology, 16(4): 361-381.

United Kingdom Anti-Drugs Co-ordination Unit (1998) Tackling Drugs to Build a Better Britain: The Government's Ten-Year Strategy for Tackling Drugs Misuse, White Paper. The Stationary Office [online]. [Accessed: July 7, 2002]. Available from World Wide Web: http://www.official-documents.co.uk/document/cm39/3945/3945.htm

United Nations Office of Drug Control (2005) *World Drug Report*, Vol. 1, Office on Drugs and Crime, Slovakia: United Nations.

United States Sentencing Commission, Special Report to the Congress: Cocaine and Federal Sentencing Policy. (February 1995). *USSC OnLine; SC-Request; RDL* [online]. [Accessed: May 18, 2006]. Available from World Wide Web: http://www.ussc.gov/crack/CHAP4.HTM

USA Today (2006) Editorial: Our view: Gifts from drugmakers damage doctors' integrity, June 7, 2006 [online]. [Accessed: May 18, 2006]. Available from World Wide Web: http://www.usatoday.com/news/opinion/editorials/2006-02-07-our-medical-ethics_x.htm

VanNostrand, L.M. and Tewksbury, R. (1999) 'The motives and mechanics of operating an illegal drug enterprise', *Deviant Behaviour*, 20: 57-83.

Wadler, G. (1999) 'Doping in Sport: From Strychnine to Genetic Enhancement, It's a Moving Target', presentation before the Duke Conference on Doping, May 7 [online]. [Accessed: May 21, 2002]. Available from World Wide Web: http://www.law.duke.edu/sportscenter/wadler.pdf

Wakeman, F. E. (1997) *Strangers at the gate: Social disorder in South China, 1839-1861*, Berkley: University of California Press.

Waldorf, D. and Biernacki, P. (1982) 'Natural Recovery from Heroin Addiction: A Review of the Incidence Literature', in Zinberg, N.E, and Harding, W.M. Eds., *Control over Intoxicant Use: Psychopharmacological, Psychological and Social Considerations*. New York: Human Science Press.

Waldorf, D. (1973) *Careers in Dope*, New Jersey: Prentice –Hall.

Waley, A. (1968) *The Opium War Through Chinese Eyes*, Stanford: Stanford University Press.

Warburton, H., Turnball, P. and Hough, M. (2005) Occasional and controlled heroin use: Not a problem? Report for the Joseph Rowntree Foundation [online]. [Accessed: June 9, 2006]. Available from World Wide Web: http://www.jrf.org.uk/bookshop/eBooks/1859354254.pdf

Wasserman, S. (1998) 'The Good Old Days of Poverty: Merchants and the Battle over Pushcart Peddling on the Lower East Side', *Business and Economic History*, 27(2): 330-39.

Webster, K. (2002) 'Drug dealer tells real deal', *The Maine Campus* [online]. [Accessed: May 17, 2006]. Available from World Wide Web: http://www.mainecampus.com/media/paper322/news/2002/05/02/News/Drug-Dealer.Tells.Real.Deal-249944.shtml?norewrite&sourcedomain=www.mainecampus.com

Weil, A. and Rosen, W (1998) *From Chocolate to Morphine*, Boston: Houghton Mifflin.

Weir, E. (2000) 'Raves: a review of the culture, the drugs and the prevention of harm' *Canadian Medical Association Journal*;162(13):1843-8.

Wendel, T. and Curtis, R. (2000) 'The heraldry of heroin: "Dope stamps" and the dynamics of drug markets in New York City', *Journal of Drug Issues*, 30 (2): 225-260.

WHO/UNICRI (1995) *Cocaine Project: Summary Papers*, March.

Wiesal, E. (1997) Public Lecture: 'Ethical Issues for Today'. Carnegie Council on Ethics and International Affairs: Louis Nizer Lectures on Public Policy [online]. [Accessed: May 21, 2002]. Available from World Wide Web: http://www.cceia.org/programs/nizer3.html

Wink, W. (1996) 'Getting off Drugs: The Legalization Option', Friends Journal. February [online]. [Accessed: May 21, 2002]. Available from World Wide Web: http://www.quaker.org/fj/wink.html#wink

Winick, C. (1962) 'Maturing out of narcotic addiction', *Bulletin on Narcotics* 14:1-7.

Winstock A, Griffiths, P. and Stewart, D. (2001) 'Drugs and the dance music scene: a survey of current drug use patterns among a sample of dance music enthusiasts in the UK', *Drug and Alcohol Dependence* 64: 9-17.

Woodiwiss, M. (1998) 'Reform, racism and rackets: alcohol and drug prohibition in the United States' in Coomber, R., (ed.) *The Control of Drugs and Drug Users: Reason or Reaction*, Amsterdam, Harwood Academic Publishers.

Young, C. M. (1988) 'Aristotle on Temperance', *Philosophical Review,* 97(4): 521-542.

Young, J. (1971) *The Drugtakers: The Social Meaning of Drug Use*, London: Paladin.

Yu, J. (1998) 'Virtue: Confucius and Aristotle', *Philosophy East & West*, 48: 323-347.

Zackon, F. (1988) *Heroin: The Street Narcotic*, London: Burke.

Zhang D, Shi X, Yuan Z, Ju H. (2004) 'Component analysis of illicit heroin samples with GC/MS and its application in source determination', *Journal of Forensic Sciences*, 4;49(1):81.

Zinberg, N. (1985) *Drug, Set and Setting*, New Haven, Yale University Press.

Index

Index of names